Elementary Health and Physical Education
A Classroom Teacher's Guide

MW01225668

Second Edition

Scott Melville
Eastern Washington University

Howard Walmsley
Central Queensland University, Australia

KENDALL/HUNT PUBLISHING COMPANY
4050 Westmark Drive   Dubuque, Iowa 52002

Credits

Figure 1.1
From *The Strength Connection: How to Build Strength and Improve the Quality of Your Life* by The Cooper Institute for Aerobics Research, Dallas, TX. Copyright © 1990 by The Cooper Institute for Aerobics Research Association, Dallas, TX. Reprinted by permission.

Figure 2.7
Adapted with permission from D. Hellison, 1985, *Goals and Strategies for Teaching Physical Education* (Champaign, IL: Human Kinetics Publishers), 6-8.

Figures 4.4 and 4.5
From *The Safe Exercise Handbook, 4th Edition,* by Toni Tickel Branner. Copyright © 2000 by Kendall/Hunt Publishing Company. Reprinted by permission of Kendall/Hunt Publishing Company.

Figure 7.8
From *Teaching Handball in the Elementary Schools, 4th Edition* by L. Marten & P. Tyson. Copyright © 2000 by United States Handball Association. Reprinted by permission.

Figures 8.1, 8.8 and 8.10
From *Fitnessgram* by Cooper Institute for Aerobics Research. Copyright © 1999 by Cooper Institute for Aerobics Research. Reprinted by permission.

Figures 8.7 and 8.14
Reprinted from *Moving Into the Future: National Standards for Physical Education* with permission from the National Association for Sport and Physical Education (NASPE), 1900 Association Drive, Reston, VA 20191, USA.

Figure 9.4
Reprinted by permission from S. Virgilio, 1997, *Fitness Education for Children: A Team Approach* (Champaign, IL: Human Kinetics Publishers), 71.

Figures 9.8 and 9.9
Adapted with permission from D. Hellison, 1995, *Teaching Responsibility Through Physical Activity* (Champaign, IL: Human Kinetics Publishers), 14.

Copyright © 1998, 2002 by Scott Melville and Howard Walmsley

ISBN 0-7872-9574-4

All rights reserved. No part of this publication may be reproduced, stored in a retrieval system, or transmitted in any form or by any means, electronic, mechanical, photocopying, recording, or otherwise, without the prior written permission of the copyright owner.

Printed in the United States of America
10   9   8   7   6   5   4   3   2

Who dares to teach must never cease to learn.

—John Cotton Dana

Contents

Chapter 8   How You Might Evaluate the Psychomotor Domain   135

Chapter 9   How Can You Change Their Habits?   169

**Chapter 10   Questions Often Asked by Classroom Teachers
about Teaching Physical Activities   191**

Preface

Without good health we are diminished, enjoyment of life is compromised and our personal and social accomplishments are limited. In this book it will become clear that despite our growing wealth, technological achievements, and advances in medicine, America is encountering major health problems as a consequence of our lifestyles. We are much less active than in the past; our diets contain more calories and are less nutritious (dangerous diets and bulimia/anorexia disorders are common); we are finding less time in our stress-filled days for restorative leisure pursuits and sleep; drug abuse and violent behaviors persist; and various health care problems remain (excessive sun exposure, unsafe sexual practices, failure to take prudent measures to minimize accidents and injuries, etc.). As a consequence, American adults are encountering high rates of disabilities such as heart attack, stroke, cancer, diabetes, obesity, depression, arthritis, emphysema, osteoporosis, fatigue, back pain, sexually transmitted diseases and trauma injuries.

Our children are facing these same lifestyle challenges and research data leads to the conclusion that they are a generation at particular risk to the adult health problems listed above. The number of children classified as overweight has risen to 25 percent (more than double what it was two decades ago). Type II diabetes—once called "adult-onset"—has increased nine-fold and is now being diagnosed more and more frequently in adolescents. Like adults, the average young person is getting much less physical activity than did past generations and his/her diet is less nutritious and higher in calories. Additionally, there are many other disturbing health practices affecting the young such as violent behaviors (perpetrated on and by them), early smoking and drug usage, excessive sun exposure, and careless sexual practices.

Given the seriousness of the above health profile of our children, action needs to be taken. It is my contention that establishing sound wellness practices is an integral part of a liberal education. If lifestyles are to be changed, schools must exert a concerted effort and you, the elementary school classroom teacher, must play a key role. Regardless of how good a physical education specialist your school might have, his/her visits are not going to be sufficient to effect the major lifestyle changes that are necessary. Most schools will have specialist visits of only once or twice a week, and significant numbers of schools do not have any specialist. The average physical education specialist might be servicing as many as 600–800 students and the trend is towards schools supporting yet fewer specialists in the future. Clearly, the specialist will be just one rather ineffectual voice crying in the wilderness unless his/her message is supported and supplemented by the other teachers, staff, and administration. Because of the close bonds that will be formed between you and your students over a year's time, you naturally become a primary influential player. Your modeling and advice will be critical.

In this book you will be given ideas of how you can work with the specialist, the administration, other teachers, parents, and community members to produce health changes in children. You will be presented a few specific overriding goals around which you can focus your planning and instruction. You will learn the basic physiological principles of exercise and the pedagogical principles of teaching motor skills. You will be given simple ideas of how to effectively manage your classes in the gym or playing field environment. You will be given many specific activity ideas, and even more importantly, ideas of how to select and modify games to make them more enjoyable and educational. You will encounter techniques for effecting behavior changes beyond the school. You will be given feasible assessment ideas for verifying learning and motivating yourself and your students. There is also a chapter on a range of questions commonly asked by classroom teachers about teaching physical activities: how to include special needs children, what are one's safety and legal responsibilities, what are physical activities which can be done in the classroom or other limited space, etc.

In this book an important amount of attention has been directed at the affective domain. If you are like most teachers or prospective teachers, you have a major goal of helping children to become better citizens. Even more than teaching them how to read and write and attain other content skills, you may wish to improve their ability to cooperatively get along with others (regardless of capabilities, gender, social status, or ethnicity), persevere at tasks, be helpful and caring, take responsibility for their actions and their role in the community. It is the authors' belief that these affective behaviors can be well taught through the avenue of physical activities. Practicing individual motor and fitness skills, participating in partner and group cooperative games, and competing in sports activities under effective tutelage can serve as an ideal laboratory for the application of good affective behaviors. You will be given workable guidelines and instructional approaches for achieving them.

Another issue closely dealt with in this text is that of competitive sports. Some of you may have had very positive experiences with sports and are thinking that you would love to offer a similar beneficial experience to your classroom children or to the youth sports teams you may coach. You remember the joy and the excitement, the close camaraderie, and the perseverance and teamwork skills learned. Others of you might have a much different recall of your competitive sports experiences. You might still feel the sting of embarrassment or ridicule that peers, teachers, or coaches may have laid on you or other unfortunates. You remember the inequality of the rewards and the frustration of working towards unattainable targets. Because we recognize the potentially powerful influence of competition, careful consideration has been devoted to it throughout much of the book. Many ideas are given to get children focusing on self-improvement-mastery goals and away from social-comparison goals. Also, various suggestions are made to insure that competitive experiences are consistent with a humanistic educational process.

At the end of each chapter are questions to check your remembrance and understanding of the major concepts covered. Also, at the end of each chapter are some laboratory exercises that might serve to promote further comprehension and application. Both the questions and laboratory exercises should be effective in promoting discussions with course instructors, classmates, and teaching peers. Finally, the back of the book contains a glossary to help the reader more quickly review significant terms and concepts.

Approximately five years have elapsed since the first edition of this book was written. I have used it in my course instruction over those years and have been pleased with the positive response of the students. I have regularly sought their feedback and incorporated many of their ideas into this second edition. Although the basic philosophy and structure of this second writing remains the same, I am encouraged to find that I have had much new to say (as I have long told my students, I can see that persistent study really does result in important change and deeper understanding). One of the significant alterations relates to a further clarification of the goals we need to be working toward. Also, the reader will find a major expansion in activity ideas and helping resources (web sites and support materials from professional and commercial organizations).

The Importance of Your Teaching Health and Physical Education

The Importance of Exercise and Health
On Immediate Quality of Life
On Quality of Life as We Age
On Length of Life

Exercise and Health Practices of United States
Exercise
Nutrition
Drugs
Sleep
Sun Exposure
Seat Belts

Why You Can Play a Crucial Role

"Those who think they have not time for bodily exercise will sooner or later have to find time for illness."
Edward Stanley

"The wise, for cure, on exercise depend.— Better to hunt in fields for health unbought than fee the doctor for a nauseous draught."
Dryden

"Health is the vital principle of bliss; and exercise, of health."
Thomson

"The goal of life is to die young, as late as possible."
Ashley Montague

Before we begin to discuss why you might play a crucial role in the teaching of health and physical education let us first consider the importance of exercise and health. Then we will look at the exercise and health status of the American people. We think that an introductory coverage of these two topics will increase your belief that elementary schools badly need to address this subject.

The Importance of Exercise and Health

"Unless you have health you have nothing!" You probably have heard this or a similar adage spoken many times. Ask anyone and they will agree that good health is your most valuable asset. Anyone who is ill or has been ill in the recent past will certainly agree. Without health a fully enjoyable and productive life is simply not possible.

Today's research provides irrefutable evidence of the enormous benefits exercise and sound health habits can have on (1) the immediate quality of life, (2) the quality of life as we age, and (3) the length of life itself. Let us briefly consider each one of these in order.

On Immediate Quality of Life

Most people do not exercise to promote the long-term quality or length of their lives, certainly not many young people. They do it for the very real benefits it can confer here and now. The most common reasons people give for being active is that it is fun, it makes them feel better, it helps them control body fat, and it firms their muscles. But research shows that activity has many other immediate consequences, any one of which would make it well worth doing. Some diverse, clearly documented physiological and psychological benefits of physical activity are: better sleep patterns, higher resistance to infections and more rapid recovery, increased perceptions of energy, better ability to cope with psychological stresses, improved regularity, better sexual functioning, reduced levels of depression and anxiety, more optimistic outlooks, stronger bones, better flexibility, less arthritic problems, and better overall feelings about physical appearance.

The late George Sheehans was a well-known physician and exercise physiologist. He stated that in the normal course of his medical practice he would have many people come to him for physical check-ups. Invariably, those patients who were not following an active lifestyle would make comments like "What is the matter with me Doc? I feel run down, lethargic, lack energy, depressed." After finding no specific, identifiable ailment he would make this diagnosis, "There is nothing unusual here. Your symptoms are the body's natural response to not exercising. You are suffering from *exercise deficiency*." Sadly, many people may have never experienced, or have forgotten, what it feels like to be active and physically fit, and they may be unaware of the myriad benefits it can bestow upon one's current quality of life?

On Quality of Life as We Age

The second valuable contribution of physical activity and a healthy lifestyle is how these can improve the long-term quality of our lives. I have a good neighbor who likes to make fun of my health conscious practices. On numerous occasions he has made only half in jest comments such as: "Why should I exercise or worry about exercising?" "Why should I follow a low-fat diet or quitting smoking?" "I don't want to live longer only to end up in a nursing home and to be a burden on my children," "I'd rather enjoy life and then some day just drop off suddenly." While I respect the opinions of my friend in many things, we need realize that his thesis in this area is not supported by recent studies. The truth is quite the contrary. People who do not exercise regularly, who do not eat properly, or who smoke, will begin to witness clear decreases in their physical capacities at rather young ages. Aerobic fitness levels begin to decline as soon as the early 20s, flexibility in the mid 20s, bone strength in the mid 30s, muscular strength losses will become apparent in the late 30s to early 40s. It is the gradual, progressive loss of these functions which begins to impinge upon the quality of one's life and limit what a person is capable of doing. Permit me to again personalize and once more pick on my neighbor. Although he is still in his 50s he cannot now do some of the yard and gardening tasks he used to enjoy. Other of my similarly aged friends who have accustomed themselves to regular robust exercise are not typically experiencing such limitations. These friends not only are doing the likes of yard and garden work but are in many cases confidently planning long distance bike and hiking trips, climbing excursions, and other adventures.

Research indicates that those who remain active can slow the inevitable aging diminution by something like 20 years. In other words, a 50 year old person who is working to maintain the various components of fitness will likely display similar capacities to that of the inactive 30 year old. If individuals in their twenties remain active, they can expect a natural aging decrease in their abilities of approximately 5 to 10 percent per decade. Although declines of these magnitudes might prevent 40, 60, and 80 year olds from winning races against those in the May-time of their youth, these diminutions are not so great as to severely curtail the activity options of people well into their latter years.[1]

At the Cooper Aerobics Institute in Dallas, Texas, some interesting data has addressed the reality of the nursing home issue.[2] Cooper's records argue that it is those who do not maintain a well balanced, active lifestyle that are the ones in far greater danger of requiring care in their old age. According to him, *morbidity* (a period of ill health) will be a reality for many of the people who are not following a balanced exercise program. By balanced he meant that the person was exercising not only the aerobic system but was also training for muscular strength and joint flexibility. After all, while some people may loose the ability to fully take care of themselves because of various cardiovascular problems, others will encounter difficulties related to functional strength and flexibility. For example, they might not maintain enough strength to get in and out of the bathtub or to

---

[1] Sometimes I like to determine whether or not research findings really do relate to me. I have run in the same race for the last ten years. When I was 40 my time was 43 minutes and 32 seconds; when I was 45 my time was 45 minutes and 36 seconds; when I was 50 my time was 48 minutes and 15 seconds. If you do the simple math as I have done you will see I was 5 percent slower each five years. Of course it is always saddening in see aging declines, but maybe we can look at the bright side; if we keep active we should still be able to be chugging along at 80.

[2] Cooper, K. *The Strength Connection: How to Build Strength and Improve the Quality of Your Life.* Institute for Aerobics Research, 1990.

carry groceries. Their flexibility might deteriorate to the point where washing their feet is impossible or they cannot turn their head well enough to safely drive a car. Figure 1.1 shows 11.5 years to be the average length of time in which a sedentary person can expect to fall below the level of independence. If poor health habits do not result in an untimely death, more than a decade of dependent living is the expected norm. Notice how this period of morbidity is almost eliminated by adherence to regular exercise (Cooper calls this *compression of morbidity*). Those who regularly exercise can generally expect to maintain functional abilities into their final years. Notice how the functional capacity curve of the active/fit individuals is maintained at a high level until pretty much the last months or year of their lives. It is also worth noting that the advances being made in modern medicine might be making this phenomenon of lifestyle compression of morbidity even more important in the future. Evidence suggest that medical care is actually contributing to an opposite trend or *expansion of morbidity*. Medical improvements have been tending to preserve life more than they have been improving its quality. Through the 1970's the life expectancy of males rose by 2.2 years, but during the same period the disability-free life expectancy rose by only 0.6 years.

On Length of Life

Finally, we need to realize that sound health practices play a big part in length of life. You may have had a friend or family member say something like; "When it's your time to go, it's time to go." "It's all genetics." "Look at that French woman who smoked her entire life and lived to be 120." While genetics obviously plays an important role in length of any individual's life, it is foolish to disregard the powerful influence lifestyle contributes. The leading cause of death in both men and women is cardiovascular disease and unhealthy lifestyle practices are the chief cause of these high

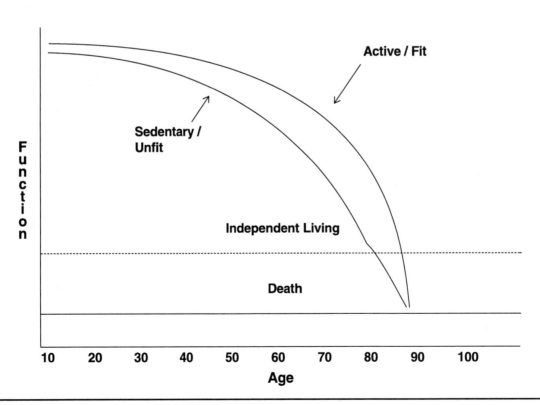

Figure 1.1. Exercise and Compressed Morbidity

rates. Cancer is the second leading killer; 65 percent of which are in part attributable to diet, smoking, and lack of exercise (lung, colon, breast, prostate cancer all correlate with these lifestyle choices). Diabetes rose by 6 percent in 1999 and now is the third leading killer. It is the leading cause of blindness, kidney failure and amputations and dramatically raises the risk of heart attacks. It kills 180,000 Americans each year. It is estimated that the rate of diabetes could be cut more than in half with better exercise and eating habits.

For the big picture, consider the overall longevity data; healthy men who do not exercise at all have a 3.44 times greater chance of dying from the three leading causes of death when compared to those who work out vigorously. This figure is even higher, jumping to 4.65 times greater, when sedentary women are compared to vigorously exercising women. When inactive individuals are compared to even lightly active men and women (walking as little as 5 city blocks a day, climbing 5 flights of stairs or engaging in 1/2 hour of vigorous sports on a daily basis) they have a 1.9 times greater chance of dying of these causes. Look at what happens to life span differences when an array of risk factors are added; the average life span is around 85 years for those who get regular exercise, maintain a low level of body fat, don't smoke, keep their blood pressure low, and control their cholesterol levels. On the other hand, those who control none of these risk factors have life expectancies only into the 60s. Of course, life is not always fair and the most fit and health conscientious of individuals could become ill, an invalid, and die young. But such untimely deaths are relatively rare. Untimely deaths are not rare in those who allow time to waste them and hope that genetics will be unusually kind to them.

Exercise and Health Practices of the United States

The opening section of this chapter verified some of the many immediate and long-term benefits sound health practices can yield. Let us now consider how well the United States' population is mining those golden benefits of health. I will state up front that I do not believe we are doing well at all. Our population has a higher percent body fat than virtually any other country. Approximately 10 years ago 25 percent of the adult population were classified as *overweight* (when defining *overweight* as having 20 percent or more body fat than what would be ideal for that individual). Now, close to 40 percent are classified as overweight when so defined. For the first time in our history our children are considered less fit than the previous generation. According to federal survey data, the number of kids who are *obese* (when defined as 30 percent or more above their ideal weight), has more than doubled in the last two decades. Studies show that an overweight or obese child has an 80 percent chance of remaining so as an adult. Also, we suffer from much higher rates of cardiovascular disease, cancer and diabetes than is necessary. The Surgeon General has estimated

Figure 1.2. Percentage of American Who Are Overweight

Males	1960–62	1971–74	1976–80	1988–94
20–70 years old	23%	24%	24%	34%
12–17 years old		5%	5%	12%
6–11 years old		7%	8%	15%
Females				
20–70 years old	26%	26%	27%	36%
12–17 years old		7%	6%	11%
6–11 years old		4%	7%	12%

that we could save 300,000 lives a year by eating better and exercising at modest levels (that is more deaths than are caused by infectious disease, firearms, motor vehicles and substance abuse combined). What a colossal tragedy we are permitting; it is equivalent to two loaded 747s crashing everyday of the year. This needlessly high rate of death and disability is even putting the economic future of our nation at risk because of the increasing cost of health care. It is believed that we could save 100 billion dollars yearly if we simply ate better and exercised more. Surely no national health care system will be less than exorbitantly expensive unless we can change our daily behaviors. When looked at from this perspective, taking at least minimal care of our bodies is a demonstration of socially responsible behavior.

Below we will survey the data collected on just some health practices. We don't doubt that you will agree that there are many areas in which health practices sorely need changing. Also, it will be obvious that these health habits are normally developed during the school years, usually the elementary years.

Exercise

Modern research data has been confirming and expanding the diverse health benefits of physically active lifestyles. Inactivity is now considered a leading risk factor and getting Americans to be more active is listed as a major goal for our country. In the age of communication, this message is being constantly sent to the population through the newspapers, popular magazines and media broadcasts. When surveyed, 93 percent of today's American adults agree that regular exercise is one of the best things that can be done to preserve their health. Furthermore, parents are increasingly concerned about their children not getting enough activity. Almost 30 percent of them are somewhat or very concerned about their children's weight. Eighty percent do not want physical education classes in their children's schools reduced for academic classes, and less than half of parents think the schools are doing enough to teach active lifestyles to prevent obesity.

Given the above views it could be expected that adults would be exercising more and schools would be upgrading physical education and health and lifestyle instruction. The reality is otherwise. Less than 25 percent of American adults are classified as regular vigorous exercisers and over 25 percent remain resolutely *sedentary*. Sedentary is defined as not doing any exercise beyond that which is required at work, and of course, most jobs require much less manual labor than in the past. Only about 22 percent are active at a level recommended for any meaningful health benefits by the U.S. Department of Health and Human Services Healthy People 2000 report on health promotion

---

Figure 1.3. Causes of Death in the United States 1,120,000 Per Year

1.	Tobacco	450,000
2.	Diet & Physical Inactivity	300,000
3.	Alcohol	100,000
4.	Microbial Agents	90,000
5.	Toxic Agents	60,000
6.	Sexual Behavior	40,000
7.	Firearms	35,000
8.	Motor Vehicles	25,000
9.	Illicit Use of Drugs	20,000

* The feature of these statistics that strikes me is the relatively large numbers contributed by the first two categories. The implication to me is that while all of these factors are resulting in tragic numbers that warrant our attention, education regarding smoking prevention and the adoption of good eating and exercise habits is especially critical. Sometimes dramatic instances of such things as a firearm event or drug over-dose can capture our attention and generate preventive school programs, but can we afford to forget about the everyday common life patterns many of our children falling into?

---

and disease prevention. These figures vary depending on what segment of the population you are considering. People earning less than $25,000 per year are 61 percent inactive while those above $50,000 are 37 percent inactive. Furthermore, current trends are towards less activity. It has been estimated that there has been nearly a 10 percent decline in adult's physical activity over each of the last two decades.

As you might expect, children with their eager supple bodies are more active than are adults. While they don't normally elect to jog or do other steady state aerobic activities for 30 minutes, they tend to be interval trainers, gleefully participating in frequent, short bursts of vigorous activity throughout the day. Young boys accumulate on average 68 minutes of activity a day and girls 59 minutes. However, we should note that the amount of activity children engage in decreases 50 percent across the school years until it is nearly down to the average adult levels by 12th grade. Most parents see their children involved in dance and/or sports lessons when they are 6, 8 or 10 years of age, but big dropouts occur thereafter until less than 21 percent of high school students are involved in even one school sport. By age 15, 75 percent have dropped out of after school sports.

Probably the best activity generalization that can be made regarding the children you are likely to have in your classroom is to say that they will be a heterogeneous group. Some of the more athletic students will be taking advantage of expanded youth sport opportunities; they likely will be extremely well skilled and trained. You might also notice that some of these more athletic children are beginning to be tracked into serious pursuit of a single sport at younger and younger ages (we will address some concerns about this phenomenon of early *sport specialization* in a later chapter). At the other extreme, for reasons discussed in the following paragraphs, you will have intermixed in your class a growing segment of children who will be decidedly less active than our society has ever before experienced. For some of them, their fitness levels may already be so low as to be perceptibly impairing their quality of life.

Overall, children's current activity trends are not good. Mirroring the adult population, children have shown a decline of approximately 10 percent over the last couple of decades. I have listed four factors contributing to this drop. The major factor is probably today's ever-present media attractions (television, videos, movies and video games). Sixty-seven percent of children watch at least two hours of television a day, and 26 percent rack up four or more hours. This 25-hour per week average increases to 40 in the summer. Such a large amount of viewing time means the supplanting of much activity. It is interesting to note that a strong positive association exists between the amount of time a child watches television and the percent body fat of the child. For every extra hour averaged above the 25-hour norm, the child's percent body fat normally will be 2 percent higher. Children who watch at least four hours daily have about 20 percent more body fat than kids who watch fewer than two hours.

A second factor limiting children's activity is the reduction in activity during the school day due to less physical education time. Required physical education has been greatly reduced primarily because of other expanded curriculum offerings. The majority of high school students take physical education for only one year between ninth and twelfth grades. In addition, 48 percent of the states allow substitutions for high school physical education. Although elementary schools have experienced smaller decreases in physical education only 8 percent of elementary schools provide daily physical education. There also has been a trend toward fewer recess periods. Currently 71 percent of elementary schools provide regularly scheduled recess for students in all grades kindergarten through fifth.

The structure of our modern society and communities is a third factor that we are beginning to recognize as degrading activity. More working parents mean more school-age children are told to stay indoors until parents come home. Bored and lonely, the children munch, watch television and play video games. More and more children are now living in bigger cities or in suburban environments. Children in the cities might engage in less leisure-time sandlot play because conveniently assessable play fields are not commonly available and the areas and surroundings may not be considered safe. For other reasons, neither are the suburban neighborhoods particularly conducive to physical play. These spread-out homes can create an isolating environment that hinders a number of children coming together for games. Also, suburban environments are designed with cars in mind and busy feeder roads can serve as access barriers to any park and recreational areas there may be. The distances between suburban homes and schools/commercial businesses tend to be long and hence so are commuting times. Not many years ago a fourth of all trips were made on foot or bicycle. Now, 90 percent of trips are made by car or bus. In the 1960s one of every two children walked or biked to school; that figure now is only one in ten.

Finally, *labor saving devices* are imperceptibly impacting overall activity levels. I think of these as unnecessary "exercise costing" devices. Each in itself would seem to play an insignificant role but even little things can accumulate over years of daily use. Around the home I am thinking of things such as electric can openers, automatic garage doors, power tools and mowers. In the community there are escalators, elevators, drive-throughs, automatic doors, people to bag our own groceries, etc.

Nutrition

Nutritional practices are now recognized as being far more important than once imagined. In the 1970s the new advocates of aerobics theorized exercise could free you to eat whatever you liked. That is not correct. We now know that eating poorly is a major ingredient in cardiovascular disease, diabetes, and in 60–70 percent of cancers, ranging from colon, to breast, to prostate, to skin.

The diet recommended by the United States Department of Agriculture (USDA) would have no more than 25–30 percent of our calorie consumption coming from fat. Three-fourth of the adults and 5 of 6 school children do not meet that minimal guideline. It also recommends as a minimum that everyone have 5 servings a day of fruits and vegetables. Only 20 percent of children do so. Only 5 percent consume a better 7 per day. One-half eat no fruit during a given day, 25 percent no vegetables, 11 percent get neither.[3] These practices result in children's average fiber consumption being approximately 5 grams, the recommended minimal level is 25 grams. You also can expect 19 percent of your children to have skipped breakfast. One-third of adolescent girls will be on a crash diet at any one time. About 3 percent of teen girls are bulimic or anorexic. Researchers say eating disorders appear to be on the rise and are affecting children as young as 8.

Children eating at a fast-food restaurant is almost a daily occurrence. In a typical week there will be a downing of three hamburgers and four orders of french fries. Cookies and other baked sweets, potato chips and other salty treats, candy and gum account for more than half the snacks consumed by kids. During the last three decades children have increased their consumption of these high fat snack foods by 200 percent and are averaging about 300 more calories a day. They are five times more likely to have a carbonated soft drink or sweetened fruit drink than fruit juice for a snack. Also, many foods available to students in school are high in fat, sodium, and added sugars. For example, 62.8 percent of all milk ordered by schools in a typical week is high in fat (whole or 2 percent milk). Forty-three percent of elementary schools, 73.9 percent of middle/junior high schools, and 98.2 percent of senior high schools have either a vending machine or a school store, canteen, or snack bar where students can purchase food or beverage. The common food offerings are soft drinks, sports drinks, or fruit juices that are not 100 percent juice. There are also salty snacks, cookies, and other baked goods that are not low in fat.

Drugs

Tobacco smoking is perhaps the health habit that has drawn the most attention in recent years and in which major reductions have occurred in the adult population. In the 1950s over half our

---

[3] Twenty-five percent of children have a least one vegetable serving a day. Which vegetable do you think is twice as likely to be eaten than any other vegetable? If you guessed broccoli or cauliflower you are in need of a reality check. The correct answer is french fries. The potato is of course good, but frying has turned it into a high fat food.

population smoked and as of 2002 that figure has dropped to just under 24 percent. However, the snake is only scotched and not killed. Adult rates have shown only slight decreases in recent years despite heightened taxes, restrictions on pro-smoking advertising, and increased anti-smoking messages. Smoking must be considered out of the worst of health habits. It has disastrous affects on those who continue to smoke (killing 450,000 yearly) and it passively damages many others.

Thirty percent of high school seniors said they smoked cigarettes in 1983 and there has been an increase in recent years. Eighty percent of adult smokers started as teenagers and the average starting age has become younger and younger until today it is at 12.5 years of age. Children by definition are immature, and are consequently most foolishly affected by peer pressure to take up the bad habit.

Overall, America's average consumption of alcohol has decreased over the last couple of decades, but are we happy with where it has stabilized? One-third of high school students have consumed 5 or more drinks in a row within the last 2 weeks. Thirteen point four percent of eighth graders reported getting drunk within the past 2 weeks.

About 1 in 20 high schoolers has used the club-drug ecstasy, and heroin use, while small, has doubled since 1991. One third of high-school seniors have used marijuana.

Sleep

It is recommended the young people get at least nine hours of sleep every night, but only about 15 percent do. A full quarter get less than six hours. Nearly 40 percent go to sleep after 11 o'clock on school nights.

Sun Exposure

Eighty percent of sun exposure occurs before age 21. Thirty-three percent of teenagers never use sun-screens and 33 percent experienced a blistering burn the previous two summers. Research also shows the skin of children is especially vulnerable to damage from the sun.

Seat Belts

We Americans spend a great deal of time in our cars. Traveling in a car is the most dangerous activity we do on a regular basis. The majority of people will be involved in at least one car accident during their lives. Use of seat belts is proven to cut the death rate and severity of injury by half. And yet, even with this danger and the many new State laws requiring seat belt use, one recent study show that only 34 percent of junior high and high school students use them when riding in the front seat of a car.

Why You Can Play a Crucial Role

The prior sections may have reaffirmed your belief that health is important and that something needs to be done to improve the exercise and health practices of Americans. Hopefully, it has also made you more aware that these habits are more often than not established during the elementary school years. But the questions you may now be asking yourself are "Why me?" "Why do I need to be concerned about teaching this subject?" "Will this not be the province of the physical education specialist?" "Will I not be too busy teaching an extremely large array of other subject matter?"

First consider the issue of the physical education specialist. It is unlikely that you will be in a school in which a physical education specialist will be available to provide daily or even frequent instruction to your children. Although there are variations throughout the States and in the different sized schools, the bulk of physical education is done by the classroom teacher; and the physical education specialists do virtually no instruction in health. The average elementary physical education instructor is responsible for something like 600 to 800 children. Furthermore, the number of physical education specialists has been decreasing in recent years because of the financial difficulties faced by schools. It would not seem unreasonable to expect schools to continue to face similar or even greater funding difficulties in the future.

The most common situation is one in which you will have a physical education specialist about once or twice per week and in some schools there will be none at all. But even if your school is fortunate to have the most effective specialist on a fairly regular basis, it is our contention that he/she will unlikely be able to single-handedly produce the size of habit changes needed. Throughout this text we will be espousing the view that the lifestyle of children will not be significantly improved unless all teachers and administrators create a concerted front.

Secondly, there is no question that classroom teachers are being asked to teach more and more. More time needs to be devoted to the basics and yet many other critical subjects of concern are demanding attention. Is it fair for one more faction or interest group to be demanding a place in the curriculum? I think that is entirely fair. I believe so, not because I think physical education and health are any more important than any other subject, but because full achievement in all other areas is contingent upon children being healthy. Children will not be as happy and they will not think and attend as well when inactive and unfit. This contention has been supported by some curricular studies. In these studies, children typically have achieved better academic performance when schools have increased the curriculum time devoted to physical education. There is good justification to be encouraging school systems to put the fourth "R" back into education—Reading, wRiting, aRithmetic, and Recreation. Daily physical activity should be given an unquestioned priority equal to that of buckling children's seat belts. It is developmentally indefensible to have children sitting for hours at school and at home, and that is what many young people are learning from our culture.

One other question you might have regarding your instructing of health and physical activity is this, "Even if I am convinced my children could benefit from instruction in this area, is it reasonable to expect that I can do it effectively if I have not had an athletic background and do not feel myself to be as physically fit as I should be?" You most certainly can! You do not need be a skilled athlete or the perfect template of fitness. Obviously, having a limited sports background will make it more difficult to teach some movement skills, but that does not mean there are not others you may be able to effectively instruct. As for health and fitness, if you believe in the importance of health and the active lifestyle, and particularly if you are making a sincere effort to realize their fulfillment, you have the essentials of being a powerful influence on the attitudes and behaviors of all those around you. There is no reason you should not be able to deliver a forceful message and one which will be credulously received by your students. I have had numerous beginning teachers come back to me and say that they initially feared teaching in this area because of perceived weakness in their motor and/or fitness abilities, but after attempting some instruction they were glad they had done so. They found the students liked and benefited from their efforts. As an added plus, some of the teachers felt as though working in an activity context enabled them to get to know and understand their students better.

If you have the will, the purpose of the rest of this book is to provide you with the way. In the following chapters we will attempt to provide you with the tools you will need: some guiding philosophy and goals, some effective teaching methods and procedures, some easy-to-use activity ideas, and some answers to questions that are commonly voiced by classroom teachers as they begin to teach health and physical activity to children.

2

Goal 1: Establish Healthy Lifestyles
    Physical Activity
    Nutrition
    Other Healthy Lifestyle Skills and Practices

Goal 2: Establish Good Social and Emotional Values

"Health and good estate of body are above all gold, and a strong body above infinite wealth."

Ecclesiastics 30:15

"Providence has nothing good or high in store for one who does not resolutely aim at something high or good.—A purpose is the eternal condition of success."

T.T. Munger

"Not less than two hours a day should be devoted to exercise, and the weather shall be little regarded. I speak this from experience having made this arrangement of my life. If the body is feeble, the mind will not be strong."

Thomas Jefferson

"Character development is the great, if not the sole, aim of education."

O'Shea

"Before supper walk a little, after supper do the same."

Latin Proverb

If you are going to be instructing in physical activity and health, or any area, it is desirable to have one, or a few, overriding goals. You need to clearly know what you want to accomplish, or more accurately, what you want the children to accomplish. Such an understanding or purpose will serve as a guide for all your subsequent curricular, instructional and evaluation decisions. It is critical for your long-term motivation. It will also help you to see how information covered in this subject area relates to the other subject goals and your overall philosophy of education. I will present two possible overriding goals that could serve to direct all our subsequent planning. It is hoped that these goals will provide a good template from which you might work.

Goal 1: Establish Healthy Lifestyles

The American Medical Association, The American Pediatrics Association and various health organizations all strongly support the goal of schools establishing good physical activity and health habits. The need is acute and no other public or private institution can possibly fulfill this objective for all children. But what specifically is meant by good physical activity and health habits? Let us first consider physical activity.

Physical Activity

Perhaps the first step we need to take in identifying our physical activity goal for school children is to consider what our final goal is for adults. *The Activity Pyramid*[1] serves as the ideal of a well-rounded physical activity lifestyle. As can be seen in Figure 2.1, the foundation of the pyramid has everyone accumulating as much light-to-moderate daily activity as possible. It advocates at least an hour a day of finding ways to get off our seats and move about. The term *Found Activities* is sometimes used for these activities which make extra steps in our day: walking the dog, taking the stairs instead of the elevator, working in the garden, walking to the store or the mail box, parking the car farther away and taking longer routes. With *Found Activities* we are also countering all those *laborsaving devices* we have programmed into our lives without thought to the accumulative negative consequences they can have on our health. Getting this amount of light-to-moderate daily

---

[1] 1996 Park Nicollet *HealthSource,* Institute for Research and Education.

Figure 2.1. The Activity Pyramid

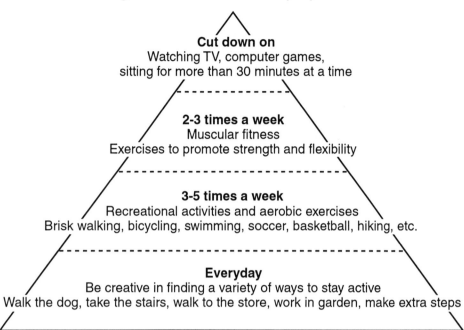

Cut down on
Watching TV, computer games,
sitting for more than 30 minutes at a time

2-3 times a week
Muscular fitness
Exercises to promote strength and flexibility

3-5 times a week
Recreational activities and aerobic exercises
Brisk walking, bicycling, swimming, soccer, basketball, hiking, etc.

Everyday
Be creative in finding a variety of ways to stay active
Walk the dog, take the stairs, walk to the store, work in garden, make extra steps

activity will promote a minimal but important level of cardiovascular fitness, muscular fitness, and healthy body composition stability (In Chapter 4 we will look in more detail at the physiological effects of light/moderate activity intensities as well as more vigorous forms of activity).

The second tier of the pyramid has the person engaging in 20 minutes or more of aerobic activities, 3 to 5 times a week. *Aerobic activities* are those which are more vigorous and the heart rate is elevated to about 60 to 90 percent above resting levels. This, of course, can be accomplished through a variety of avenues: recreational sports such as soccer, hiking, basketball, tennis, martial arts, dancing; and exercises such as brisk walking, cross-country skiing, bicycling, swimming, jogging. These higher intensities contribute to higher levels of cardiovascular fitness, muscular fitness, and calorie burning for fat control.

The third tier sees the individual doing exercises 2 to 3 times per week to promote muscular fitness in the major muscle groups. While the activities done at levels 1 and 2 will be developing some muscular strength and flexibility, all the major muscles groups may not be being used, or may not be overloaded sufficiently to maintain strength, muscle mass, and a balanced range of full motion. Calisthenics, weight training, stretching, and yoga, are the kinds of exercises that meet these needs.

The small peak of the pyramid is there to remind people of the sedentary activities that they may need to reduce. Excessive television watching, computer usage, driving around, are examples of common sedentary behaviors. Breaking these kinds of activities up every 30 minutes or so is recommended.

If we accept *The Activity Pyramid* as our optimal goal for adults, it follows that we should be attempting to motive our children in the direction of realizing it. By the time they are graduating high school seniors they ideally would have it integrated into their life patterns and would be reaping all the benefits it has to offer. However, while I completely endorse the pyramid as final target, it might not be a reasonably appropriate goal to set for most adults and children. As the data made apparent in the previous Chapter, the movement habits of American adults are not robust and hence are nowhere near conforming to the pyramid. I would confidently estimate that less than 10 percent of the population would meet the combined minimum criteria of an hour a day of moving, 3 aerobic work-outs per week, and both strength and flexibility exercising 2 to 3 times per week. Would it really be effective to be holding up *The Activity Pyramid* in its totality to the nearly one half of the population that is sunk in its totally sedentary ways, or even to those who are making some good efforts at being active? Consider yourself and those around you. Would it be feasible for you right now with all your university work, job and family responsibilities? Maybe, maybe not. How about for your parents and all your aunts, uncles, cousins and peers?

My view is that for too long we have tried to demand a model of vigorous physical activity that is either unfeasible or intolerable to much of our population. Ever since the 1960's, when Kenneth Cooper's first Aerobics book[2] came out we have told Americans they need to exercise vigorously enough to get their heart rates up into a training zone and they must maintain it there at least 20 to 40 minutes. Most everyone has tried adopting this at one time or other, but few have persisted. Perhaps we would be more successful in getting people to move, and continue to move throughout their lives, if we told them that exercise does not have to be painfully vigorous to be good for them. I am not alone in calling for a new adult physical activity goal that focuses on light/moderate activities. The new physical activity recommendation from *The U.S. Centers for Disease Prevention and Control* (CDC) and *The American College of Sports Medicine* (ACSM) is concisely stated: "Every U.S. adult should accumulate 30 minutes or more of moderate-intensity physical activity on most, preferably all, days of the week." In recent years, many national, state, and local organizations have been marketing this sort of message.

What are the specific reasons a refocusing of our goal from the higher tiers of *The Activity Pyramid,* to the advocating of light/moderate daily activity, might be a more successful approach to improving the health of our society? Firstly, we need to recognize that the greatest health benefits are realized when people move from a sedentary stage to engaging in regular light to moderate activities. The sedentary, or nearly so, make up an increasingly large portion of our society and they are accounting for the vast majority of untimely morbidity and mortality rates. Their maladies are greatly reduced when quite modest levels of activity are maintained.[3]

Secondly, what are the specific reasons the advocacy of light to moderate activity is a more feasible health goal? When we survey adults about why they quit exercising, the top reasons are (1) they do not have time, (2) they are too tired after a long day at work, (3) they do not like to and lack sufficient motivation, and (4) life stressors interfere (these are schedule disrupters: injuries, colds, pregnancies, unavailability of facilities, etc.). If these are the barriers, think how much more attainable is the goal of an accumulation of 30 or 60 minutes of daily, light to moderate activity. All the major reasons for not doing activity are blunted if not annihilated. The problem of finding time is still a real one but far from insurmountable. Major blocks of time for preparation, vigorous continuous activity, and cleanup are not required. *Found Activities* throughout the day, when diligently planned and made into routines, can add up to a significant amount of moving. The making clear that strenuous activity is not necessary, and that light activities are acceptable, goes a long way in countering both the arguments of not having enough energy to exercise or not liking to do so. Light intensity activities are simply not onerous and should be found to be enjoyable by most everyone. Walking type activities tend to be much more enjoyable and less fatiguing than those activities demanding sweating and a pounding heart. And *Found Activities* are far less susceptible to all those schedule disrupters such as illnesses, injuries, equipment and facility needs. Unless you are confined to bed there are probably movement possibilities.

---

[2] Cooper, K. *Aerobics*. Bantam Books, 1967.

[3] Undeniably there is further worthwhile benefits to be gained when exercisers add more vigorous aerobic and muscle fitness exercises. These benefits will be covered in Chapter 4.

What then should be our activity goal for school children? I would argue that just as we are coming to believe for adults, we will be more successful in getting all children to continue moving when we make it plain that any level of activity is good for them. The essential thing is that children enjoy moving, any kind of moving, and are encouraged and afforded the opportunity to do so on a regular basis each and every day. *The Children's Lifetime Physical Activity Model (C-LAM)*[4] is worthy of our goal adoption in that it advances this philosophy with well-defined criteria the frequency, intensity and time expectations for children's physical activities. As is outlined in Figure 2.2 the frequency, intensity and time of the children's activity expectations are clearly specified. The model calls for at least an hour a day and that the activity is dispersed over three or more activity bouts (600 calories +). The rationale for setting a bare minimum of 1 hour of activity per day is as follows. We know that activity levels tend to decrease across the school years and life span. It therefore seems wise to shoot for more than the minimal 30 minute a day activity goal we set for adults. Also, children, with their young supple bodies are naturally more ready and interested in physical activities. And developmentally they are in need of ample activity; copious movement experiences contribute to diverse physiological formations ranging from growth of bones and muscles to changes in brain development that are related to cognitive functioning and body/spatial awareness skills.

The specification of 60 minutes a day of a combination of moderate and vigorous activities should be adding up to over 600 calories being burned each day. To give this guideline some relevance, let us translate that into tangible activity for an adult or child? A touchstone could be to think of a 150-pound person walking one mile. Doing this amount of activity would burn approximately 100 calories. Hence we can see that our 600-calorie guideline is calling for the person to engage in about 6 mile of walking everyday or comparable actions. Think how many miles you might cover on the golf course or while playing a game of tennis and you will have a fair estimate of caloric work done. If a child weighed half the 150 pounds of the adult, he/she would necessarily need to

Figure 2.2. Energy Values in Kilocalories per Hour of Selected Activities

	Weight (pounds)					
	95	125	155	185	215	245
Slow walking	86	114	140	168	196	222
Walking, moderate pace	172	228	280	336	392	555
Hiking	258	342	420	504	588	666
Jogging	430	570	700	840	980	1,110
Running	480	770	945	1,134	1,323	1,499
Heavy housework	194	256	315	378	441	500
Sweeping	108	142	175	210	245	278
Scrubbing	237	313	385	462	539	611
Tennis	301	399	490	588	686	777
Golf (carrying clubs)	237	313	385	462	539	611
Golf (in a cart)	151	200	245	294	343	389
Swimming (light laps)	344	456	560	672	784	888
Swimming (hard laps)	430	570	700	840	980	1,110

[4] Developed by *The President's Council of Physical Fitness and Sports.*

cover almost twice as much distance to consume equal calories. See Figure 2.2 for a list of calories burned in different activities. Also, it should be known that whether or not the miles are covered in a slow walk or in a more vigorous running like fashion, as long as the total distance is equivalent, it does not make a big different as far as calories go. Doing activities at higher intensity levels produces other desirable physiological results that we will address more fully in Chapter 4.

The *C-LAM* specification of 3 or more activity bouts everyday is recognition that it is developmentally inappropriate to have children's movement restricted for extended periods during a day. They naturally want to move unless we over time have cribbed, cabined and confined it out of them. Regretfully both schools and home environments have been becoming more and more guilty of doing this.

As for the intensity level of activity, the *C-LAM* designates that children should be engaging not only in light/moderate activities but also in some vigorous bouts interspersed with rest periods. This shows a cognizance of the innately high energy and excitement levels of children. In addition to moderate activities, they are generally receptive to numerous vigorous movements in games and challenges as long as they are provided with needed rests. Experience has taught me that elementary aged children tend to be what I call *Interval Trainers*. That is, they are eager to launch into high intensity episodes and then they quickly tire; but in the next instant they once again are up and running full blast. Pacing is a concept almost entirely lost to them. A mixture of high and low intensity levels is good for them and we should be encouraging it.

Finally, perhaps a defense of the adoption of the *C-LAM* as our goal is in order. There are those who might see acceptance of it as a softening retreat or lowering of goals. They see that we are simply putting less stress on vigorous aerobic activity and muscular training because so many adults and children are doing next to nothing. These critics are aware that the physical fitness levels of children are becoming significantly lower and feel that lessons of disciplined hard work in the form of more calisthenics and steady-state aerobic experiences are in order. My response to this perspective is as follows. I would like to think that by the time of high school graduation each student would know, appreciate, and be applying *The Activity Pyramid*. Of course, that means that in addition to amassing good amounts of light paced found activities; they are participating in recreational activities, sports, or aerobic exercises to achieve higher levels of cardiovascular fitness; and they are doing specific exercises to develop muscular strength and flexibility. I also view it as desirous for them to have formulated an activity plan appropriate to their interest to take beyond the school into early adulthood. However, I do not believe that having *The Activity Pyramid* as our goal for the high school level means we should be equally promoting all aspects of it in the younger grades. Certainly primary level kids just need to be given abundant opportunities to move and have fun doing activities. I want the kids to have the attitude that they like to move. Doing calisthenics and conditioning exercises, either within games or as separate entities, is only okay if all of them think it is fun and just another way to enjoyably move. Perhaps by the intermediate grades some discussion of participation in exercises for exercising sake can be begun. But even here I think our focus needs to remain on the foundation of enjoying a regular combination of light and vigorous games and activities, and that is precisely what the *C-LAM* is stating.

Nutrition

In addition to establishing regular physical activity as a key ingredient in the lives of children, there are many more health practices we will wish to inculcate. Of these other health practices good nutrition is of fundamental importance and deserving of major goal status. In the 1960's when research unequivocally began to document the various health benefits of aerobic exercise, many of the authorities were claiming that here was a panacea for the rampant cardiovascular diseases the our nation. Dr. Kenneth Cooper, the author of the first aerobics book and considered the father of the aerobic movement, once believed that adherence to aerobic activities would actually have the benefit of allowing you to indulge all your dietary inclinations. Because activity would be burning those fats and calories you could eat pretty much as much as you wanted, and whatever you wanted. It was just one of the joyous freedoms conferred by doing aerobics. Since those early days our knowledge of the benefits of physical activity has continued to expand but so has our appreciation of the critical role of sound dietary practices. To be truly healthy, physical activity and a sound diet must compliment each other. Many Americans, even if regularly active, will not be able to avoid cardiovascular diseases, diabetes, excessive body fat, cancers and other impairments if their nutritional practices are bad.

You have heard many divergent views about what foods are good for you and which ones are bad. No doubt, friends and family have vowed, modeled and advised you as to the benefits of extremely different dietary practices. Each year new diet programs, supported by famous scientists and/or the testimonies of celebrities, are marketed in the popular media. The newspapers periodically have articles on some revolutionary nutritional data published in *The New England Journal of Medicine* or some other prestigious source. How do we know what is correct and incorrect for us and our children? It is necessary to say up front that nutrition is a complicated field and admit that there is much that researchers do not yet fully understand. As a consequence, we must realize that any model that is put forth will be necessarily subject to revisions as science progresses. Nevertheless there is a great deal that we have learned from decades of nutritional research. In light of this data, all the various health organizations are in agreement that the fundamental structure of *The Food Guide Pyramid*[5] holds the best hope for healthy living. There is a wealth of date supporting this as the best model of nutrition for Americans ages 2 through geriatrics. Refer to Figure 2.3 for the depiction of *The Food Guide Pyramid.* In the next paragraphs we will clarify its recommendations.

The broad base of the pyramid emphasizes regularly consuming significant amounts of complex carbohydrates (6 to 11 servings). The major sources of these are breads, cereals, rice, and pastas. Overall, these foods should account for approximately 60 percent of total calorie intake. They are a good source of essential vitamins, minerals, and dietary fiber. Complex carbohydrates are our best source of sustained energy supply for the muscles. Whole grain breads, cereal and rice are better than simple sugars because they provide a longer energy supply, contain more fiber, and usually retain more of their vitamins and minerals. Highly processed foods like Twinkies and donuts are carbohydrates but they have been processed down to simple sugars and hence tend to give only short-term energy and are pretty much devoid of all that is good in the form of vitamins, minerals, and fiber. This is why they are referred to as "empty calories" and are classified at the peak of the pyramid under sweets. High intake of sugary foods and drinks correlate strongly with obesity and diabetes.

Fruits and vegetables form the second tier of the pyramid. As you can see the recommended number of servings is 5 to 9. Most fruits and vegetables are also largely made up of complex carbohydrates and as such play the same multiple useful roles in supplying energy, fiber, and different vitamins and minerals. *Five-A-Day* is a useful motto for setting a goal to meet the minimal serving standard for daily fruit/vegetable consumption.

The third tier consists of milk products, meats, beans and nuts. Among other things, foods in these groups supply much of proteins, fats and calcium that we need. Proteins are particularly important for lean tissue/muscle growth and maintenance. Fat is necessary for such things as insulation of internal organs and neuron pathways, brain functioning, and the building of cell membranes. Calcium is well known to be essential for the formation of strong bones and newer evidence is indicating that it plays a role controlling hypertension, obesity, and fighting some types of cancer. The suggested guideline is that proteins account for approximately 10 percent of total calorie intake while fats should not be between 20 to 30 percent. A basic concept of the pyramid is that many Americans exceed the recommended number of servings in these categories and thus they should strive for some moderation (2 to 4 for dairy products, 2–3 for meats, beans and nuts). The

---

[5] U.S. Department of Agriculture, Human Nutrition Information Service, August 1992 Leaflet No. 572.

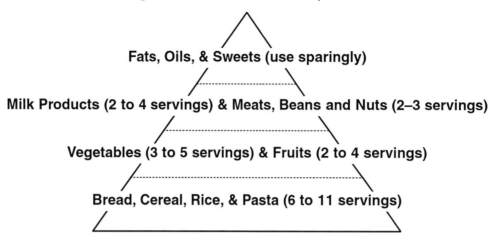

Figure 2.3. Food Guide Pyramid

Fats, Oils, & Sweets (use sparingly)

Milk Products (2 to 4 servings) & Meats, Beans and Nuts (2–3 servings)

Vegetables (3 to 5 servings) & Fruits (2 to 4 servings)

Bread, Cereal, Rice, & Pasta (6 to 11 servings)

WHAT COUNTS AS A SERVING?
* Note: this food guide pyramid is the same for children 6 years of age through adulthood
* Note: this food guide pyramid is also recommended for children age 2 to 5. Their serving sizes should be reduced by about a third.

Bread, Cereal, Rice, and Pasta
Adults and children over age 6:
    1 slice bread or 1 dinner roll
    1 ounce ready-to-eat cereal
    1/2 cup cooked rice, cereal, or pasta
Children under age 6:
    1/2 slice bread
    1/2 ounce ready-to-eat cereal
    1/3 cup cooked rice, cereal, or pasta

Vegetables
Adults and children over age 6:
    1 cup raw leafy vegetables
    1/2 cup cooked or raw chopped vegetables
    3/4 cup vegetable juice
Children under age 6:
    2/3 cup raw leafy vegetables
    1/3 cup cooked or raw chopped vegetables
    1/2 cup vegetable juice

Fruits
Adults and children over age 6:
    1 medium apple, banana, or orange
    1/2 cup cooked or canned fruit
    1/4 cup dried fruit
    3/4 cup fruit juice
Children under age 6:
    1 small apple, banana, or orange
    1/3 cup cooked or canned fruit
    3 tablespoons dried fruit
    1/2 cup fruit juice

Milk, Yogurt, and Cheese
Adult and children over age 6:
    1 cup milk or yogurt
    1 1/2 ounces natural cheese
    2 ounces process cheese
Children under age 6:
    Same serving sizes as for adults

Meat, Poultry, Fish, Dry Beans, Eggs, and Nuts
Adults and children over age 6:
    2 to 3 ounces cooked lean boneless meat, poultry, or fish (3 ounces of meat is approximately the size of a deck of playing cards)
    1 to 1 1/2 cups cooked dry beans
    2 to 3 equivalents of 1 ounce of meat
Children under age 6:
    1 to 2 ounces cooked lean boneless meat, poultry, or fish (3 ounces of meat is approximately the size of a deck of playing cards)
    2/3 to 1 cup cooked dry beans
    1 to 2 equivalent of 1 ounce of meat (1 egg or 2 tablespoons of peanut butter is equivalent to 1 ounce of meat)

most direct problem with protein rich diets has to do with dehydration and its toxic effects on the liver. Concern about too much fat intake is a particularly complicated subject. The primary worry here is the impact it might have on the cardiovascular system. There is evidence that high fat consumption is related to clogging of arteries and the resulting disability of heart attacks and strokes. There are also concerns about fats' association with Alzheimer's disease and various cancers (colon, breast, prostate). A major division in the types of fats is that of *saturated fats* and *unsaturated fats*. *Saturated fats* are the ones most correlated to the above disabilities and therefore are the ones thought best to be limited. Limiting them to no more than 10 percent of total intake is encouraged. Foods that are high in *saturated fats* are the meats and milk products, while the fats in nuts and beans tend to be unsaturated.[6] Vegetable oils are more highly *unsaturated fats* (corn, olive) except for the *topical vegetable oils* (palm and coconut). It follows that cooking with olive and corn oil is more in accordance with the food pyramid than using the *tropical vegetable oils* or lard or butter.[7]

Although over consumption of high fat dairy products can be a problem, some adults and children may not be getting enough calcium. Low fat milk and yogurt are good sources of this calcium and a striking trend exists towards lower consumption of these foods. Figure 2.4 illustrates a pronounced decrease in milk consumption over the past fifty years. This reduction can be accounted

Figure 2.4. Milk and Soft Drink Consumption Over the Past 50 Years: Gallons Per Capita

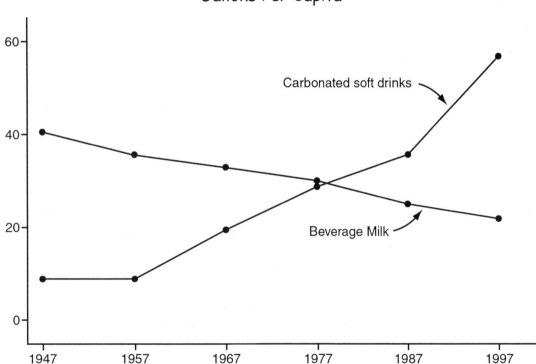

[6] I tell kids to "Go Nuts!" Contrary to popular opinion nuts are not junk foods. They are a great source of protein and other nutritional goodies. People who eat them regularly are less likely to die from heart disease.

[7] If butter is high in the bad saturated type of fat, where does margarine fit in? Margarine brings up a whole new complication. Margarine and many process foods have undergone a process known as *hydrogenation*. At this stage of scientific investigation the effects *of hydrogenated* fats and oils has not been found to be good. We are probably best off trying to stay away or minimize these. Olive oil is better than butter, butter better than margarine.

for by the supplanting of milk with ever increasing imbibing of soft drinks. Get this, the average yearly consumption of soft drinks has risen from around 10 gallons per capita to over 50 gallons. And if that is not disturbing enough, it is worth noting that this Figure 2.4 graph ends at 1997. Since that time we know there has been a great increase in "supersizing" of soft drinks so that it is probably reasonable to assume that the chart is actually understating the current day situation.

Roughly 5 percent of Americans now follow a meatless/fishless diet for one or a combination of reasons. One reason could be a laudable concern for the environment. It indeed requires vastly greater resources and energy to raise animals as opposed to eatable plants. A second reason might come from an increased awareness of animal rights and "speciesism" issues. Finally, some might have adopted vegetarianism in the belief that such a diet is the healthiest and/or a good way to lose weight. When you have vegetarian students in your class, or see fit to discuss it as part of our coverage of nutrition, the *Vegetarian Food Guide Pyramid* in Figure 2.5 should be a helpful model. Such a vegetarian diet can provide complete nutrition and a sufficiency of carbohydrates, fats, and proteins. Concerns about not getting enough proteins in such a diet need not be warranted if adequate levels of beans, milk, cereal, and nuts are being consumed. Cultures that have followed this type of diet have had typically lower rates of cardiovascular disease, obesity and cancer.

Although I believe that adoption of vegetarianism is a good and acceptable alternative diet, healthy adherence to it requires both discipline and knowledge. A child will need instruction and monitoring to see that he/she is getting the needed daily variety of foods such as beans, nuts, tofu, soy, seed oils. Students whose chief motivation is to lose weight are especially prone to violate the principles of the model. And so are those who might be subscribing to the stricter form of vegetarianism known as *veganism. Veganism* precludes not only meats but also all dairy products. Such a diet makes it extremely difficult to achieve a nutritious, balanced diet, and I believe it requires more constant judicious planning than what should be expected of children or, for that matter, most adults.

Finally, I would like to make a few including observations about *The Food Guide Pyramid* serving as our goal. Although we saw in Chapter 1 that the majority of children are happily munching ever so far from the pyramid's criteria (only about 2 percent of children are regularly in full compliance), I sincerely believe that it is an achievable diet that can be sustained for a lifetime. Most other diet plans proscribe certain foods, be it specific food items or all of fats, or all of carbohydrates. This of course is indefensible from a nutritional perspective, but also is impracticable ad-

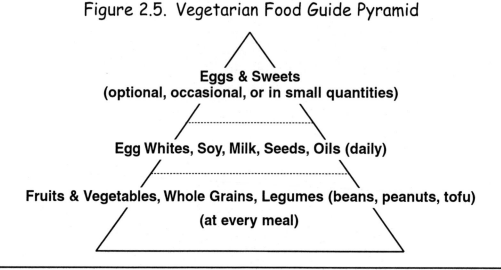

Figure 2.5. Vegetarian Food Guide Pyramid

Eggs & Sweets
(optional, occasional, or in small quantities)

Egg Whites, Soy, Milk, Seeds, Oils (daily)

Fruits & Vegetables, Whole Grains, Legumes (beans, peanuts, tofu)
(at every meal)

herence wise. We know that diets that prohibit certain foods and that promise and produce rapid weight changes are inevitably doomed. The pyramid, although it requires the very real labor of modification to increase or decrease certain types of foods, permits and even calls for foods of all kinds. Its essence is variety and nothing is forbidden. Sweets are allowed as part of the plan. So are the occasional fatty foods. We don't have to be *fat phobic*. You can sometimes have that donut and chocolate cake. It embodies what is known as *The 80-20 Diet Ratio*. This means that the pyramid is not an unmerciful diet. It allows for 20 percent of your calories to come from treats if you are more vigilant with the other 80 percent. It is just that we have to get away from the regular consumption of the same high fat foods: daily hot-dogs, french-fries, and ice cream, etc. And we must upgrade certain foods, notably fruits and vegetables.

I have told my students that it is easy for me to comfortably get at least 7 servings of fruits and vegetables before the day is even half over. The first practice that helps me do this, and this is a worthy stand-alone goal to set for children, is to not skip meals so as to have three meals a day.[8] For my normal breakfast I begin with a glass of juice,[9] have raisins or berries and a banana with whatever (hot or cold cereal, toast, pancakes, etc.), and for a desert something like dates or dried plums. For my normal lunch, besides a bagel or sandwich and maybe some trail mix, I will take one piece of fruit, a can of juice such as V8 juice, and a small bag of vegetables to snack on (carrots, celery, etc.). If you add things up you'll see I made it. Although I then always try to have some fruits or vegetables with my dinner, if I should happen not to I am still above the minimum. The point is that it is not hard if you develop a system and make sure you plan for it when you grocery shop.

Other Healthy Lifestyle Skills and Practices

In order to meet the goal of establishing healthy lifestyles our discussion, to this point, has been limited to promoting two things: regular physical activity and sound nutritional practices. We explained why each was thought to be of overriding importance and models with specific guiding criteria were offered. Although admittedly the current practices of many of our children are far below the standards set forth, these objectives are attainable if they are kept foremost in our minds. They are attainable if the entire school is determined to bring them about.

Our decision to keep things simple by concentrating on physical activity and nutrition in no way means that there are not other worthy objectives to be accomplished in the field of physical and health education. Below are listed other goals that can be accomplished through physical education, and other health habits that good health education can inculcate. It is my philosophy that changes in lifestyle are never easy and hence teachers frequently will need to choose their battles. Changing everyone's peer-influenced behaviors requires both thoughtful instruction and sustained reinforcement. What might be best for you, the beginning teacher, will be to look over this list of potential positive outcomes and identify those for which you have particularly strong feelings. Then direct your efforts towards accomplishing one or two. Over time and experience you will be able to refine your instruction and perhaps broaden your scope somewhat. You know what my two major health lifestyle goals are. I keep them foremost in my heart and mind and planning; and I constantly evaluate the success of my teaching in light of them. Nevertheless, this focusing does not preclude me from hoping, and from finding opportunities and strategies, to change other skills and behaviors.

---

[8] Breakfast is especially important. Evidence exists that children do better of exams when they have had breakfast. What the child eats for breakfast is also important. A meal composed of protein, fat, starch, and sugar will prevent drops in blood sugar for several hours, whereas a breakfast of just starch and sugar will sustain a child for only one to two hours. A drop in blood sugar is associated with a decline in energy and the onset of hunger symptoms.

[9] Any glass of whole juice, except apple juice, counts as a serving. Having the actual fruit is slightly better because of the extra fiber.

Other Goals of Physical Education

✳ Acquisition of fundamental movement skills such as running, leaping, dodging, throwing, striking and catching: These help children develop both body awareness skills and directionality and laterality understanding of the environment. They also lay the foundation of learning of sport specific and recreational skills.

✳ Acquisition of team sport skills, individual sport skills, and recreational skills: These allow children to more readily experience the thrills, excitement, challenges, and camaraderie found in games, sports, and recreational pursuits.

✳ Improve the physical fitness of the students: The basic components of physical fitness are muscular endurance, strength, and flexibility; cardiovascular fitness, body composition.

✳ Develop creativity skills through movement exploration.

✳ Develop appreciation of the games and dances of other cultures.

✳ Acquisition of relaxation skills, problem solving skills, and trust and confidence skills through recreational activities.

✳ Provide a new realm for the integration of other subject content.

✳ Simply provide a break from sedentary classroom activities: Allow children to blow off steam and to stimulate blood flow to their minds.

Other Goals of Health Instruction

✳ Develop good sleeping habits: Children should be getting at least 8 to 9 hours a night.

✳ Develop the habit of keeping the body well hydrated: The basic guideline for adults is 8, 8 ounce glasses of water a day. For children I would moderate that level to something like 3 glasses a day. A good goal would be to get them to substitute some of their sugary drink consumption with water.

✳ Develop the habit of washing hands to reduce the spreading of bacteria.

✳ Develop the habit of regular brushing and flossing of teeth.

✳ Develop the habit of three meals a day, especially breakfast.

✳ Develop safety practices when riding bikes, scooters, and skateboards: This relates to both riding skills and equipment usage such as helmets and kneepads.

✳ Prevention of drug use: Smoking and chewing would be primary topics.

✳ Prevention of violence: Anger control techniques and avoidance of danger from others might be covered.

✳ Prevention of over exposure to the sun.

✳ Develop the habit of seat belt use.

Goal 2: Establish Good Social and Emotional Values

Our second overriding goal is not subject specific. If you were asked why you are studying to become a teacher of elementary children you might give some responses relating to knowledge attainment in various content areas or certain intellectual skills. But I bet that just as frequently, and quite possibly more often, you would give answers such as; "I would like to help children become better people; get along better; be responsible citizens; strive for goals and persist; work well with others no matter the gender, race, economical background; feel good about themselves; be benevolent caring persons." It is the desire to achieve these traits at which my second goal is directed. As much as I value developing healthy lifestyles, and I have made it my life's work, nothing can be more rewarding than helping a child to become a better human being.

Although children can be delightful people with whom to work, it is idyllic to think of children as all little angels. Children are immature and are capable of being self-centered and cruel. It is not uncommon to have children criticize others because of their appearance, performance, or just because they are different in some way. They may choose not to interact with others. They may ostracize the opposite gender, persons with disabilities, or people who are merely not dressed according to an excepted fashion. They will not always play safely, win graciously, accept unsuccessful attempts with equanimity, persevere at tasks, help others, cooperate, etc. I contend that it is the important responsibility of all adults and teachers to educate the young that such behaviors are wrong and to model and instruct them as to what is right and appropriate. For children to learn these correct behaviors the teachers throughout the school will need to be planning and taking advantage of every opportunity to reinforce.

I also believe that the physical education environment is a unique laboratory opportunity for teachers to address the above inappropriate behaviors and to instill desirable ones. When children are participating in emotionally charged physical activities and games they will constantly have to interact with others and to deal with personal responsibility. They are provided with a real test of putting into practice what everyone has been advocating and instructors are positioned to provide timely encouragement and corrective feedback.

Don Hellison is a well-respected physical education teacher who has had extensive experience in teaching social and emotional values to children with behavioral problems. Figure 2.6 shows the six levels of his *Personal and Social Responsibility Model*.[10] Like me, many teachers have used and found the model to be effective in codifying their social and emotional goals. As can be seen, it advances a system for codifying specific levels of children's social and emotional functioning. It provides an ultimate goal of helping children become caring people and it spells out what that entails. Also, understandable interim steps to reach that goal are outlined.

In conclusion, I have kept this chapter short and have presented only two goals: the establishment of (1) good physical activity & health habits and (2) good emotional & social values. Furthermore I narrowed our definition of these goals to 60 minutes of daily activity, adherence to *The Food Guide Pyramid,* and the self-responsible/caring behaviors as outlined by Hellison. I have offered these limited goals in the hopes of illustrating a simple to remember guiding focus. It has not been my intention that you must necessary adopt these exact goals or models. Rather, I hope you will consider them as a possible foundation for your own philosophy and goal formulation. If you know your purpose, then as the chapter introductory quote by T.T. Munger said, you have the ". . . eternal condition of success."

---

[10] Hellison, D. *Teaching Responsibility Through Physical Activity.* Human Kinetics, 1995.

Figure 2.6. Personal and Social Responsibility Model (PSRM)
Six Developmental Levels

Level 0: Irresponsibility
Students who are unmotivated and undisciplined. Their behavior includes discrediting or making fun of other students' involvement as well as interrupting, intimidating, manipulating, and verbally or physically abusing other students and perhaps the teacher. They make excuses and blame others for their behavior and deny personal responsibility for what they do or fail to do.

Level I: Self-Control
Students who may not participate in the day's activity or show much mastery or improvement, but are able to control their behavior enough so that they do not interfere with other students' right to learn and the teacher's right to teach. They do this without much prompting by the teacher and without constant supervision.

Level II: Involvement
Students who not only show self-control and respect for others, but are involved in the subject matter.

Level III: Self-Responsibility
Students who learn to take more responsibility for their choices and for linking these choices to their own identities. They are able to work without direct supervision, eventually taking responsibility for their intentions and actions.

Level IV: Caring
Students who are motivated to extend their sense of responsibility by cooperating, giving support, showing concern, and helping.

Level V: Outside-of-Class Caring
Students who apply the upper levels outside the program - on the playground, at school, at home, on the street.

How You Might Get Children to Enjoy Physical Activities and Conditioning Exercises

3

Getting Children to Enjoy Physical Activities
    Exposure to a Wide Variety of Activities
    Facilitating Successful Perceptions
    Teaching Perseverance

Getting Children to Enjoy Conditioning Exercises
    Sanctioning All Intensity Levels
    Setting Self-Performance Goals

"Stop thinking of exercise as more of that self-improvement stuff and start thinking of it as rescue: private time, a tranquilizer (and energizer), an antidote for the poisons of modern life . . . Exercise: how badly that term fails to capture the excitement and reward that hard use of the human body can bring."

John Jerome

"True enjoyment comes from activity of the mind and exercise of the body; the two are ever united."

Humbolt

"I wish to preach, not the doctrine of ignoble ease, but the doctrine of the strenuous life"

Theodore Roosevelt

"Such is the constitution of man, that labor may be styled its own reward.— Nor will any external incitements be requisite if it be considered how much happiness is gained, and how much misery escaped, by frequent and violent agitation of the body."

Samuel Johnson

When I speak of *physical activities* I am referring to a continuum of movement experiences; highly organized competitive sports would be at one end, informal endeavors such as leisurely walking or gardening would be at the other. Normally we participate in these because we enjoy something about the activity itself. Any physiological conditioning benefits we might incur from these activities may be important to us, but are generally secondary to our intrinsic interest in the activity. On the other hand, I am defining *conditioning exercises* as movement endeavors which are done not primarily for the fun of the activity itself, but for the physiological benefits that will be derived. We might do conditioning exercises so as to facilitate the ability to play sports better and lessen chances of injury. Or we might do them simply to improve or attempt to maintain general physical capabilities for everyday healthful living and appearance. Calisthenics would normally fall into this category as would weight training and stretching exercises. Clearly, in using these definitions, there is no fixed demarcation between *physical activities* and *conditioning exercises.* Many people might jog and participate in aerobic dance classes solely for physical benefits and would quit if they thought their fitness would not suffer too much. But there are others who might come to enjoy the doing of these same activities for the rhythmic feelings, the sheer joy of moving, the psychological rewards, and for social reasons.

If we expect people to lead active lifestyles which will promote their health, it is essential for them to have at least one, but better yet, a range of physical activities they enjoy. Surely finding and integrating physical activities into one's life is best achieved at young ages. Children will normally choose to be active given the opportunities and encouragement. But if movement skills and habits are not learned and enjoyed during the childhood years the likelihood increases that such a lifestyle will become foreign to them and adoption will be more difficult.

In addition to participating in physical activities, people eventually need to realize that incorporating physical conditioning exercises into their lives may be necessary if they wish to maintain well-rounded, balanced health. Most activities will not develop or maintain all of the important components of health. Also, as we age, exercise becomes more essential for safe and successful continuance of the activities we enjoy. Did you ever hear the adage, "I do not play sports to condition myself, rather I condition myself so I can play sports." This may be slightly over stating the role of conditioning, but it does have some validity. Finally, we should be aware that adults typically will find it difficult to devote as much time to physical activities as they were able to when younger. The mature demands of work and family will typically abbreviate the perhaps long hours of youth spent at the gym or playing fields. Encountering these time constraints will necessitate a greater reliance upon time efficient conditioning exercises. In my younger years it was not uncommon for me to play sports for two or more hours most very day. Now I must assiduously schedule my time for my goal of about an hour a day; and because of that reduced time, I feel it has become more necessary to concentrate that activity and devote much of it to balanced conditioning rather than more leisurely physical activity.

It is probably unnecessary to put much stress on conditioning exercises when working with primary level children. At this stage we hope that the children will be becoming accustomed to being active, enjoying moving and performing movement skills, being creative and explorative, and playing simple non-competitive games. It is probably too early for them to be much concerned about doing specific activities for fitness reasons or attempting to do exercises in a prescribed manner. Telling children to exercise for the sake of "staying healthy" simply isn't very effective. Long-term health is about #63 on a child's priority list. Fun is #1. However, during the intermediate grades, while major emphasis should still be directed at exploring enjoyable physical activities, some introduction to conditioning exercises would seem appropriate. Children at this age are beginning to play sports more vigorously and thus it is important for them to begin to understand the need for achieving minimal levels of fitness to do those sports successfully and safely. While we do not favor children being heavily involved in weight training and long demanding aerobic workouts to achieve high levels of performance in a specific sport, the learning and practicing of warm-up and cool-downs, some stretching and calisthenics such as curl-ups makes sense. They should be beginning to appreciate activities for the indispensable contributions they make toward cardiovascular, musculoskeletal, and body composition fitness. It is not too soon for them to learn that they need to begin taking care of their bodies.

Getting Children to Enjoy Physical Activities

There are three things teachers can do which will result in children coming to enjoy regular physical activity. (1) They need to encourage and expose children to a wide variety of activities. By so doing it is hoped they will encounter those activities which are well suited to their unique physical abilities and temperament. (2) When students are experiencing a new activity the teacher must attempt to insure that they will be reasonably successful or, more importantly, perceive that they are successful. This is because the students normally will want to continue participating in activities in which they feel competent and often will not remain with those where they see themselves incompetent. (3) The children may also need to be taught a certain degree of perseverance. Many physical activities require serious practice before the skills can be effectively performed. Individuals who have not learned to persevere may give up during the early difficult goings.

Below we will separately discuss ideas for how you might accomplish these three things.

Exposure to a Wide Variety of Physical Activities

If children are not exposed to a wide variety of activities many of them may not discover those they would find most rewarding. The breadth of activities encountered in and out of school is frequently quite narrow. Not uncommonly, curriculums may only emphasize a few different team sports. While these sports will be attractive to many students they are not necessarily the best solution for decreasing the hypoactivity of American children. When you think of all the diverse kinds of movement activities, everyone should be able to find one, if not many activities, he/she would enjoy doing on a regular basis (see Figure 3.1). In support of this view, we should realize that most people probably have some movement abilities which would allow them to be fairly successful at certain types of activities. Research tells us that there are many kinds of relatively specific

Figure 3.1. Some of the Activities Children Have Enjoyed in Elementary School

Walking and Hiking

Skating (roller-skates, roller-blades, skateboards)

Bicycling (bicycling safety, on-grounds obstacle courses, off-grounds community rides)

Cross-country jogging

Dance (folk, square, country, creative, jazz)

Step aerobics

Kickboxing

Circus activities (juggling, footbags, unicycles)

Frisbee games and activities

Tumbling

Jump rope

Tennis

Badminton

Golf

Relaxation-imagery

Judo

Challenge courses (ropes, obstacle, climbing walls)

Orienteering

Traditional team sports (volleyball, softball, basketball, flag football, hockey)

Track-and-Field

Swimming

motor abilities and that it is wrong to think of people as being either athletic or not. This is known as the *specificity of motor abilities hypothesis*. The implication of this concept is that different types of activities and sports draw on different abilities. For example, children who do not have the abilities and/or temperament to excel at basketball or soccer could do very well and enjoy roller-blading, dance or swimming. Cross-country jogging or yoga may fit the hidden talents of others. Even people with severe physical disabilities might still have other abilities that allow them to skillfully participate in certain movement skills; sight impaired individuals have been Olympic track performers and wrestlers; people who have lost significant use of their legs have won national championships in archery, gymnastics, and many others sports.

Although most sports require some degree of ability to perform well, it is important to make the point that it is not necessary for people to be athletically gifted in order to live an active life. I think this is a lesson of which all young people need to be made aware. I have a number of friends who would not be considered athletic at all, and yet they regularly enjoy moving and are healthy as a consequence. They do things like walking, cycling, inline skating, backpacking, and lifting weights. Walking probably has the greatest carryover potential of any activity for keeping many Americans active. We must dispense with the idea the "walking is whimpy." It probably is the most reasonable of all long-term activities and to my mind we should be regularly walking kindergarders, twelfth graders, and everyone in between. What if you established the routine of taking your class on a daily walk? You might not have the skills or abilities to run and jump rope but you can successfully walk and so, barring a serious disability, will all your students. You would be role modeling an active lifestyle right alongside your kids. Any academic subject you might be teaching in the classroom could be reinforced on the walks. Many of the children may have never experienced 10 or 20 continuous minutes of rhythmic aerobic exercise before reaching the sixth grade. A healthy practice, like a fun walk, could become etched in a kindergartner's mind for life. Figure 3.2 charts some reasonable guidelines for that would be good for the younger children.[1] Figure 3.3 presents a number of games to sometimes spice up walking or running activity. Be sure to look them over. They can be so fun and easy to do by all, and yet so beneficial.

Figure 3.2. Reasonable Distances (Round-Trip) for Walking Field Trips

	To start with (miles)	Later in the year (miles)
Kindergarten	½–¾	1–1½
First Grade	¾–1	1½–2
Second Grade	1–1½	2–3
Third Grade	1½–2	3–4

Figure 3.3. Fun Run-Walk Activities

Conversational Jogging
This is the official name of the activity but I have also called it RUNNING AT THE MOUTH. Students are asked to find a friend and to begin jogging (this works great as a walking activity as well). As they complete a lap or so the teacher holds up a sign indicating a topic of conversation: "your favorite book," "what I'm doing for the holidays," "my favorite animal," "my best sport's experience," etc.).

Following the activity is a good time to talk to the students about the run or walk. Hopefully some students can be made to realize that these activities can be made enjoyable by conversation and that the time went rapidly

Time Estimation Run
The perimeter of a full size basketball court equals 288 feet; therefore 18.33 laps equals 1 mile; 9.16 laps = ½ mile. Everyone initially estimates how long it will take him or her to run a mile (or whatever distance selected). They keep track of their laps and tell the teacher when they reach the finish line. He/she whispers the time to them. As they are cooling down they must calculate the number of seconds between their estimated and the actual time. When everyone has finished the instructor surveys to see how well everyone paced themselves.

---

[1] R. Sweetgall & R. Neeves, *Walking for Little Children.* Creative Walking, Inc. 1987.

I have done this run at Halloween and called it the PUMPKIN RUN. The students with the closest estimates won pumpkins.

Nature Walk

I am amazed at how little most children, and even adults, know about the natural environment around them. Ahead of time, all or some of the students are given a specific topic that they are to learn to identify. They must also find out some interesting information pertaining to it. These topics are natural things that will be likely encountered on the hike you have selected. Possibilities in your neighborhood park might be an oak tree, lilac bush, house sparrow, starling, crab grass, basalt rock, and ladybug. If the student sees his/her assigned subject on the walk, the student stops the class and tells some interesting fact about it. Sometimes it might be fun to take along binoculars or even a camera.

Another nature option would be to take along a checklist and see how many different birds, trees, mammals, insects, or flowers could be identified.

Good Citizen Clean-Up Walk

I am also amazed that many children are careless about dropping wrappers, cups, etc. When I go for a walk I generally make it a habit to pick-up at least one bit of litter. It seems to me a good environmental lesson to have the kids do the same. A garbage bag and some plastic gloves would be good to take along.

Card Run

Children are to run a course, maybe for 15 minutes. Each time they pass the teacher they get a playing card. A figure 8 shaped course works well because the students pass the teacher more frequently and thus accumulate more cards. After the time is up and everyone is cooling down, some games may be played with the cards: anyone with three of a kind gets a reward, anyone with two pairs gets a reward, etc. You can see that the more cards someone has earned the better he/she is likely to do in the card games.

Alphabet Walks

Students try to spot objects whose first letter spells out the 26 letters of the alphabet. Students should report them in alphabetical order and actually see them. Can you or your team go from A to Z in 20–30 minutes?

Walk Across America

Keep a map on your classroom wall and plot your daily progress using your classes' total miles. Using your daily averages, how many days would it take to walk across America? Where would you be by a certain date such as Memorial Day? Could you do it in 80 days?

If 30 of your children averaged about 10 minutes of walking daily (a half mile each), then by the end of the school year your class would have totaled 3,000 miles walking—the distance from Independence Hall in Philadelphia, Pennsylvania to The Space Needle in Seattle, Washington. And all along the way you could be discussing our nation's geography, history and culture while practicing mileage addition.

Walk with the Principal

Each week one of the students in the school is rewarded for doing something good. The reward is the privilege of walking with the Principle on Friday afternoon.

I read were an elementary school principal had a policy of inviting two students outside at lunch for long walking conversations every day. It was an offer her students could not refuse. After several weeks, she selected two new children to accompany her. This rotation would go on throughout the school year. Everyone got a chance to walk. Being selected was not a punishment either. It was simply this principal's way of controlling her weight and finding out what was really going on in her school.

While I think it would be great if you could get your principal to participate in this way, an alternative might be to schedule it yourself, WALK WITH THE TEACHER.

The Calorie Run

In preparation for this run, you need to list a variety of foods, determine the calorie content of each food, and figure out how far your average student would have to run to burn off the calories in each food. You can use a burn rate of 20–25 calories per quarter mile to estimate distance. Write each food name, calorie content, and distance on a separate card, and put all the cards in a box. Each student draws a card and then runs the required distance to burn the calories. Once students understand the assignment, you may hear them say they want an apple or orange instead of a candy bar!

pad of butter	45 calories	1 tablespoon of mayonnaise	99 calories
orange	64 calories	10 french fries ($3^1/_2$")	214 calories
banana	101 calories	baked potato	145 calories
carrot ($7^1/_2$")	15 calories	potato chips (10)	114 calories
raised doughnut	124 calories	broccoli ($^1/_2$ cup)	20 calories

The Straw Walk

Challenge your students to walk at their fastest maintainable pace on a $^1/_4$-mile track. Reward students with one soda straw for every lap they complete. After 15 minutes, whistle everyone to stop. Have all walkers measure their heart rates, then record their own straw walk scores (the number of straws collected plus any fractional lap, e.g. 4 straws + $^1/_2$ lap = 4.5 straw walk score = 4.5 mph pace). Every straw represents 1 mph in speed because everyone is moving on a $^1/_4$-mile track for $^1/_4$ hour.

The Little Straw Walk

The primary purpose of The Little Straw Walk is to get children moving at their fastest aerobic walking pace for a sustained period of time. The course can be built on a fairly small playground area. Make a circular or oblong track using 10 cones. The cones are placed $17^1/_2$ yards apart so that you end up with a 175-yard or 1/10th of a mile course.

Line the kids up at the starting line. Blow a whistle and start your stopwatch. Reward them with straws each time they complete a lap. Blow a final, 6-minute whistle to freeze everyone in place. Since The Little Straw Walk is a 1/10th-hour walk on a 1/10th-mile loop, the score turns out to be your exact mile-per-hour walking pace. Thus, if Johnny is standing next to the 5th cone on the course with 3 straws in his hand when the whistle blows, that means Johnny is a 3.5-mph walker.

How Fit Are Your Little Walkers?

	3 Straws	3½ Straws	4 Straws	4½ Straws	5 Straws
Kindergarten	G	VG	E	O	O
1st grade	G	VG	E	E	O
2nd grade	F	G	VG	E	

The Pacer

The PACER (Progressive Aerobic Cardiovascular Endurance Run) is an aerobic running challenge for K on up. The objective is keep up with the music. The children run back and forth across a 20-meter distance. The music is slow to start with but it gradually gets faster and faster. To do this one you will need to order the tape, but it is not expensive and would be worth the effort. The children will love it and you will be able to use it many times. (The FITNESSGRAM, developed by The Cooper Institute for Aerobics Research, Dallas, TX. 75230, (214) 701-8001.

Landmark Orienteering

Students may be given 15 minutes to get to as many control points as possible. With a partner (joined at the wrist) they are to locate each control point as described below. When reaching each control point they are to identify the appropriate information in the space provided and then move on to the next point. A 1-minute grace period to return to the staring point will be given.

1. What is the street number on the building to the West of the school building?

   _____
   10 pts

2. How many windows are there on the front of the school building?

   _____
   5 pts

3. What is the inscription on the softball fields backstop?

   _____
   20 pts

4. How many trees are in the field next to the soccer field?

   _____
   10pts

5. What color is the door of the utility shed next to the playground equipment?

   _____
   5pts

Cross Country Orienteering

Each student is given a marker and his/her own copy of a map of the area. A number of checkpoints have been marked on it. The task is to find all of the checkpoints as quickly as possible. Each checkpoint has attached to it a small plastic bag with a cardboard model of one item (symbol, anima, vegetable). The student records the item and returns to the starting point.

Kids Marathon

Kids run a marathon? Yes, but not all at once: Here's how it works:

The Seattle Kids Marathon is a non-competitive running or walking event. Maybe you could use some of their ideas to create something.

* Establish a measured safe, route that is easily accessible to participant

* Participants run, or walk, the course to total 25 miles within a 6 week period

* Students keep journal entries of their training experience

* Students who complete the 25 miles qualify for the culminating event

* The event is a 1.2 mile run or walk to the Finish Line of the Seattle Marathon

* Students receive milepost awards, a certificate and a T-shirt

For more specifics: http://www.seattlemarathon.org/kids.asp

Ironkids Triathlon

Another way to spice up a running program would be to tie it in with biking or even swimming. This obviously would require some significant organization but it could be great fun. The basics of the National IronKids Triathlon are listed below to give you some ideas. The competition is divided between boys and girls, and then by age. The kids can get friends and compete as a relay team so that everyone does not have to do each event. Although I think it would be great to have swimming as part of the event, organizing a Biathlon would be more feasible compromise.

Age: 7–10 years
   Swim: 100 meters
   Cycle: 5 km/3.1 miles
   Run: 1 km/ .6 miles

Age: 11–14 years
   Swim: 200 meters
   Cycle: 10 km/ 6.2 miles
   Run: 2 km/ 1.2 miles

For more specifics: http://216.15.198.22/html/tria/tria_info.html

---

Undoubtedly there are things that will limit your ability to introduce many other activities to your classes: your knowledge and skills, your facilities and equipment, your preparation time. However, it might make a big difference to some, if each year you could have your class participate in at least one or two new things beyond what they normally encounter in their traditional curriculum. If actual participation is unmanageable, it may be worthwhile discussing and listing various activity possibilities. An enthusiastic talk from you might be enough to get some of the children to give it a try outside of school. You could personalize and explain the different activities you and your friends like to do. Also, ask the students what kinds of activities they do to be regularly active and praise them for it. I have known many children and adults who as a result of unsuccessful attempts at a limited range of activities have concluded that they were "not athletic" and did not enjoy sports. A little timely encouragement from you could make the difference. Inviting guest speakers from the community and various clubs might be effective. Many individuals and groups (bicycle clubs, karate clubs, volts marchers, etc.) are ready and eager to introduce their favorite activity.

Facilitating Successful Perceptions

Encouraging and providing children the opportunity to participate in a wide variety of activities, that range from light-paced non-competitive experiences to vigorous challenges, will result in most of them finding some movement experiences enjoyable. But another reason some will not find activities enjoyable, even when an activity is potentially suited to their likes and abilities, is how well they can initially do the skill or how well they feel they are doing (of course this is more of a risk in the games and sports requiring more skill and fitness). In Chapter 6 you will be given many ideas about how to design the learning environment to make skill performance easier and more successful. For now, let us address the basis upon which children form perceptions about their successfulness. This is important because even though they may be reasonably accomplishing a task, they still could be dissatisfied with their performance and hence discontinue its pursuit. Being overly self-critical of one's performance, along with being too tenderly sensitive to what others may think, is arguably the greatest cause of failing to pursue a new activity.

Normally children in the primary grades judge the goodness of their performance on the feedback they receive from significant adults, most commonly their parents and teachers. They want the adults' attention and if they are given praise for their performance they will accept it and conclude they are doing good. Since most parents and teachers are supportive and encouraging, young children typically have high self-concepts of their abilities. It is not uncommon to hear remarks such as, "I am the strongest boy in the world, feel my muscle!" "I can run fast!" "Watch me!" Children enjoy most activities at this stage because they are told, and faithfully believe, that their performance is good. The obvious recommendation for teachers hoping to further these attitudes is to be liberal in their praise of the children's attempts. We should be encouraged by the extraordinary influence we have at this stage in the child's development, but it is also a weighty responsibility. Sadly, the

Word of Caution about Conditional Praise

I stand by my recommendation to praise children for their early performance efforts as a means of facilitating their successful perceptions. However, we must always be watchful that in employing operant conditioning techniques that we do not unintentionally undermine the inherent motivation to enjoy an activity. Consider this story of an old man whose sleep was disturbed each Saturday morning by the regular early morning pick-up baseball games of the neighborhood kids. One Saturday he goes to the sandlot and tells the kids how much it warms his heart to hear them playing their game. In fact, he likes it so much he gives them a twenty dollar bill and asks them to be sure to come back next Saturday and hoop it up. Of course, the next Saturday the games are started early with everyone in full throat and vigor. As the games are finishing the old man comes out and again praises all of them. But this time he says he is a little short of cash and gives them a ten-dollar bill. The players are still pleased and promise to return in seven days. Events are much the same during the third week but the old man now can only afford to part with five dollars. The enthusiasm of the children is not nearly as great but they take it and plan on meeting again. Finally week four arrives as do the kids and play occurs. The old man appears and maybe you guessed it, while he enjoys the games he announces that he is out of money and can no longer pay them. When he asks if he can plan of their return the following week one of the children pipes up, "No way, I am not coming to play for nothing!" And other voices of rebellion agree.

Our highest objective is for the children to be *intrinsically motivated*. I think it is fun to walk, or run, or play sports and that is the long-term attitude I want the children to develop. When we continually make our praise and rewards contingent on performance some children might become controlled by it, as were the children in the story of the old man. They see that they are doing the activity for those things, not for the activity itself. They are *extrinsically motivated* and when the rewards are gone, they see no further reason to do the activity for its own sake. Perhaps the best approach to avoid this undermining of intrinsic motivation is to always begin and continue to stress the inherent worth of the activity. Remember to convey the expectation that the activity is interesting and fun to do; that you or others like it and look forward to doing it. As for praising and rewarding performance, try to do so only when you think some individuals are encountering difficulties and are not yet seeing the enjoyment of it. Hopefully, as they continue you may be able to fade the use of rewards and praise. The lesson is that if the students are having a good time just doing it, let it sell itself. That is where we want to end up.

powerful influence of adult feedback can be all too well documented in those children who have had abusive and unsupportive parents or teachers. Young people in such environments often have extremely low perceptions of self-worth and capabilities. Of course, it is doubly important for us to give encouragement to individuals who have had this kind of debilitating background.

As children move into the intermediate grades their basis of reference begins to change. They typically are no longer wholly accepting of elders. Now you might hear, "Come on Dad try, you are letting me win!" Teachers are less likely to hear, "Watch me." Increasingly the children become more aware of the performance of their peers and begin to value their acceptance above all else. They become more realistic, discovering themselves to perhaps not be the strongest or fastest. The feedback peers give each other is sometimes not as kind and diplomatic as it should be. This social comparison process results in an inevitable lowering of self-concepts for some. This is a major factor in why children are no longer quite so unanimously pleased with new activity endeavors and why large numbers begin to be less enthused with sports programs and may completely drop out. Everyone cannot be first-place winners, and if enjoyment is viewed as being contingent upon performing as well or better than others, one's activity options are unnecessarily limited.

The appropriate role for the teacher at this stage in the children's development, as well as later, would seem to be to attenuate or soften this social comparison process. Some believe that many overzealous parents, teachers and coaches do just the opposite. They create *hypercompetition* by always keeping scores, recording ranking and giving special recognition to top performers. Charts are posted depicting which skills have and have not been accomplished by whom. The intent of these efforts is to provide extra incentives to make the children strive harder and be happier with awarded successes. The danger is that many are taught to think even more along social comparison lines. Also, I would argue that the students who will receive the most positive recognition are going to be the top performers who are oftentimes least in need of it. They are more likely already sold on the activity. On the other hand, the message provided to a large number of other students, whose liking for the activity could go either way, is a discouraging one. These tender growing shoots see that social comparison is to be valued and that, in this instance, they are only average or sub par. Euphemistic scales ranging from good to above average to great should not be expected to disguise this reality from them.

The implication to be drawn is not that we should never put children in competitive sports and other social comparison situations. These activities can be excitingly fun and they have the potential of teaching many lessons. However, there also are good reasons for having the children participate in physical activities and exercises where the focus is on self, rather than inter-student comparisons. Learning to direct attention to one's own physical performance is a more necessary lesson than always worrying about beating or being beaten by some else.

Regardless of how socially competitive the learning environment is, the feedback you habitually provide is also a factor in whether or not social comparisons will be promoted or reduced. Its intent should be to direct the students' attention toward their own performance and its progress. You want the students to realize that enjoyment is found in doing and self-improvement and is independent of others. This means that as children are sampling new activities and accessing their performance, you should try to avoid saying things like, "How many reached 20?" "Did you win?" "Who could do it?" Rather, say, "If you gave it your best, you should be proud of your effort and progress." "Lets see if everyone can do more than last time." "Don't worry about what others are doing, be your best." "Sure it is difficult, that is part of the challenge and fun." "Did you have fun?" "Did you learn?" If through persistent feedback we could sway them to adopt some *performance goals* rather than thinking only of *outcome goals* where they are concerned about who is better than whom, enjoyment of activities should be open to many more people. I have known many people to truly enjoy participating in sports even though their level of play was much below average. It did not much matter to them, and indeed why should it. Pleasure was in the doing and the benefits were just as rich.

Also, because the feedback the child gets from the other children is coming to have great valence, we need to emphasize their social responsibility of helping and caring. Being laughed at or criticized by peers can be devastating to one's feelings about their skills or appearance. We simply cannot permit such to occur. We need to be constantly rewarding good interactions and informing them of why unkind behaviors are hurtful. I will have more to say about this in Chapter 9.

Teaching Perseverance

Perseverance is one of the important moral lessons that participation in physical activities is well suited to teach. Many physical skills cannot be accomplished immediately, but if continued effort is put forth, rewarding, tangible results will soon occur. What can you do to help children persist long enough at an activity, to get through the rough going, and experience the joy of achievement? This is an important question because persistence is characteristically low in many children.

They simply have not learned the necessity of working and delaying need gratification. I have had many children make a few attempts at a task and then say quite resignedly, "I don't like this." "I can't do it, I tried but I can't do it."

There are a number of things you can do to facilitate persistence. To begin with when introducing a skill make clear to the students that it may well require lengthy practice before they will be completely successful. Tell them it will take some people longer than others. When a skill is being demonstrated either by you or another skilled model, be sure to explain how much practice was required to reach this level of proficiency. Whenever I give a competent demonstration of a gymnastic stunt, a throw, a jump-rope skill, I make it a point to explain that thousands of trials and often years of practice have gone into mastery. If possible I also give a brief account of the initial difficulties and frustration. In fields of endeavor as diverse as chess, sports, and music, there exist what is known as *The Ten Year Rule.* A substantial body of evidence suggests that elite performers require about 10 to 12 years of regular quality practice to acquire the necessary skills and experience to perform at an international level. The very best violinists have been found to have spent over 10,000 hour in "deliberate practice" (deliberate practice is defined as an effortful activity mo-

Supplement Story

This discussion of perseverance brings to mind a personal experience. A number of years ago I decided to take a watercolor class through the city's recreation department. I had little knowledge of my abilities in this area but I figured it might be fun to try something new. The first night the instructor gave a slide presentation of his painting career. We all knew that he was an excellent professional painter and the slides of his later works confirmed that in all our eyes. He also showed examples of some of the paintings when he was beginning art school over twenty years ago. These early works were not at all impressive and he good-naturedly admitted that to be the case.

I struggled throughout the eight weeks of class. My paint ran where I did not want them, my colors were muddy, and my shapes were unerringly distorted. Many times I thought about quitting and I noticed that about two thirds of the class members had done so by the last night. That last night of class, the painting I was doing turned out a good bit better than my pervious ones. I was cautiously proud of it and my instructor and remaining classmates were kindly congratulatory. That small success and timely encouragement was enough to keep me painting following the cessation of the class. I have continued to pursue this hobby over the years and have derived much reward from it.

Although the instructor and student praise was important, I believe that the early slide show was an indispensable key to my continuing to paint throughout the class and beyond. I wanted to skillfully paint like he did, but my performances were so inferior to his demonstrations. What kept me going was recalling the weakness of his beginning efforts. I convinced myself that maybe my attempts were not all that discouragingly bad; my messes were about as good as his, and it took him twenty years to get where he was today.

Today, when I am teaching physical skills, especially to children, I attempt to apply this valued lesson learned from my art instructor. I don't rely upon praise alone, I make it a habit it let beginners know how much time has gone into the skills I or others are demonstrating. And if I cannot give them visible evidence of how much weaker the initial attempts were, I at least can attempt to describe some of those difficulties.

tivated by the goal of improving performance). The average intermediate level violinists have spent "only" 8,000 hours. Estimates are that basketball players have performed over one million shots before they get to the professional level. The lesson is clear, if your kids want to be like Michael Jordan, they have to "Practice, practice, practice." "But, hey! what could be more fun?"

As the children are engaged in the activity you need to keep reinforcing the persistence theme. Rather than directing verbal reinforcement toward best performances, habitually look for effort and publicly recognize it. Those who truly tried hard are deserving of all your kudos, regardless of their level of performance or even if they did not improve. Those who easily succeed do not need much praise and are not necessarily deserving of it. When you see effort flagging tell them you have confidence that they eventually can get there. When you hear the dispirited, "I can't," and you regularly will, apply *The Yet Principle.* You cannot do it 'yet' but you will if you keep trying. William James said "Effort is the measure of a man." We must teach children this precept.

Finally, we can foster stick-to-it-ness by helping the children detect any performance improvements that may be occurring. Sometimes the students will not know that their technique is becoming more fluid and efficient, or they may not remember that their performance outcomes were worse than what they have now become. For some skills, assessment and/or charting might lend credence to our encouragement or make you aware of advances being made that you had not detected. Plotting out the number of times targets have been hit over a week, two weeks, or over a much longer time frame could make for a good exercise. This could be done for individuals or groups. Repeated recording of times needed to get through an obstacle course or the number of minutes and seconds of successful rope jumping would be other examples. In a later chapter the idea of having students keep portfolios will be introduced. These graphings of performance over a period of time would make a nice project.

Getting Children to Enjoy Conditioning Exercises

Is it possible to get children to actually enjoy conditioning exercises? If we adhere to the definition presented at the beginning of this chapter, physical conditioning exercises cannot really be enjoyable, if they become enjoyable they are no longer conditioning exercises but pass into the realm of physical activities. This sort of desirable transition is sometimes feasible. I know people, myself included, who over a period of time doing exercises such as swimming, jogging, and stretching have actually reached a point of truly enjoying those activities. So much so that they would do those activities even if no physical health benefits were concomitant. Hopefully a high degree of liking would develop for some of your students. More probably for most students it is unrealistic to expect that physical conditioning exercises will be actually relished. They will remain conditioning exercises and may not become especially enjoyable physical activities. But recognizing this reality does not mean that most need to view exercising with loathing or even dislike. I know many people who have learned to accept exercises as a not unpleasant aspect of their normal routine. Indeed, virtually all those people who have developed the habit of exercising over an extended time period seem to have achieved this status. If exercise is truly onerous to somebody, it is the exceptional person who would long persevere at it.[2] Let us look at two things we can do which may help to make exercise enjoyable, or nearly so.

---

[2] Allow me a small philosophical excursion. I have read some of Eastern teachings which stress living in the presence, life is short and every moment and activity is precious. They advocate cultivating an enjoyment of sitting quietly, eating, talking, working, etc. My application of this belief has taught me to appreciate exercise for itself and not be doing it solely for some future benefit. I see exercise as a "celebration of life" and think it important that I do what I can to help others develop such a perspective.

Sanctioning All Intensity Levels

One factor strongly related to the enjoyment of exercise is how strenuous it is. Generally, although the relationship does not apply to everyone, the more strenuous the exercise the less pleasurable it is perceived to be. There is a wealth of evidence showing lower intensity exercise programs such as walking and hiking are rated as being more enjoyable than jogging, aerobic dance, step aerobics, and aerobic swimming activities. As a consequence, the more vigorous exercises are not maintained nearly as well. Only about 10 percent of the population are successful in long-term adherence to these more heart thumping pursuits. This evidence should teach us that if we place all, or even most of our instructional emphasis upon high intensity exercise, we are doomed to be unsuccessful with many children. Most people simply will not subscribe in the long run to a strict "no pain, no gain" philosophy.

My recommendation is that we sanction all intensity levels of exercise: vigorous, moderate, and light. All are good for you and you need to find those with which you can be comfortable. We should expose all the children to some vigorous conditioning exercises and explain the special health benefits they confer (In Chapter 4 we will be explaining guidelines and benefits of vigorous exercise). Many children are very energetic and can become quite enthused about exercise given the encouragement and right environment. Likely you will have students who are eager and will prefer moving at high levels. A goal for these children is to keep them interested and to accustom them to regular practices.

Some of your students will find it more difficult to savor vigorous conditioning. These children need to be of special interest to us because it is they that are at greatest risk of becoming sedentary and suffering health problems in the long run. For those people I do not feel that unremitting admonishments to do it anyway, to push and pick-up the pace, should be the teacher's response. To express your dissatisfaction with their difficulty and lack of intense effort may just make these activities all the more trying and distasteful to them. Rather, the message might be that it is okay to do less vigorous exercises, they are good for you too, and the initial most important thing is to keep doing at any level. You need to find what is comfortable for you so that you can make it a regular part of your lifestyle. If you choose more moderate and light activities the benefits may not be as great as the more vigorous sweat producing activities, but they still are very important.

I heard someone once go so far as to say "exercise is that gentle pastime in which we coax subtle changes from our bodies." This mild philosophy may not produce great athletes but of course that is not our purpose. It could greatly profit many sedentary people. They need to develop the attitude that exercise is not something to dread doing. It is something we do for ourselves, not to ourselves. When you have the children stretch you might tell them that they don't have to make it hurt; just hold the stretch at a point were pulling can be felt. When you are running everyone does not always have to be worried about times and improving; as long as you are doing it that is okay. Tell them to find a friend to talk with as they go or just take in the scenery (see Figure 3.3 for a description of these and other ideas). Do walking and hiking events in addition to runs or other options. Find a comfortable carpet or mat to do your curl-ups and it is okay to stop after those muscles start to become fatigued, it is good if you want to work harder to be able to do more, but sometimes it is all right just to maintain, and a lot less difficult. Faster, longer, higher might be a good creed for Olympic athletic achievements but can become burdensome.

Setting Self-Performance Goals

We pointed out earlier that physical activities might be enjoyable to more people if social comparison worries were minimized. We believe the same applies to physical conditioning. The actions of many teachers would suggest they believe just the opposite. They employ many practices that socially compare the fitness performance of students and then provide rewards to the better performers. For example, they will ask which students were able to do 30 or 35 curl-ups, they may provide normative data on a running test, they may display charts and graphs depicting individual performances, and extra praise, rewards, or even better grades are given to the higher performances. They justify these practices on the grounds that they will provide extra fun and motivation for the students to improve their fitness; the students meeting those standards will be receiving extra positive vibes, the students not achieving them will be motivated to strive harder to reach those levels and achieve awards.

My view is that the incentives based on comparisons of social outcomes do not always work in this manner. There is no question that rewards to those students achieving standards will act as an extra incentive. However, a couple of questions need to be asked. Firstly, are extra incentives all that important to those already performing at the upper end of the class? Most of these people are frequently already sold on fitness. Secondly, more often than not, good outcome fitness goals are not as much the result of effort and practice as they are of natural ability and early maturation (this issue will be discussed more fully in Chapter 8). If this is the case, we may be rewarding some who are not deserving because they are not necessarily developing the lifestyle practices for which we are striving. They get the message that, "Hey, I am fit, therefore I must be doing all that I need to."

As for the other students whose outcomes are below par, it is very questionable that they, in response to this information, will work harder, catch-up, and receive positive recognition for doing so. Undoubtedly this happy scenario could be true for some, however, there will be many more others that will receive the poor information and simply be discouraged by it. They will feel bad and wish only to avoid all thoughts of conditioning exercises in the future. They will feel it is impossible for them to reach the standards of others. And what of the students who are motivated to labor diligently so as to catch-up? Because of the overriding significance of developmental rates and genetic differences, physical fitness outcomes in children are in only very small part due to effort and lifestyle. Consequently, many, no matter how conscientious their effort, simply will not perceptibly close the performance gap with their peers. This means that we may be setting impossibly difficult goals for them. If this is the case, we are guilty of one of the great sins of teaching. We in essence are setting the children up for failure and failure isn't fun. In some individuals it does not take too many such experiences before they acquire the attitude of *learned helplessness* towards not only exercise but perhaps other aspects of their schooling as well.

The alternative to encouraging social comparison goals is to get people to direct their focus primarily upon maintaining or improving their own performance. Here we are again advocating *performance goals* as opposed to *outcome goals*. *Performance goals* tend to be more realistic for all the children. The top students should have challenging goals as well as the lowest. Such goals are more under their control and thus less stressful and threatening to many. The criterion now being taught is based upon their own relative performance. The teacher makes it a habit to say things like "Who was able to do as many or more than last time?" "You all know how long it took you to complete the circuit yesterday. Set what you think would be a good time for you today." Striving for your "personal best" or "maintaining your fitness zone" would be typical directives.

When students set goals of doing 25 curl-ups, touching their toes, or jumping rope for three minutes, they are striving for a certain standard of performance. Even though these self-referenced *performance goals* may be reasonable ones for their individual abilities, even here there is still some inherent stress. Some people may find always having to work towards criteria is onerous and adds an unpleasant aspect to exercise. When someone exercises, is it always necessary to be counting and timing oneself and worrying about those scores? "Feeling the need to always do better." The answer is no. What about simply having *performance goals* that simply specify doing a certain amount of activity without concern for meeting any criterion? I, and many of my friends who maintain satisfaction with chronic exercise, generally operate this way. Our goal is to do certain amounts of exercise: getting a minimum of three aerobic work-outs in this week, stretching each day this week, weight training two or three times. Notice that when thinking this way people do not need to be monitoring and being concerned about how fast they are running or how far they are stretching. They can cut a workout a little short on some days they don't feel their best; at least they are disciplining their lives and consistently exercising. Why worry and bother? Are they not after all doing what is reasonably necessary? Will fitness therefore not take care of itself? Will conditioning not be more enjoyable?

Physical Fitness and the Physiological Principles You Need to Know about Physical Activity/Exercise

4

What Is Physical Fitness?
Component of Cardiorespiratory Fitness
Component of Flexibility Fitness
Component of Muscular Fitness
Component of Body Composition Fitness

Physiological Principles You Need to Know about Physical Activity/Exercise
F.I.T Principle
    F.I.T. Principle applied to improving cardiorespritory fitness (Aerobic)
    F.I.T. Principle applied to improving cardiorespritory fitness (Anaerobic)
    F.I.T Principle applied to improving flexibility fitness
    F.I.T. Principle applied to improving muscular fitness
    F.I.T. Principle applied to reducing body composition fitness
    Qualification of the F.I.T. Principle
Overuse Principle
Reversibility Principle
Readiness/Trainability Principle
Warm-Up and Cool-Down Principle

"What a piece of work is man, how noble in reason, how infinite in faculties, in form and moving how express and admirable, in action how like an angel, in apprehension how like a god! The beauty of the world, the paragon of animals."

William Shakespeare

"Science teaching (for children) should begin, not with the mythical body in rest or uniform motion, but with the human body."

J.B.S. Haldane

"Everyone agrees with the educational catchprase 'A child's mind is a terrible thing to waste.' But what about the hearts, lungs and legs of those same young bodies?"

Tom Weir

If one of our goals is to establish good physical activity & health habits in ourselves and in our children, it would be helpful for us to know what we mean by physical fitness and what are some of the basic physiological principles of physical activity and exercise.

What Is Physical Fitness?

We could divide physical fitness into two levels. The *health fitness level* would represent minimal fitness for which everyone should strive throughout his or her life span. Those in possession of it would have sufficient physical fitness to carry out their daily activities without pain or significant restrictions. They could shop, climb stairs, mow and trim the yard, garden a small plot, clean the car or house, and even hurry after the bus without undue risk of injury or sore muscles. They would not feel run down and exhausted by the end of the day. They could live physically comfortable, independent lives, free of the degenerative *hypokinetic diseases* associated with an inactive lifestyle (cardiorespiratory diseases, type II diabetes, excessive body fat, lower back pain, etc.).

The *performance fitness* level would permit us to go beyond our everyday tasks. We would be capable of expanding our movement horizons to include recreational/sports activities. These activities could vary from long neighborhood walks and golfing to climbing mountains and competing in ironman length triathlons. *Performance fitness* would enable us to safely enjoy these challenges and reach the fullest physical potential for which we might strive. This level would yield a higher level of protection again *hypokinetic diseases* and might also afford greater psychological benefits such as better self-concept, body image, and anxiety reduction.

Regardless of which of the two levels of fitness we are striving, physical fitness must be thought of as being made up of a number of components. To have *health fitness* we must possess a minimal degree of certain components of fitness; other components and higher levels of those components may be needed for *performance fitness*. Below we have listed the major components of physical fitness and have explained the role of each.

Component of Cardiorespiratory Fitness

The cardiorespiratory system can be divided into two basic components of fitness: *aerobic* and *anaerobic*. In simplified terms, the word *aerobic* is referring to "with oxygen." When we exercise we breath faster and deeper to take in more oxygen, and the heart beats faster and more forcefully to transport that oxygen from the lungs to the needful working muscles. It is obvious that we want a strong, efficient aerobic system in order to perform vigorous sports and activities, which last for a period of time. In fact, a good aerobic foundation is considered essential for all sports/recreational activities and *health fitness*. A sound aerobic capacity is an indispensable underlying energy system if we are going to comfortably complete everyday tasks. Furthermore, the leading causes of death and disability are a result of a deteriorated aerobic system. Narrowed and hardened arteries restrict oxygen flow to virtually all the body organs and is associated with numerous impairments as diverse as strokes, heart attacks, decreased mental alertness, sexual disfunctioning, and loss of skin suppleness. An efficient aerobic system can play a role in reducing chronic high blood pressure and its concomitant health problems. There are good arguments for saying that *aerobic* capacity is the most critical component of health fitness. The two foundation levels of *The Activity Pyramid* are there primarily because of their contribution to aerobic fitness.

Anaerobic refers to "without oxygen." When the body is called upon to exert a large amount of energy in a short period of time the cardiorespiratory system does not have the capability of providing adequate oxygen to the muscles: kayaking in a particularly swift patch of water, swimming a fifty meter race, or sprinting to hit a number of tennis shots in quick succession would be examples. The body has a short-term means of accomplishing such tasks by producing energy through chemical reactions that do not require oxygen. However, these reactions can only be maintained to up around 90 seconds before an "oxygen debt" is incurred, byproduct lactic acid builds up in the blood, and activity falters and stops. Although a good functioning anaerobic system is not important in more moderately paced sports/recreational activities, the above examples attest to its importance in others. Anaerobic fitness is not considered to be nearly as important to *health fitness* as we saw aerobic fitness to be. Unlike aerobic diseases, we do not have to worry about degenerative disabilities as a result of anaerobic problems and it is rare to be faced with anaerobic tasks in our normal daily routines. Nevertheless, it is well to recognize that even in our humdrum existence there arise emergencies when we may wish to vigorously push a car out of a snow drift or sprint some place when we or others are in danger. *The Activity Pyramid* does not specifically dictate anaerobic experiences although many recreational sports experiences might have anaerobic aspects to them.

Component of Flexibility Fitness

Here we are, in an oversimplified way, referring to the ability of the joints to move smoothly through a full range of motion. The major factor limiting the normal range of movement in a joint, other than the bone structure of the joint itself, is the tightness of the tendons, ligaments, and other muscular connective tissues involved. It is hard to unequivocally say what is a desirable level of flexibility. In the past it was an entrenched acceptance that higher levels of flexibility were always to be preferred. The logic was that this would allow the muscle to move more unrestrictedly with less soreness, and when encountering a full stretch at the end of a range of motion, it would be less likely to suffer the trauma of a tare or detachment. Recent research efforts have brought these assumptions into question. A high degree of flexibility has been found to be related to instability of the joint and an increase in injuries. Studies show higher injury rates in athletes who are classified in the highest 20 percent of the flexibility distribution. Also, the evidence does not generally show decreases in either injuries or muscle soreness when flexibility programs are employed.

The general consensus in scientific circles is that a modest level of flexibility is desirable for performing everyday activities and most sports. Regularly moving through the range of motion required in these activities is probably sufficient, whether it is done simply by doing the activity or by stretching exercises. In sports such as gymnastics, dance or rock climbing, where unusually flexible positions must sometimes be achieved, supplemental stretching exercises are advisable. Some postural problems such as rounded shoulders might be traced to over tightness in the chest area. Chronic neck pains and lower back pains are sometimes attributed to tight extensor connective tissues in these regions. Larger losses in flexibility accompanying more sedentary aging can pose safety problems and restrict even self-care movements. The third tier of *The Activity Pyramid* specifies that some stretching exercises should be done 2 or 3 times per week.

Component of Muscular Fitness

The muscular system can be divided into two basic components of fitness: *muscular strength and muscular endurance*. These components are not completely unrelated to one another in the sense that developing one will have some developmental effect on the other.

Muscular strength is determined by how much resistance someone is capable of moving. Bench pressing as much weight as possible would be a test of the strength of the chest and arm extensor muscles. Squeezing a hand gauge with maximal force would be a measurement of hand contraction strength. Muscular strength may come into play in weight lifting, wrestling, rock climbing. A child may not have enough strength to swing a bat or shoot a basketball with proper technique. As for general health, muscular strength is only minimally important. Moving the refrigerator, loosening the bolts to change a tire are a couple of examples of when strength is required around the house and garage. My elderly mother has difficulty twisting off jar lids.

When a resistance must be repeatedly moved we are relying on the component of *muscular endurance*. This ability is needed in virtually all sports-recreational activities. Running distances demands that our legs continually thrust the body upwards and forward. When swimming the arms must pull through the water again and again. As do the majority of sports/recreational activities, hiking, paddling, biking, and swinging rackets all require sustained, repetitive movement. When muscular endurance wanes, skilled performance is impaired. Muscular endurance affects our daily health in more ways than just walking about; it plays a crucial part in posture. For instance, while standing, abdominal muscles must maintain a degree of tautness to keep the hips from rotating too far forward and letting the abdomen protrude. Likewise, having strong thigh muscles (quadriceps) sometimes are helpful in preventing knee pain. According to *The Activity Pyramid* muscular fitness exercises (strength/endurance) are to be done 2 to 3 times each week.

Component of Body Composition Fitness

Body composition is considered another component of fitness. Here we are referring to the body's percentage of body fat relative to lean mass. The lean mass is primarily made up of bone, muscle and connective tissue. Fat is chiefly necessary for protection of internal organs, brain function and transmission of neural messages, insulation to preserve body heat, and as a reservoir of energy supplies. For most all sports-recreational activities it is good to have a relatively lower percentage of body fat because any more than is necessary results in extra weight that must be moved. The extra weight will reduce the speed with which we can move and it also places greater stress on the cardiorespiratory system. Furthermore it will result in greater forces being placed on joints thus increasing the chances of muscle and joint injuries. A couple of sports where a somewhat higher percentage of fat may be beneficial would be distance swimming in cold water, because of the need for insulation, and football linemen, where the greater weight of the individual would make it more difficult for an opposing player to apply enough force to move them out of the way.

With regards to health, it is very important that children or adults do not accumulate more fat than necessary. We saw in Chapter 1 that the percentage of affected Americans has been rapidly increasing. Excess body fat makes all daily activities more fatiguing and is associated with cardiovascular diseases, type II diabetes, arthritis, some kinds of cancer, and low back pain. Excess body fat is also the most readily observable of fitness components and is generally viewed negatively. Because many people hold an unfavorable view, being overfat frequently has restricting social and psychological implications. Of course, all of the activities of *The Activity Pyramid* contribute to the burning of calories and hence to fighting excessive fat accumulation. A primary purpose of the pyramid is to ensure that people have a good quantity of movement, at least an hour a day of *found activities* in addition to aerobics and muscular fitness activities.

But having a healthy body composition is not always about burning calories and reducing body fat. Having too little body fat is not nearly as common a health problem as is having too much but it can have serious, even life threatening, consequences for those affected. Because of the prevalent negative views that society has toward fat, some adults and children do acquire anorexic, bulimic, and excessive exercise behaviors. The message needs to be one of moderation. The role of *The Activity Pyramid* is to promote adequate activity with some room for rest and recovery. The role of the *Food Pyramid* is to moderate excessive fat and sugar consumption, not eliminate it.

Physiological Principles You Need to Know about Physical Activity/Exercise

We now know that physical fitness is multifarious. To be physically healthy we must achieve, and maintain throughout our lives, a minimal level of functioning in a variety of components of fitness: aerobic, muscular endurance, flexibility and body composition. For the fuller athletic life, higher degrees of functioning in those components may be necessary. Additionally, well-developed muscular strength and anaerobic cardiorespiratory capacities will be required in some sports and recreational activities. We shall now direct our attention to some physiological principles relating to the development and maintenance of each of the components of fitness that we have been discussing. An effort has been made to keep this coverage focused on the bare essentials. The principles should be easy to comprehend and remember, and yet be a fully sufficient guide for leading a healthy life of physical activity and exercise. Not only do you the teacher need to understand these principles, to some level you must be able to communicate them to the children. Students in the upper elementary grades need to be beginning to take some degree of responsibility for their own physical fitness. That will not be possible without them having some basic appreciation of the relationship between physical fitness and different kinds of physical activities and exercises.

The F.I.T. Principle

F.I.T. is an acronym for Frequency, Intensity, and Time. Frequency refers to how often someone needs to exercise, intensity refers to how hard or vigorous that exercise needs to be, and time relates to how long the exercise must persist. Figure 4.1 contains a listing of the generally recommended minimal training guidelines for each of the components of fitness discussed above. Justification for the above guidelines is derived from research studies showing that when people follow them over a period of weeks, months, and years, significant improvements can be clearly verified. The gradual progressive stresses of these magnitudes, when placed on the body as a result of these guidelines,

---

Figure 4.1. Minimal Training F.I.T. Guidelines for Various Components of Fitness

	Frequency	Intensity	Time
Cardiorespiratory (Aerobic)	3–5/week	60–80% max HR	20–30 min
Cardiorespiratory (Anaerobic)	2/week	near max HR	sport specific multiple bouts
Flexibility	2–3/week	point of slight discomfort	30 seconds or 6 deep breaths
Muscular Strength/ Muscular Endurance	2–3/week	near exhaustion	1 bout of 13 or more repetitions
Body Composition	daily	low to moderate	one hour

will result in adaptation in the cardiorespiratory, musculoskeletal, and body composition regulatory systems.

F.I.T. Principle Applied to Improving Cardiorespiratory Fitness (Aerobic)

The recommended minimum guidelines for achieving a more efficient oxygen delivery system is to exercise with an intensity sufficient to elevate the heart rate into a target training zone, maintain it in that zone for a time of 20–30 minutes, and repeat such an exercise routine at a frequency of 3 or 5 times per week. The *target heart rate zone* is usually defined as having the person exercise at an intensity, which will elevate the heart rate to between 60 and 80 percent of maximum heart rate. *Maximum heart rate* is simply how many beats per minute a person's heart will achieve when that person exercises as strenuously as possible. *Maximum heart rate* varies from individual to individual but a rough way of approximating it is to use this simple formula, maximum heart rate = 220 – age. Using this formula it would be determined that a 20 year old would have a maximal rate of 200. A 40-year old would be able to achieve a maximum rate of about 180. You can see that as people age their hearts gradually loose some capacity to beat rapidly. Now to determine the target zone for the 20 year olds we would multiply their maximum 200 by 60 percent (.60) and 80 percent (.80) and come up with a range between 120 and 160 beat per minute. The zone for the 40-year old would be 108 to 144.[1]

F.I.T. Principle Applied to Improving Cardiorespiratory Fitness (Anaerobic)

As you may recall, anaerobic processes occur when exercise is very vigorous and the cardiorespiratory system cannot supply adequate oxygen to the muscles. Preparing the body to function under anaerobic conditions dictates that training intensity needs to be very close to maximum. The most common activity is to have the performers do sprints; other examples would be near all out execution of certain drills or calisthenics. The T of the *F.I.T. Principle* is usually determined by the specific activity for which you are preparing. If the softball player might face 30 seconds or less of sustained effort in the game as he/she rushes about the bases, then that is considered the best length of time to make the training bouts. But of course, that does not mean that the whole anaerobic workout ends after just one 30 second bout. The concept of repeated bouts or sets is used to promote greater physiological training effects. The softball players might be required to sprint or go near full speed on a drill for 30 seconds, allowed to recover by walking it off for about a minute (twice as long), then go again and again, doing a series of repeats (maybe 5 or 10 or more). This type of training is called *interval training*. See Figure 4.3 regarding specific suggested interval training lengths for some common sports.

Because anaerobic interval training is difficult and stressful on the body, the F.I.T. Frequency guideline is to keep the workouts for young adults to twice a week. While aerobic training is thought best to do year round, four to six weeks of good anaerobic training has been found to be sufficient to achieve anaerobic peaking. Thus, interval training is often begun in the weeks of preseason and then periodically during the season. If the performers are regularly performing anaerobicly as a result of game play then it may not be necessary. But if there are breaks in the schedules and players are not getting full game time, it may be needed. With regards to prepubescent children, many authorities caution us against an over emphasis on anaerobic training due to its demanding physiological and psychological nature. Perhaps significant moderation of the F.I.T. standards would be appropriate. Having the youngsters do a bout or two on an occasional basis

---

[1] Although I believe it is good to teach both children and adults how to monitor their exercise heart rates and determine whether or not they are exercising in their prescribed training zones, the calculations involved in using the *F.I.T. Principle* might be more complex than what is always necessary. Also, calculating one's zone from the 220 minus age method is only a rough estimate and can have an error of as much as 17 beats for some individuals. A much simpler way of determining appropriate aerobic training intensities is to use the *1–10 Perceived Exertion Scale* shown in Figure 4.2.

Figure 4.2. Perceived Exertion Scale

This simple 1–10 scale allows people a quick and easy way to estimate the intensity of their aerobic activities. Here the children are told that if they are feeling they are exercising somewhat hard (4,5,6,7) they are in a good heart training zone, if they are below it they might want to go just a little faster. If they are above it, be careful because they might not be able to keep it up. Your chart might also place greater emphasis on facial diagrams rather than verbal descriptors.

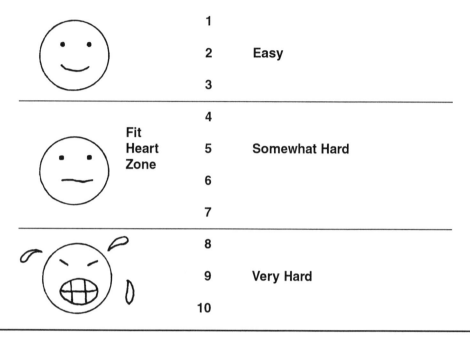

might be sufficient to give them an idea of the potential importance of anaerobic fitness for future performance. Later in the chapter under the heading of readiness, I will have more to say about children and anaerobic training.

F.I.T. Principle Applied to Improving Flexibility Fitness

There are two basic types of stretching exercises. *Ballistic stretching* is characterized by bouncing and lunging to reach as far as possible. Although this sort of stretching can improve flexibility and is used by some coaches, it is not now normally recommended because of potential injury to the muscles, tendons and ligaments. *Ballistic stretching* creates high peak forces in the muscles that

Figure 4.3. Interval Training Guidelines for Common Sports

Sport	Interval Training Recommendations
Softball and Football	Short intervals of 30–60 sec.
Basketball, Wrestling, Tennis	Medium intervals of 1–2 min.
Soccer, Lacrosse, Middle-distance Swimming	Long intervals of 2–10 min.

can result in muscle stiffness. An effective and safer way to stretch is to do it statically. *Static stretching* means that we slowly and gradually move to the limit of the joint and then hold that position or only very gradually extend it. As can be seen in Figure 4.1, the recommended intensity level is listed as "the point of slight discomfort." As long as you extend this far you will be placing sufficient stress on the limiting connective tissue; going further and making it hurt is not necessary and is proscribed because of possible trauma. If we apply the T of the principle to the time of which the stretch is held, 30 seconds is suggested as a minimum. Instructing the performer to take 6 deep breaths is a means of achieving this time guideline without the necessity of counting seconds. Doing one bout of the stretch is adequate but doing multiple bouts would promote more rapid gains and would not be overly stressful. As for the frequency of the stretching, 2 or 3 times per week is considered a minimum. Figures 4.4 & 4.5 show eight basic healthy lifestyle stretches recommended for the major muscle groups. Research on stretching demonstrates a 5 to 20 percent increase in static flexibility is possible within 4 to 6 weeks of stretching.

Although you may still see it commonly done, exercise physiologists no longer recommend *static stretching* as a warm-up to activity. Stretching cold muscles carries some risk of injury as it is being done, and has not been shown to reduce injury rates in the subsequent performance. Furthermore, it has been surprisingly determined that static stretching prior to an athletic event has the effect of reducing the amount of force the muscles are capable of producing. For example, groups who have warmed-up by *static stretching* have been shown to have significantly lower vertical jump scores than other groups who did not stretch beforehand. It seems that the preferred way to prepare for performance is to warm the muscles by engaging in several minutes of light movement to elevate the body temperature. The time for stretching appears to be following the athletic performance. Stretching through a full range will be easier because of the muscles are already warm, and the slowness of the stretching will afford a good tapering cool-down period.

F.I.T. Principle Applied to Improving Muscular Fitness

As you will recall, there are two basic types of muscular fitness: strength and endurance. Normally, different F.I.T. guidelines are set when adults are training for *muscular strength* as opposed to

---

Figure 4.4. Four Basic Stretches for the Lower Body

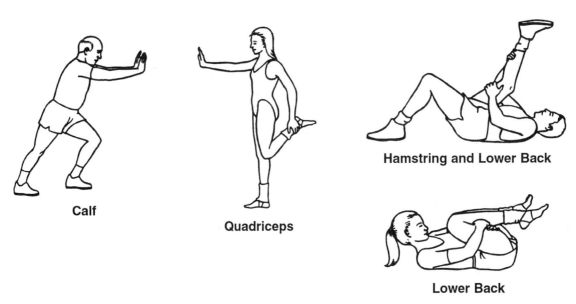

Calf

Quadriceps

Hamstring and Lower Back

Lower Back

Figure 4.5. Four Basic Stretches for the Upper Body

**Shoulder
and Triceps**

Shoulder

Chest

Head

muscular endurance. The difference lies in the number of repetitions the resistance is to be moved. When working on strength, the recommendation has been to have a resistance heavy enough so that it can only be moved 6 to 12 times. This appears to be the optimal range to increase muscle size and its ability to complete one repetition with a heavier weight (which is the definition of muscular strength). For developing muscular endurance the guideline calls for a lesser load, one that the exerciser can move 13 or more times before becoming fatigued. Such training prepares the muscle for being able to continue functioning over a longer period of time (which is the definition of muscular endurance). If a student did 25 curl-ups and was nearly incapable of doing any more, this would be an example of a muscular endurance exercise done according to F.I.T. prescription. But also, if a runner's legs were beginning to become heavy and wobbly after a mile run, this too would be evidence of a good muscular endurance workout for his/her specific sport.

When dealing with elementary aged children it is unnecessary to make separate time or repetition guidelines between muscular strength and muscular endurance training. Children 5–12 years of age have been found to develop both better strength and muscular endurance when doing 13 repetitions or more. This working with more moderate loads also has the advantage of decreasing the possibility of injury. While there is no evidence that resistance training is physiologically harmful to children,[2] having them straining to move very heavy weights does not seem prudent because their lifting techniques might be poor and they might not always appreciate the amount of caution required.[3]

Before leaving the issue of repetitions a word should be said about exercise bouts or sets. Recall that when training the anaerobic system our Figure 4.1 guidelines specified doing multiple bouts. Traditionally the same idea of multiple bouts has been recommended for strength training. It has been a long accepted practice that doing around 3 sets of exercises was best for strength gains. Notice that our Figure 4.1 guidelines do not require repeated sets for the development of muscular strength and endurance. The reason for this deviation is that some recent research has not shown repeated sets to result in significantly greater increases in strength when compared to single set procedures.

---

[2] In the past there has been a concern that heavy resistance training could damage the soft growth plates of children's bones. No evidence has been found to support this thesis. In fact, children's bones, like those of adults, respond to the stress by becoming denser and less susceptible to breakage.

[3] It is never recommended to have children straining to see how much they can bench-press on one attempt, or how heavy an object they many be able to pick up. Such efforts even pose a health risk to adults who are physiologically mature and trained, and who are well-versed in proper mechanical techniques.

According to many exercise physiologists, doing the extra work of repeated bouts might produce some small extra strength gains, but the key ingredient in stimulating muscle growth seems to be if the muscle has had to contract at, or near, maximal force.

As outlined in Figure 4.1, the I of the F.I.T. demands a fairly high intensity level or "near exhaustion." This means that you do not have to go until you cannot move that muscle any more, but on the other hand, you should be approaching that threshold. Only as you draw near that threshold will measurably significant muscle fiber adaptations be stimulated. Remember, any level of activity will develop some strength, but maximal gains occur with maximal effort and muscle overload.

The F guidelines are for 2 to 3 bouts per week. The reason for this is that when you exert the body to near exhaustion levels it is important for the body to have a day or two of recovery time (remember how highly stressful anaerobic training was also recommended only twice per week). Some serious weight trainers who lift everyday do so by varying the muscles they work. They might train their upper body muscles one day and the following do exercises for the lower body.

In Figures 4.6 and 4.7 I have diagramed a few basic *isotonic* muscular strength/endurance exercises. They are designed to exercise the major muscle groups of the body. You will note that there

Figure 4.6. Muscular Strength/Endurance Exercises for the Upper Body

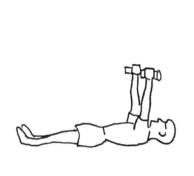
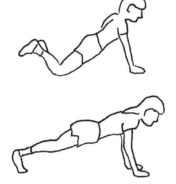

Upright row: pulling toward the front
Muscles used: upper back (trapezius) and front of upper arm (biceps)

Bench press and push-ups: pushing to the front
Muscles used: chest (pectoralis) and back of upper arm (triceps)

Curl-ups: pulling rib case down
Muscles used: stomach (abdominals)

Back extension: extend the back
Muscles used: back extensors (erector spinae)

Overhead press: push above the head
Muscles used: shoulders (deltoids) and back of upper arms (triceps)

Pull-up: pulling down
Muscles used: back (latissimus dorsi) and front of upper arm (biceps)

Figure 4.7. Muscular Strength/Endurance Exercises for the Lower Body

Calf raise: extend the ankle
Muscles used: calf (gastrocnemius)

Forward lung and squat: extend the hip and knee
Muscles used: buttocks (gluteals), and front of upper leg (quadriceps)

is a balance between the exercises; for example, one exercise will employ the muscles used to push and extend away from the body, another exercise will call on other muscles to make the opposite movement of pulling and flexing towards the body. This is called strengthening the opposing or *antagonistic muscles* in a balanced fashion. More and more schools are acquiring weight-training pieces of equipment and even weight machines. In my diagrams I have tried to show that when such equipment is not available calisthenics can be done and makeshift weights can be improvised. Plastic drink containers that are about a quart in size, when filled with water, can make a reasonable resistance.

To this point in our discussion of muscular fitness we have been talking only of moving resistance through the range of motion. This type of training through a movement range is called *isotonic training* and is the most common means of training. There is another type of muscular strength training known as *isometric training*. Here we are referring to training without movement. Examples would be a student forcefully pushing his/her hands together or pushing mightily against a wall or against the offsetting force of another student. This kind of *isometric* training can be as effective as *isotonic*. A couple of major draw backs of it is that the student might not as readily witness muscular gains as would be seen in accomplishing a greater number of pull-ups or being able to move a resistance a greater number of times. Also, the muscular strength gains made in *isometric* exercises seem to be quite specific to the joint positions used in training. Therefore, either the exercises need to be executed at a number of joint positions or significant strength gains at other joint angles can be expected to be small. Perhaps a good place you could utilize isometric exercises is in the classroom. As an activity break to get the blood flowing you could design a few exercises in which the students push and pull against himself or herself or against a partner

F.I.T. Principle Applied to Reducing Body Fat

For the reduction of body fat, the F.I.T. guidelines call for an hour of daily, low to moderate exercise. To understand the rationale for these guidelines some fundamental knowledge of calorie burning is useful. To begin with, assuming our body composition is at a stable level and we are not going to alter our caloric input by making any dietary changes, to lose one pound of body fat a person must do an extra 3,500 calories worth of exercise. Remember that relationship, *Three thousand five hundred calories must be burned to lose one pound of body fat.* Next, realize that if a 150-pound individual walked a mile on level terrain, he/she would burn approximately 100 calories above the normal resting metabolism rate. This figure would not vary much from individual to individual because, barring disabilities, most everyone walks with comparable efficiency. The only factor, which would pronouncedly effect this caloric figure, would be the weight of the person. A 300-pound person would burn about twice as much and a 75-pound child might burn half as much. If you are impressed with the above figures as I am, you are probably thinking, "Wow, a lot of walking must be done just to lose one single pound of fat." The 150 pounder must walk 35 miles, the 300-pounder 17.5 miles, and the 75 pounder nearly 70 miles.

Now consider the caloric burning when our three people have run a mile. Because of the greater work inefficiencies in running compared to walking, our people would consume more calories during the activity: the 150 pound person would burn approximately 120 calories, the 300 pound person 240 calories, and the 75 pound person 60 calories. However, the net caloric effect of vigorous activities like running is not quite so simple. When people engage in vigorous activity their metabolisms get revved up and remain elevated for a period of time following the cessation of movement. You probably have noticed how your rate heart is somewhat higher and your cheeks and skin glow with the stronger flow of coursing blood. The more intense the exercise has been, the more this affect occurs. The metabolism can be thought of as a revolving wheel, the faster you get it going the longer it will continue to go after the applied forces have been terminated. Researchers have labeled this post-exercise calorie burning, due to a stimulated metabolism, *residual calorie burning*. Before we become overly excited about the benefits of residual calorie burning, we need to recognize that its contribution to total calorie expenditure is probable rather limited. The metabolism seems to be only significantly elevated following sustained high intensity exercise and even then it quickly returns to baseline levels within an hour or two. While it is difficult to calculate precise figures, and investigators are not yet in full agreement, most estimate that only around 20 to 40 residual calories will be burned up following robust aerobic efforts. If we return to our three runners once again we might come up with a best guess of their calorie usage by allotting each a mid-range figure of 30 residual calories. Doing so would see our 150 pounder consuming 150 calories as a result of the mile run (120 during + 30 residually); our 300 pounder 270 calories (240 during + 30 residually); our 75 pounder 90 calories (60 during + 30 residually).

So what are the implications we might draw from the above information? Firstly, as we already noted, a great deal of walking miles must be covered to lose just one pound of body fat (35 miles for the 150-pound person, 17.5 for the 300-pound person, and 70 for the 75-pound person). This is a sad fact of life that we need to understand, *the amount of weight you lose through exercise is grossly exaggerated.*[4] You probably have to walk a mile to burn up the calories consumed in a bite-size Snickers (95 calories). Secondly, it is apparent that exercising more strenuously, given the same distance is covered, does not radically increase the total number of calories used. More will be burned during and following exercise but still, the 150 pound person might have to run at least 30 miles, the 300 pound person 13 miles, and the 75 pound person 39 miles. An initial despairing reaction you might have to the above data could be to conclude, why bother! Exercise, even vigorous exercise, seems so ineffectual in fat loss. Why put out such a great amount of effort for so small a return? Although such a response is understandable, there is a more optimistic counterpoint to be made. Granted, exercise, either light paced or vigorous, will not produce large reductions in body fat in the short run, but let us look at the situation with a more long-term eye. What happens when we adhere to *the F.I.T. Principle* for body fat reduction over a period of time? Say our 150 pounder did an hour of walking or a comparable light-paced activity. We already know that an hour of steady walking would net about 3 miles or 300 calories. Now if this was done 7 days throughout the week, as the guidelines suggest, we would be talking about 2,100 calories. The weight scales would not yet show rewarding evidence of a pound of fat loss, but the needle would be wavering in that direction. Next assume that we have habituated this week's walking regimen and have continued it faithfully for the next 52 weeks. Now we are talking about real calories and fat loss, 109,200 calories and over

---

[4] It is indeed a sad fact of life if we are hoping to exercise so as to lose excess body fat. Our ancestors who were scrambling to find enough food to eat certainly would not view it as a sad fact. The efficiency of the body deserves to be appreciated.

31 pounds. The moral of this story is clear. A lifelong active lifestyle will make a difference. Application of the *F.I.T. Principle* can be an effective, long-term approach to fat loss. People normally gain unwanted body fat over many months and years and we need to go about reducing in the same manner.

Perhaps a concluding point is warranted pertaining to the *F.I.T.* recommendation of light and moderate activity vis' a vis' vigorous activity. It should not be construed to mean that vigorous activity could not be effectively used as an avenue for weight loss; a better interpretation is that it is not a necessity. Light to moderate activity is suggested because, given equal amounts of total work, nearly as many calories are expended in light as in vigorous movements, and because data show that more people enjoy lighter paced activities and tend to better persevere at them for extended periods of time. But realize that participation in vigorous activities has its advantages. Those who become accustomed to and can enjoy more robust activities will be effectively burning calories and will also be deriving additional benefits. Training at more vigorous aerobic heart rate zones can give rise to greater psychological gains and to physiological gains in the cardiorespiratory and muscular fitness systems. Another benefit of higher paced activities is that more calories are burned in a shorter period of time and hence, for the same caloric loss, less time needs to be devoted to exercise; a 3 mile jog can be completed in probably half the time of a walk. This can be an important factor when we consider that lack of time is by far the most common reason given for not exercising. Figure 4.8 quantifies how, when time of exercise is held constant, modestly increasing the vigorousness of activity will significantly up the number of calories burned.

Qualification of the F.I.T. Principle

In concluding our discussion of the *F.I.T. Principle* as it relates to each of the components of fitness, a qualifying point is worth making. While the *F.I.T. Principle* provides a good training guideline and has scientific support, we need recognize that failure to fully comply with these guidelines does not mean some fitness improvements will not take place. Any amount of exercise, even though far below *the F.I.T.* guidelines, is good for us. Would no aerobic benefits be achieved if a person's target heart rate zone was 120 to 160 and he/she exercised at 119 beats per minute? Of course not, the body does not operate in an all or nothing manner. In fact, research documents that people who regularly engage in activities such as walking and gardening derive important cardiorespiratory benefits. Those people are not exercising at 60–80 percent of their maximum but at more like 20 for 30 percent. Likewise, should we expect no gain in abdominal muscle strength if the sit-ups were terminated before a near maximal effort was reached? No, the gains would be greatly lessened but some strength and muscular endurance improvements would take place. If someone is in the habit

Figure 4.8. Calories Burned by Walking or Slowly Jogging for One Hour

MPH	Weight					
	100	120	140	160	180	200
3.0 (20 min/mi)	180	220	260	300	340	380
3.5 (17 min/mi)	220	260	300	340	380	420
4.0 (15 min/mi)	250	300	350	400	450	500
4.5 (13.3 min/mi)	280	340	400	460	520	580
5.0 (12 min/mi)	320	380	450	530	610	690

of holding stretches for 15 seconds instead of the recommended 30 seconds, small benefits are undoubtedly going to be conferred when compared to doing nothing at all.

Perhaps we should think of exercise as having a *dose effect*. That simply means that small amounts of exercise and low intensities will produce small benefits, be they improvements in fitness components, protection from *hypokinetic diseases,* or many diverse psychological aspects of our lives. Larger doses of exercise will produce larger benefits. Figure 4.9 depicts a linear dose effect relationship established between a disability and different levels of exercise. Such linear relationships are not always found when exercise levels are increased to quite high levels. For example, one study showed that for every additional mile run per week—up to 50 miles a week for men and 40 for women, the subjects had better blood pressure, better blood cholesterol, and less estimated risk of heart disease. Beyond 50 and 40 miles no further improvements were found. Another study found that subject who were moderately fit had half the risk of early death as those who were not fit. Those who had attained high fitness fared even better, but not to quite the same degree—their premature death rate were 10 percent to 15 percent lower than the moderately fit group. And sometimes, when exercising to very extreme levels, a point of diminishing returns may be passed and health could be negatively impacted. That topic of overuse will be addressed in the next section.

Perhaps the most balanced stance to take relative to the *F.I.T. Principle,* is to see it not as unbendable requirements, but a useful guideline. I believe that teachers should make students aware of the *F.I.T. Principle* and the consequences of complying with differing degrees. Very little activity is bad, some regular activity is good, more regular activity is better. We should then let them know

---

Figure 4.9. Dose Effect of Exercise as It Relates to Incidence of Stroke

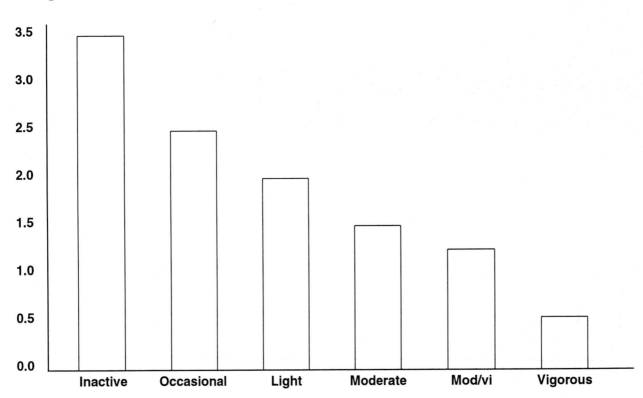

The height of the columns represent the number of stroke incidence per 1,000 people each year. Subjects studied were men aged 40 through 50 years old.

---

that they are responsible for the level of activity they choose to follow. I do not think it fruitful in the long run for us to be martinets and demand strict compliance. Such an approach may be discouraging to many whose exercise histories are many fathoms below these prescribed levels. Some of these people may never become comfortable with vigorous activities. And yet, if given an encouraging okay, they will be able to find light and moderate activities that can be a joy and benefit to their welfare.

Having given my imprimatur to backing off of the *F.I.T. Principle* so as to stay in one's comfort zone, a cautionary word is in order. People must be aware that authorities view the guidelines as minimal standards that need to be followed if a fully healthy life is to be attained. If a person does 30 minutes of light activity each day he/she will indeed be much healthier than the person who chooses to be sedentary, however, this level of activity will not produce a well-trained cardiorespiratory and muscular fitness system. Nor will it likely be sufficient to enable the maintenance of an ideal or even good ratio of body fat. Our genetic inheritance is a product of physiological beings that survived by almost constant and unrelenting physical exertion, supported by an unreliable and worst than plain diet. Is it therefore unreasonable to expect that we need provide ourselves with at least an hour a day of moderate/vigorous activity to partially compensate for hour after hour of sitting, and plate after plate of succulent foods? Considered in this light, is one or more hours, out of 16 waking hours, really so exorbitant and unnatural?

Overuse Principle

The *Overuse Principle* is the simple statement that more is not always better. We need remind ourselves that most health behaviors, if advocated and taken to the extreme, can actually be harmful to well being. Attempting to reduce fat intake down to near zero is not a good idea; being obsessively worried about sun exposure, germs, or other environmental hazards can also become needlessly debilitating. There is often wisdom in moderation and virtue in the mean.

With regards to exercise, it is important to remember that more is not always better. Generally speaking, unless there is a specific physiological problem, exercising at intensity levels well beyond the *F.I.T.* guidelines does not need to be dangerous. Joy and peak physical fitness benefits can be safely found even in long arduous training sessions, running Marathons, climbing mountains, and competitively lifting heavy weights. However, it should be obvious that the stresses on the body may be too great if workloads are not slowly and progressively increased; and it is always essential to listen to warning limits of the body. When coaches and athletes operate according to the motto of "no pain, no gain," they are dangerously pushing the very upper limits of training intensity and injuries are not an uncommon consequence. If we are running and dancing with painful knees, and throwing with sore arms, we must know that our muscles and joints are saying that excessive trauma is occurring; the body is not successfully adapting to the strain and is in danger of breakdown. Overtraining without adequate recovery times can also effect more than limbs. Chronic fatigue and weakening of the body's immune system to colds and other stresses may occur. It is a good habit to regularly check one's resting heart rate. An unusual elevation may be a sign of overtraining or infection.

Finally, prepubescent children are more susceptible to overuse. They may become hyperenthused about activities and poorly monitor warning signs. Additionally, their physiological defense systems are immature and less capable of coping with large forces and prolonged poundings. I have already made the point that children should not be seeing how much weight they can lift. When they do resistance training they should have a weight that can be safely controlled for at least a number of repetitions. As for determining how far it is safe to have a child walking or running the following *Children's Walk/Run Formula* is useful: miles to walk/run = age divided by three. This means a nine-year-old should be able to buildup to 3 miles but be careful about much exceeding that. As with any such standard, still pay attention to individual differences. Children with disabilities, excessive body fat, etc., may need an individualize standard.

Reversibility Principle of Training

The Reversibility Principle simply means that physiological adaptations will not long be maintained following the cessation of training. It is a sad tale but true, you cannot store fitness. This is probably the most violated of all exercise principles. We all have at one time or other engaged in activities that have resulted in improvements to some component or components of fitness. Maybe we worked at a job that required heavy lifting and we noticed a significant increase in the strength and endurance of our arms. Maybe we played regular racquetball one term and could tell that both aerobic and anaerobic fitness had advanced. When we terminated these activities, and were not doing others that taxed those particular component of fitness, it was not long before those gains were lost. It is easy for researchers to document the reversibility process, it is not easy to say exactly how rapidly it occurs. The level of fitness that had been achieved, the component of fitness involved, the person's age, and innate individual differences can effect the rate of loss. A rough estimate might be something like a 10 percent decline of capability each week until the return to baseline. Although the exact rate of loss is not always clear, it is clear that no significant chronic effects should be expected. If an adult attributes his/her well-developed shoulder muscles to a youthful swim team experience, he/she is not correct. Either he/she is continuing to do some exercise which is maintaining it, or he/she naturally has a larger than normal baseline level for big shoulders.

The moral of the *Reversibility Principle* is that if a certain level of fitness is acquired or possessed, and we wish to maintain it, then we must habituate ourselves to lifelong continuance of comparable activity. Children need to understand that gains made in school or during a sports season will be quickly lost if they become inactive over holidays or the summer months. Riding bicycle in the summer will not produce aerobic fitness throughout the winter months. Physical fitness is a dynamic process, a way of life.

Readiness/Trainability Principle

We have been saying that the various fitness components will respond to progressive training loads. However, this *readiness* to adapt to the stresses of exercise depends upon maturity. Before puberty, children do not fully possess the physiological mechanisms that will enable them to acquire the degree of fitness gains that can be garnered by post-pubescent children and adults. They are not nearly as *trainable* or amenable to exercise effects. When we see pre-pubescent children make improvements in fitness activities we must attribute most of that to their simply learning how to do those skills better; they are demonstrating more effective neuromuscular changes in technique, pacing themselves better, and/or benefiting from more self-confident motivation. Particularly little gains should be expected in the components of fitness requiring high intensity efforts: strength and anaerobic fitness. For those components, *muscle hypertrophy* (increased muscle diameter size) is a major factor for improvements and young children do not yet have all the hormones to simulate this growth.

What is the implication of low *trainability* in young children? To my mind, it means the improvement of elementary children's physical fitness levels should not be a priority goal. Any efforts here will be of limited avail, particularly with regards strength and anaerobic fitness. However, it does not mean that young people should not be learning the importance of exercise and should not be formulating the exercise habit.

Warm-Up and Cool-Down Principle

Warm-up activities can be most any light or moderate paced activities or exercises that you do at the beginning of the lesson. Warm-ups should precede any strenuous activity because it increases respiration and blood flow and helps to guard against muscle, tendon, and ligament strains. As said earlier, newer research has suggested that stretching might not be a good activity for this purpose.

Gradually going from walking to jogging to running is effective. And doing the same activity at a slower intensity takes advantage of the specificity of training principle.

Slower paced activities have long been advocated as a cool-down. The thought has been that if someone suddenly stopped moving following vigorous effort the pumping action of muscles would stop. That in turn would result in many bad things happening. Metabolic waste products such as lactic acid that built up in the muscles during exercise would not be removed as well and the result would be greater muscle soreness and slower recovery from fatigue. It was also thought that heart arrhythmia, that is more common immediately following strenuous efforts, might be lessened with a more gradual tapering of movement.

Upon close inspection of the research literature there is little evidence that these things actually happen. Differences in muscle soreness and recovery time from fatigue have not been documented between those who immediately sat down following exercises and those who did cool-down procedures. Nor is there evidence of differences in abnormal heart behaviors.

My conclusion is that each of us should do whatever feels best. If you like to move about that is fine, if you like to collapse, that too is all right. With your classes I still do advise ending with slower paced activities. It gives everyone a chance to cool off a little and to settle down. I always like to have a discussion at the end of class to summarize what was learned. By having a slower activity and a reflection time you will find that you have better behaved students in the hallways and back in the classroom. Vigorous exercise can promote more attentive and calm behaviors in the classroom but the transition should not be expected to be instantaneous.

Useful Management Procedures

Starting Class

Establishing Class Rules

Other Teacher Techniques

Management Games

Correcting Misbehavior

"Men should be taught as if you taught them not, / And things proposed as things forgot."

Alexander Pope

"The teacher who is attempting to teach without inspiring the pupil with a desire to learn is hammering on cold iron."

H. Mann

To accomplish our goals it is obvious that we need an instructional environment conducive to learning. You undoubtedly already have some ideas of management rules and procedures you will be using in the classroom. Appropriately, for continuity sake, you will be wishing to apply those same management techniques when you take your children beyond the classroom; you will be expecting the children to continue to display certain behaviors on field-trips, when attending assemblies, and during recess and gym instruction. This chapter will introduce some management procedures that may be especially useful in the gym and on the playground. When you have children participating in movement activities, management procedures become ever so important for a number of reasons. Those environments often have many distractions to which children are especially susceptible. You will have more difficulty making yourself heard because of generally poor acoustics, the greater dispersion of the students, the high noise levels of the activities, and the great excitement and laughter of the students. The children face greater inherent physical risk during movement activities and thus you must be able to quickly start and stop the action. Finally, because the children often experience high levels of physical and psychological arousal as they participate in games, undesirable behaviors will inevitably result unless good control structures are in place to prevent or quickly correct them.

Starting Class

When children are taken into a gym or other play space they naturally are excited by the environment and the prospect of physical activity. If little teacher control is present, they in all probability will begin racing about and screaming and shouting. Experienced teachers have found two basic procedures effective for avoiding this problem. One is to simply have a clearly established policy of the children moving to a set area and sitting down to await instruction. The other method is that of *instant activity.* The concept of *instant activity* is that the children know they are to engage in activity has soon as they enter the area. The activity could be in the form of a routine such as jogging a few laps and/or completing certain exercises or activities. As soon as those activities have been finished they know to move to a prescribed area and sit for the lesson's instructions. Another instant activity regimen is where the students know that when entering the area they will encounter written directions. These directions might be posted on a bulletin board or given to the students in the classroom. The prescribed activities might be conditioning in nature or they may be skill related to the previous or ensuing lesson. Figure 5.1 offers a couple of examples of instant activity assignments. Notice how the directions can be written so that all the students will not be assigned the same task. This procedure might be desirable because it makes better use of equipment and space. Also, it instills the habit of all the students reading the instructions for themselves rather than just following the lead of what the others are doing.

I particularly like the idea of *instant activity* instructions for three reasons. Firstly, the students are learning to read directions and become self-learners. Secondly, it directs them immediately into purposeful activity. And thirdly, it serves the management goal of releasing some of their pent-up energy and thus makes them better listeners for the beginning of class.

Figure 5.1. Example Instant Activity Directions

1. Everyone find a personal space and practice a set of curl-ups and 3 different stretching exercises we have learned. Remember that each stretch should be held for at least 6 deep breaths.

2. If your last name begins with A-L get a ball, find a personal space and practice your stationary dribbling skills.
   If your last name begins with M-Z get a partner and one ball, find a space and practice your passing skills.
   When the music stops, put the balls away and sit your squads.

3. Draw a playing card from the stack, look at it, and put it back.
   Hearts and Diamonds: get a hoola-hoop and see how well you can spin it around your, waist, wrist, and neck.
   Clubs and Spades: get a rope and see how well you can jump with a forwards and backwards spin; and on one foot.

Another small but possibly useful point to consider is the arrangement of the children when beginning the lesson. Simply having everyone sitting in a group is probably the most used formation. Being close together makes it easier to hear and sitting reduces shuffling and bumping. However, having the students assigned to squads has some advantages. With the students sitting in straight lines of about six per squad you can often utilize those divisions to quickly form teams or make station assignments (having an even number of students per squad is a good rule). Also, with squads you can have student leaders. Squad leaders can be given duties to help you in many ways. They can help with the distribution and collection of equipment, assignments, and exams. They might be given the charge of monitoring and recording their group's effort. Whatever the role you might see them fulfilling, it is probably a good idea to have a system where most everyone has the opportunity to qualify for this coveted leadership role.

Establishing Class Rules

Most educational authorities recommend that class rules be a short list of simply worded positive statements. They should be carefully established at the very beginning of the school year. The teacher might choose to have a prepared listing that is introduced and discussed with the students. Or the teacher may engage them in the process of democratically formulating the rules. This latter procedure has the potential advantage of creating a high level of student ownership and hence more willing compliance. Regardless of which approach is taken it is important that everyone understands the rules and ascents to the necessity for them. Once the rules have been written they should be posted where they will be frequently seen.

Although you have introduced the rules, discussed the need for them, and even gained good student concurrence, you should not expect that everything will run smoothly ever after. The behaviors that the rules are specifying are skills that must be practiced and learned. As immediately as possible after the children are exposed to the rules it would be good to begin this practice. Let us say that you have three class rules: (1) good listeners, (2) fast reactors, and (3) friendly people. You explain a simple tag game of some sort. Before starting the game you insert the comment about how you are pleased that everyone was good listeners and how that is allowing us to get started playing this fun game. After the game has been in progress for a short period you give a clear stop command.

As everyone comes to an immediate halt you enthusiastically congratulate him or her on their fast reaction skills and applying the class rules. You might also remind them of how important that is for safety. After they again have played a brief while you stop them and comment proudly on their running and dodging. Everyone stayed under control and did not crash into anyone else. You tell them that that is part of being "friendly people." You also mention that behaviors such as rescuing people who have been tagged are instances of "friendly people" and this makes the game enjoyable for everyone. The point being made here is that you are concentrating on teaching and reinforcing the application of the class rules. I believe that this should be the primary purpose of the teacher during the first week or two of physical activities sessions. The other fitness and motor skill goals might be considered of secondary importance at this stage. If the children first learn the class rules you will be able to accomplish all other content goals much better over the year. Also, it will make life infinitely easier on you and the students.[1]

The task of working on the class rules does not end after the first week or two. Even if you get your class off to an excellent start, the phenomena of *slippage* will occur. This is where the students will drift or slip away from adherence to the class rules unless they are periodically reviewed and reinforced. For instance, part of being fast reactors was the expectation that the students would stop immediately on your command. During the first weeks the students were faithfully stopping within 3 to 5 second but later on you noticed that you and the class had to wait significantly longer for some to settle down. This is *slippage* and the best course for you to take is not to allow it to continue and invariably grow worst. If you do not deal with it now, you will have to deal with an entrenched problem later. The recommended course to take is to avoid becoming angry with the group or any individual. Rather patiently await the full attention of the class and say something like, "We seem to be starting to forget one of the rules. We are not being fast reactors and stopping quickly. Remember how we agreed that we needed to do so for safety reasons and because it would permit us to have more time for fun activities. Let us start this activity again and when I give the command we will impress ourselves with an instantaneous stop."

Other Teacher Techniques

There are a variety of other management techniques which experienced instructors have found particularly useful in the physical education setting. The first technique is simply that of *teacher movement*. You may have been already taught the educational benefits of moving beyond the front of the classroom and circulating between the desks. Moving about the play area while games and practices are in progress will make a big difference in keeping all the children on task. Not only will it enable you to provide more direct verbal reinforcement but also it puts you in a position to provide personalized demonstrations and feedback. Timely physical guidance help can also be offered in the form of helping someone through the correct throwing action, spotting a gymnastic landing, or repositioning hands on an racket or club.

When you are engaged in teacher movement and drifting about the area, it is good to be near the perimeter most of the time. This better permits you to have general supervision of all the action. It also lends itself to your employing the *back-to-the-wall principle*. This principle states that when you wish to address the class you should position yourself at the perimeter of the group. Your back should not be to any of the students because they will not be able to hear you as well and they more likely may be off-task while out of your sight. This must sound like such an obvious technique but I find beginning teachers often do not think to do it and encounter poorer student responses as a consequence.

---

[1] A useful idea might be to develop the class rules fashioned around Hellison's *Personal and Social Responsibility Model* (PSRM). This model was introduced in Chapter 2 and will be further discussed in Chapter 9 in the section dealing with the teaching of affective habits.

Another management technique is what I have coined the *When I say . . . Principle.* The idea here is to preface your instructions with "When I say go," "When I say begin," "When I say walk," etc. This procedure avoids the inevitable rushing of some children to begin an activity before you have finished your explanation. For example, suppose you wished the children to get a piece of equipment from a supply box and then, without swinging the implements, spread out in a personal space. If you began these directives by saying "Get a piece of equipment and then . . ." That likely is as far as you would get before at least some of the students would be hurrying to the supply box. With the ensuing movement and noise it would not be unusual for the remainder of your message to go largely unheard. This confusion and unwanted behavior could have been avoided if your instruction had begun with "When I say walk, we will get the equipment from the box and then . . ." The forethought of attaching this one small but significant preface might save you one small but significant headache.

Yet another technique for heading off potential or incipient management difficulties is the use of *proximity control.* As an example, you are beginning to instruct the class and you suspect that a given individual may not be the best of quiet listeners, or perhaps he/she is already talking out of turn. You exercise *proximity control* by happening to move in the direction of that student or danger zone. The intent of your getting closer to the student is to correct behavior without disrupting your instruction or having to say anything negative. Just by being closer to the student will hopefully be enough. My experiences have been that if the students are used to you floating about during the lesson it will not be apparent to them that you are engaged in exerting attention to a particular misbehavior. Of course, we are not saying that your looming presence alone will nullify every problem, but if you'll abide the pun, it is a good first preventive step in the right direction.

Finally, you might want to think of using music as a management tool. Music can energize activities and make movement more fun. Simply having a collection of upbeat tapes or CDs ready for use can make a major difference. Many of the best physical education instructors I know use music as a matter of course, some even when outside. Often they have established it as a management cue, the children know that they are to be engaged in activity when the music is playing and to stop and listen when the music stops. If you do find yourself using music extensively, acquiring a remote control on-off devise might be worth the investment. Some good physical education specialists have even discovered the significant benefit of regularly using a microphone system. Not only does this make their instructions vastly more dominant and effective, it also saves on the stress of having to project in a loud voice.

Management Games

Management games can be used in many ways to facilitate adherence to class rules. Among other things, these games can make it fun for the students to quickly follow your commands to begin an activity, stop an activity, find a partner, and form a circle or other formation. They can help you rapidly pick teams or gain the students' undivided attention when they are off-task. Below I have listed some such games that have been effectively used by other teachers and myself.

Back to Back: The teacher has the children locomotoring around an area and when the "back to back" command is given, everyone finds someone with which to get back to back. Everyone should pair with the nearest free person (it is not being a "friendly" person if you avoid anyone). Those who cannot find someone are told to go to the center where the "lost and found" area is located. To solve the problem of someone being left out, I sometimes join in the action when there is an odd number of students. This game can be varied in many ways. Different body parts can be called out: toe to toe, biceps to biceps, elbow to back, knee to knee to knee (three people). Numbers can be shouted out with the understanding that groups of that size are to be formed. How about integrating math problems: 5 minus 3 or 12 divided by 4.

Silent Shapes: The teacher calls different shapes and groups of students attempt to position themselves in that formation as quickly as possible: the number 7, the letter S, a square, a circle, a trapezoid. The task is easier for smaller numbers of students but eventually it is hoped that the entire class could be able to correctly arrange themselves. You can see how their being able to do this would be a usable management tool for you. You want to play a circle game and they can quickly form it. You call out the number 11 and they are there ready for a two-sided game. The game is called Silent Shapes because they are not allowed to say anything as they make the shapes. For fun and increased activity, I usually have them perform the version called *Moving Silent Shapes*; this is where I specify that a movement such as jogging or skipping must be maintained throughout.

Shipwreck: The teacher is the captain of the ship and the children are the sailors. The sailors must ensure a taut ship by carrying out all commands with alacrity. Orders of "bow," "aft," "port," and "starboard" sends the sailors scurrying to those sides of the ship. "Sharks" has them rush to the center to cover their heads. "Leaky ship" has everyone madly pumping out the water with push-ups. A partner activity is called to "abandon ship"; here two people do a rowing exercise. All right, you can take it from here. The idea is to instill the habit of responding to the teacher and making it fun. I have heard of this same game played with a variety of interesting themes and activities: Christmas, Halloween, Star Wars, Cowboy & Cowgirls, Travel time.

Popcorn: The teacher calls popcorn and everyone must start jumping up and around as if they were popcorn being popped. On the "sticky popcorn" command each is to pop over to somebody, stick shoulder to shoulder and keep popping. This is of course a quick way to form partners for a subsequent partner activity. If you wished groups of 4 or 8, "stickier popcorn" and "super sticky popcorn" should produce the popcorn ball sizes you desire. Sometimes it is fun to have them all stuck together and then have everyone melt into a gooey mess.

Cue Words: All that is involved here is having designated cue words for various desired formations. For instance, I have used the cue word theme of "Fruits and Vegetables." Whenever I said "bananas" the students were to go bananas and spread out so each had some personal activity space. When I said "potatoes" they knew to sit down. "Celery" meant stand-up. "Kumquats" meant pairs and "grapes" directed everyone to come and sit in a clump in front of me. You might find that a list has a tendency to grow. I once began to make a remark about a "potato" which was lying down as I was talking. His clever riposte was that he was a "mashed potato." Immediately a popular new word was added to our class lexicon.

Attention Getters: The above games were primarily designed to produce fast responding to the teacher's commands. Occasions sometimes arise then the students' attention is elsewhere and they may not be mentally set or focused on you. It is at these times that a clearly recognizable *attention getter* is an asset. Of course, a shouted "Stop!" or whistle blast may serve this purpose but there are other more effective fun ideas. A good procedure is to give some well-known distinctive signal to which the students have a set response. I knew one teacher who would forcefully say, "Are you ready!" and this cued the students to give an arm pump and shout "You bet!" Even if a given student did not catch the teacher's signal the shouted response of the other students would be distinctly heard and understood as a cue to pay attention. Another teacher used a unique hand clapping pattern (slow, slow, quick, quick, quick) which the students could not help but notice and to which they would have to respond which a practiced unison clap. How about this one for generating a fun student response? Whenever the teacher said, "Where am I?" the students rapidly recited the following poem while simultaneously touching the corresponding body parts, "Here I am! Head, shoulders, knees and toes, ankles, thighs, heart and nose!" Can you not see how this practice would have the effect of drawing everyone into the chant and away from what they were doing? At its completion all eyes and minds will be on you.

101 Ways to Pick Teams: A common physical education situation is the lining-up of the children and the picking teams. I am sure we all remember that. Quite likely you may have counted off by 2s or 4s. Or maybe captains were designated and they in turn selected who would play for them. Both these time worn methods have shortcomings. Neither is very rapid. Counting off is oftentimes confusing to the younger students and sometimes there is even some shuffling of positions in the hopes of being counted on the same team as a best friend. As for selection by captains, I call this the *slave market approach*. I have heard many adults say that the thing they recalled and hated most about physical education was the sinking feeling of being picked last. Even Ann Landers has received many testimonials of this kind.

Here are some concepts that should provide you with 101 or more ways of almost instantaneously breaking your group into the number of teams you want. (1) Simple body gestures or positions could be used; "Clasp your hands together. OK, everyone who has his/her right thumb on top step forward." Or "Cross your legs. OK, those with their left leg in front take three giant steps forwards." Or "Inspect your finger nails. Those whose palms are turned upward move over here." (2) Specifying different actions or shapes will work; "Swimmers think about doing either the back crawl or front crawl. When I say swim, do four strokes. OK, ready swim." Or "Think of making either an X shape with your body, like this, or an O shape like this. When I say shapes, go. Ready, shapes." (3) Favorite things can work. "Think which you like best, crunchy or smooth peanut butter. OK, smoothies over here." Which movies, books, sports, colors, etc. (4) The names of the students can be used. "Anyone whose first name begins with A through L . . ." "All whose first name has four letters or less . . ." (5) Birthdays are known by even the youngest. Winter people with birthdays in December, January, and February, form a snow drift on this line . . ."

By now you must have the idea how you can get to 101 or beyond. When your initial division tactic does not yield equal divisions don't panic, it's easy to move a few students from one team to another. A quick survey of clothing is one sure way to do it. Those in this group wearing shorts, hats, red, belts, rings . . .

Correcting Misbehavior

By far it is best to head off behavioral problems before they happen. Successfully doing so is the lion's share of the battle. Throughout this chapter, and scattered elsewhere throughout this book, I have offered ideas that should serve this purpose. Nevertheless you know that problems will arise. Handling these problems is the number one concern of beginning teachers. I do not have all the answers for what you may face but can describe a few procedures that have been useful to other teachers and myself.

In your education courses you undoubtedly have or will be introduced to a number of the most current recommended approaches. Whichever procedure you adopt for classroom management should be carried over into the gymnasium and playing-field setting; consistency has the advantage of producing clearer expectations for both teachers and students. To my mind, it is ideal if the entire school has a coordinated assertive discipline plan. If your school has such a plan, I suggest you give your full effort to supporting and working with others to make it the best it can be.

When misbehavior first occurs I would prefer to deal with it positively, without any element of punishment. The discipline technique I have in mind is known as *Overcorrection* (see Figure 5.2). The first step *in Overcorrection* is to tell the child about the incorrectness of his or her action, why it was incorrect (not in accordance with class rules), and what would have been appropriate behavior. If the class were engaged in activity I would not normally stop the flow of action, but rather communicate privately, one-on-one. If the incident occurred in the full view of everyone, it might be appropriate and instructive to stop the class and verbally correct the child. It would be best to emphasize that it was the act that needed to be changed, not that you were personally criticizing the individual. Hopefully the lesson would be learned, the behavior remedied and *Overcorrection* completed.

If the misbehavior reoccurred, the verbal explanation would be repeated and the student or students would also need to do *over* the incorrect behavior in the appropriate manner. For example, if a student ran into the gym and slid across the floor, he or she would be required to go back to the

Figure 5.2. Overcorrection Procedural Steps

1. Tell the student that he or she is behaving inappropriately.

2. Provide systematic verbal instruction during overcorrection activities.

3. If necessary, physically assist the practice of overcorrection.

4. If the student was removed from class for overcorrection, return him or her to the class activity immediately after the overcorrection activity has been successfully completed.

5. Reinforce the first appropriate behavior the student displays

gym entrance, walk into the gym, and take his or her assigned place quietly, and maybe have to do it more than once if you thought further reinforcement and practice might be needed. The same could be done for the entire class if they entered in an unruly manner. Another example might be where a student throws down his or her jump rope in a tangled mess and moves on to something else. You would explain the correct behavior and he or she would of course be required to pick up the rope and hang it away properly. He or she might also be required to straighten up all the ropes or any other pieces of equipment. If you had the help of a paraprofessional, that person could be used to monitor the student's practicing of the behavior while you moved on with the class.

Hopefully at this stage the appropriate behavior has been instilled and as soon as you notice the individual or the class demonstrating the correct behavior it would be wise to reinforce it with praise. But what if *Overcorrection* does not work? Maybe you did not feel like you had the time to deal one-on-one with the situation? Maybe at the moment of the occurrence you could not think of a good *Overcorrection* activity for the student to perform? Maybe the misbehavior was quite aggressive and needed to be more strongly addressed? Or simply that the misbehavior continued?

The commonly advocated *time-out procedure* has been generally found to be the most effective punishment technique for elementary physical education teachers. Elementary children usually are eager to participate in movement activities and a warning or short denial will serve as a strong incentive. Even if removal from certain physical activities might not be adverse to a particular child, very likely there are other greatly valued activities that will be. In such a case, the disruptive child needs to know that some of the time-out can be carried over into a more attractive, future activity.

There are four basic recommended steps of the *time-out procedure*. (1) A first misbehavior warrants one clear warning; it is not a personal attack but rather a statement that a behavior was inappropriate. For instance, a firmly controlled statement such as . . ." Kevin, you are forgetting to stop immediately on command, this is a warning that that behavior is not permissible." The concept of having only one warning should be stressed and known by all the students. Repeated threats are a downward road not to be traveled. (2&3) A reoccurrence of the misbehavior results in a removal to a time-out area that is safe, easy-to-monitor and non-reinforcing (e.g., the corner of the gym). Some teachers like to make the first visit to the time-out area of duration regulated by the student. The student is to remain there until he/she feels ready to re-enter the class activities and abide by the rules. "Kevin, you must go to the time-out area. When you feel that you can return to the class activities and follow the class rules, you will be welcome to join us." Other teachers skip this student-determination phase and set the length of time of return. The suggested length of time is five minutes or less, yet the average length used by educators has been tracked to be 12 minutes. Some pedagogists have suggested that a student should remain in time-out for one minute for each year of his or her life. Most educators agree that a timer should be used to determine the end of a time-out. It is so easy to loose track of time when you are involved with a lesson. (4) If the child returns from time-out and continues disobedient the final step is removal from class. The student might then experience personal counseling with the teacher, school psychologist, principal or some combination. Generally the parent(s) are informed and involved at this stage. This is where an agreed upon school policy is particularly helpful.

While on the topic of discipline procedures, something needs to be said about two other practices you undoubtedly have seen or experienced: (1) the use of exercise as punishment and (2) punishing the entire class for the actions of some of its members.

For as long as I can remember, physical education authorities have been admonishing against using exercise as punishment. The reasoning is an easily understandable one that goes like this, "If we want children to learn to value and enjoy exercise we cannot associate it with something that is disliked and to be avoided." I know many people who have said that they want no more of running, push-ups, or doing other similar exercises because they remember being punished with them years ago in school or the military. But in spite of the logic of not using exercise to punish, and in spite of educators delivering this message over the years, many teachers and coaches still rely on it to one degree or another. They probably do so because it has become a tradition modeled by many in the field, because it is easy to use, because it will generally produce some quick-term results in curbing undesirable actions, and because the instructor has not developed a clear set of time-out or other alternative procedures. I can only add my voice to the chorus of authorities who advocate other punishment avenues . If we keep our ultimate goal of developing enjoyment of activities and exercise in mind, we simple must find other ways. I knew a coach once who had his players so convinced of the importance of hard work and training that he was able to effectively punish individuals by not permitting them to participate in some of the conditioning drills. They had to sit and watch and miss out as the rest of the team improved themselves by determinedly running stairs and the like. While achievement of such an ethos may not be realistic in your teaching environment, it does epitomize the kind of attitude for which each of us should be striving.[2]

Much that has been said about exercise as punishment can also be said about whole class punishment practices; both have long been discouraged by those in higher education but they continue to be frequently used by practitioners. Those using group punishment feel that is a potent tool because it results in classmates putting pressure on the truant children to conform to class rules. Counter-argument would be that although it can sometimes be effective, at other times the offending student or students will rebel and lash out at their not always so diplomatic, criticizing peers. My feeling is that creating such a situation is hardly conducive to the establishment of a friendly class milieu where we wish children to learn to help and positively encourage one another. Here again, use of it is probably indicative of a failure to develop and apply a sounder technique along the line of the fore-mentioned time-out procedures.

In Chapter 9 we will be advocating the teaching practices of awareness talks and reflection times. They can be further tools in addressing misbehaviors.

---

[2] If a child suffered some physical or psychological trauma during physical punishment you would have no educational objective for a defense in court. Rulings typically have been in favor of the plaintiffs.

Useful Procedures for Teaching Movement Skills

6

Introductory Instructions and Demonstrations

Practice

Feedback

Review

"Improvement depends far less upon length of tasks and hours of application than is supposed. Children can take in but a little each day; they are like vases with a narrow neck; you may pour little or pour much, but much will not enter at a time."
Jules Michelet

"If, in instructing a child, you are vexed with it for want of adroitness, try, if you have never tried before, to write with your left hand and then remember that a child is all left hand."
J.F. Boyse

I strongly believe that education is a most worthy profession and that you can become a good teacher if you deeply wish it. Regardless of your personality and background, if you have the desire, and persevere at developing effective teaching procedures, you will be able to make it happen. In this chapter you will be introduced to some teaching skills that master teachers regularly demonstrate. If you practice these techniques you will see things falling into place, violate them and potential problems will be likely. The procedures offered specifically pertain to teaching movement skills but you will see that many of the concepts are generic to teaching regardless of subject.

A theme stressed in Chapter 3 and elsewhere in this book is that we need get children regularly moving and ensure that it is an enjoyable experience. Having the attitude that a person likes to be active is even more important than how athletically skilled he or she is. I have a number of adult friends who are not particularly skillful and yet they still regularly enjoy physical activities and exercise. Conversely, I know former athletes who now are quite sedentary. Nevertheless, data shows that people who acquired good movement skills when young tend to remain more active than do those of low abilities. The purpose of this chapter will be to introduce you some teaching procedures that will help children learn movement skills safely and successfully.

Introductory Instructions and Demonstrations

To better insure that students will be attentive to your instruction and demonstration you should consider the following preliminaries. Firstly, if at all possible, have the students seated. They are often naturally fidgety and it will be unlikely that unseated children will refrain from shuffling feet and bumping others. Secondly, if they have been given any implements such as balls, bats, paddles, rackets, hoops, or jump ropes, get those things out of their hands. A good procedure is to always establish a *Home Position* at the very beginning. For instance, the children know that on the "stop" or "home position" command, they are to place the ball at their feet, stand inside the hoop, stand on the jump rope, etc. Without *Home Positions* there will be some inevitable juggling and swinging of things. It is so much better to have a positive environment and thank everyone for remembering the correct *Home Position* rather than having to nag them about being still. Thirdly, attempt to have the students facing away from the sun and distracters. Of course, looking into the sun will make it harder to see your demonstration. Distractions are common in the gym and on the playground and children are particularly susceptible to them. Finally, before beginning to give instruction regarding the skill, it is often good to remind yourself of establishing an *Anticipatory Set*. This means setting the stage for the skill you will be teaching. Make the skill sound interesting by being enthusiastic. Explain why this skill will be fun to learn and the possibilities to which it may lead. If it is a sports skill, present a reason why possession of this skill is prerequisite to successful enjoyment of the game.

The instruction itself should be kept short, two minutes or shorter is normally a good rule. For coding purposes we will call it *The Two-Minute Warning*. If your talk is much longer than this you are likely covering more than what will be retained in long-term memory. A useful procedure is to stress one *Learnable Piece*. This means that with each instructional bout you are focusing on one observable objective that everyone should be able to accomplish or review. For example, suppose you wished to help the children with their overhand throwing. Decide what might be one important aspect of the throw you would like all to have. Maybe "stepping forwards with the opposite foot to your throwing hand" or "following through across your body" would be the *Learnable Piece*. These would be good because they are do-able and worthy of practice by all, and they are specific things both the students and we should be able to monitor. The point is that we should not attempt to accomplish indeterminable, grandiose things in one day; "Today we are going to learn to become good volleyball players" or "We will get good at jumping rope." These things will not be accomplished in many periods let alone one period, and you and the students may not be clear on what denotes good serves and rope jumping, and what specific actions are required. A better developmental, less frustrating, approach is to learn one thing at a time and then to build off of that in future lessons. This gradual adding to a previous day's learning is called *Scaffolding*. One day we have an objective of leading with the opposite foot and the next day, if they seem to have mastered that aspect, we add the next objective/learnable piece of the cross-the-body follow-through.

Demonstrations are the best way to convey movement skills. They, like pictures, are indeed worth a thousand words. The most essential thing about a demonstration is that it shows the skill correctly performed. If you can do the skill reasonably well that is great. You should not feel that it must be done with great power and precision, as long as it is done with fundamentally correct form. If you cannot do the skill correctly there likely will be a student in class who can. If none of your students can, it may be worth the effort to see if you can recruit the services of someone from outside of the class. Even if you can do the skill it is not a bad idea to supplement your demonstrations with student demonstrations. When the students see others of their age and gender successfully performing, it can effectively convince them that they too might be capable. Remember that good demonstrations do more than provide information of how the skill is executed, they serve to convince that mastery may be within their means. This believing that you are capable of accomplishing a specific task is called *self-efficacy* and having it is an extremely important determinant in attempting, persevering, and mastering skills. I would like to make one more point about your modeling of motor skill; don't feel inadequate if you cannot demonstrate some skills. Admit to the students that you have not yet learned to perform a skill and make it an opportunity to convey the message that physical skills require lengthy practice and no one can be expected to master them all. Remember the point I made in Chapter 3 regarding *The Ten-Year Rule* and the huge amount of practice that sometimes is required.

Even the best of demonstrations may not result in a full conveyance of desired information. There is much going on during a demonstration so it is not to be unexpected that important aspects of the movement might go undetected. The student may have been watching the feet, the arms, the face, the implement, or simply might not have been vigilant and paying attention at all. There are a number of procedures that could help. Firstly, make sure you have cued the key elements; "Watch the feet, notice how I step with the foot opposite the throwing arm." Concepts need to be given labels if they are to be stored in memory. Experienced teachers have learned this and often use catchy, vivid cues to abet the retention process (see Figure 6.1 for some examples). Secondly, demonstrations should be performed a number of times at both full and slow speed. Doing the skill at full-speed should serve to represent the actual patterning and timing. Surprisingly it is common for instructors to not repeat or even give a full-speed execution. Adding a slower-motion performance is obviously good in that it sometimes can make it easier to see. Thirdly, changing your position, or that of the onlookers, so that the skill will be viewed from more than one perspective, might yield a clearer image. Finally, if the skill has a rather dramatic outcome like achieving a target or distance goal, be aware that the children will be easily distracted and may attend to the goodness of the outcome instead of focusing upon relevant parts of the technique. When this is the case, a good policy might be to first perform the skill and allow the students to initially view the outcome of the movement.

Figure 6.1. Learnable Pieces and Corresponding Vivid Cues

Learnable Pieces	Vivid Cues
when running, have the elbows bent and the arms swinging forwards and backwards in opposition to the legs	"pumping steam engines"
when dribbling a basketball, let your fingers give with the ball, don't slap it	"pet the kitty"
when catching a ball, eyes on the ball, arms extended in preparation, and elbows bending to absorb force	"look, reach, give"
when fielding a ground ball, get in front of the ball and use both hands	"make a tunnel"
during aerobic exercise, keep the feet constantly moving	"happy feet" "ten toes clubs"
when swinging, follow-through high	"air the armpit"
when doing a backward roll, stay tightly tucked	"knees near nose"

It can be motivating to see how far the ball can be kicked or how accurately it can be shot. But then, to better insure attention on the movement objective, remove the target by shooting or kicking against a wall or without a target; or even doing the skill without the implement such as pretending you are kicking a footbag or serving a ball.

Practice

It is best for skill practice to begin as soon after the explanation-demonstration as possible. You want the explanation, image and verbal cueing fresh in their minds. As soon as practice commences you should always alert yourself with the *SOS question.* This means that you judge the appropriateness of the practice by asking three things in this order: Is everyone Safe? Is everyone On-task and active? Is everyone being Successfully challenged?

Of course, safety needs to be the first concern of any movement experience. Look to see if the children are adequately spaced from each other and from dangerous obstacles such as poles and walls. Make sure they are not performing on a hard abrasive surface if they are at high risk of falling down. Are they adequately under control and watching out for others? If you can foresee a real potential for accidents it is your duty to immediately stop the action or make alterations. Just use your good judgment. The law expects you to be *reasonably prudent.*

Is everyone On-task and active? For practice to be effective it is imperative that all the children get to execute the skill many times. Of all the variables that effect the learning of motor skills, the most powerful determinant is simply how many times the skill has been attempted. Minimal skill development will result if only a few children are performing and the rest are standing in lines waiting turns. In the past, when the students of physical education teachers have been observed it has not been unusual to find that they are only active 10 to 30 percent of the time or even less. We should be able to do much better than this. A good rule of thumb is to strive to have children actively engaged in movement for at least a *50 Percent Activity Standard.* Meeting or exceeding this standard is easier when teaching some activities as opposed to others. It should not be difficult to keep everyone performing at near 100 percent when teaching aerobic activities and circuit training. Instruction in gymnastics and softball skills present more of a challenge, but still can be done with good planning.

Having enough equipment for everyone, or at least for every two or three students, is critical for high participation rates in many activities. What would you do in your classroom if you had only a few textbooks, computers, microscopes, paint brushes, etc.? Would you form lines and expect students to fold their arms and serenely wait their turn to read the book or use the equipment? Obviously that would not be educationally sound. You would either go to lengths to get more equipment or you would design your instructional approach so that students would have other stations at which to work until the needed equipment was not in use by classmates. Having and acquiring balls, racquets, jump ropes, hoola hoops, beanbags, beach balls, balloons, for all or half of the students may not be as improbable as it first would appear. Most schools have sports teams whose equipment could be made available; many children might be able to bring their own items from home; the physical education specialist might have available equipment or avenues of procuring some; many outside organizations would be glad to make a small contribution to this sort of worthy cause. I have known classroom teachers who, through various means, were even able to gather a significant number of more expensive items such as roller-blades, unicycles, bicycles, and tumbling mats. Another point relative to equipment is that it does not always have to be officially correct to be a serviceable learning aid. Different kinds of playground balls might do as substitutes for soccer or basketballs. I have had students make their own beanbags and jump ropes. I once used crunched-up milk cartons for a soccer dribbling lesson and it turned-out great; they were easier to dribble around cones and pass short distances.

If you cannot procure sufficient equipment or space to permit a high rate of practice of the skill, plan other activity stations to reduce downtime. Many teachers have learned that *Circuit Training* is a time efficient teaching method; while some students are learning the new skill others are simultaneously reviewing and practicing other skills at one or numerous locations around the gym or play space. The workstations can be spread out to reduce congested safety concerns and yet you can still have general supervision of everyone. Posting instructions and teaching the students to independently read and carryout the activities can be a good educational process. Figure 6.2 offers an example of instructions for an individual and partner circuit. Notice how different levels can be listed to accommodate differences in ability. Music can be effectively used both as a pacing and motivational tool. When the music begins the students know that they are to be active. When the music stops it is a cue to stop and to move to the next station. The use of music tends to energize and make the activities more fun. I have many tapes with breaks placed in the music at 30 second, 45 second, 1 minute, and 2-minute intervals. This saves me from having to watch clocks and blow whistles. I know other physical education specialists with remote control devices for turning the music on and off.

The third letter of the *SOS* mnemonic stood for Successful. Is everyone being Successfully challenged? It is not good to have a situation in which the children are experiencing repeated failure. Nor is it good if the skills are too easy and therefore fail to challenge. As a general rule it is best to have a *Learnable Piece* at which everyone has something in the realm of a *80% Success Rate.* Because your students will have different experiences, abilities, disabilities and maturational levels, some individualization of instruction will be necessary to achieve this level of success for everyone. To achieve individualization of practice, remember the principle of the *Long Slanty-Rope.* Here is what it is. Imagine you had one end of a long rope held on the ground and the other end pulled taut and

Figure 6.2. Circuit Training Instructions

Individual Soccer Circuit

Sole Trap
level A. toss ball off wall, allow two bounces then trap

level B. toss ball off wall, allow one bounce then trap

level C. toss ball off wall, trap before it bounces

Head
level A. toss ball above head, and head it

level B. toss ball above head, and head it twice in a row

level C. toss ball above head, and head it as long as you can

Shoot at goal
level A. score as many goals as you can from the short line

level B. score as many goals as you can from the middle line

level C. score as many goals as you can from the long line

Dribble around cones
level A. strive for 10

level B. strive for 15

level C. strive for 20

Partner Circuit

Throw-in & Trap
level A. short distance line

level B. middle distance line

level C. long distance line

Passing
level A. 10 passes

level B. 15 passes

level C. 20 passes

Dribbling through cones
level A. 5 circuits

level B. 10 circuits

level C. 15 circuits

Corner kicks & goalie catches
level A. 10 ft. line

level B. 20 ft. line

level C. 30 ft. line

raised to a height of three feet. The children's task is to practice their leaping skills. As they are practicing they can choose to jump over the rope at the section suited to their abilities and confidence. Because the rope is an extra long one, all the students can practice at the same time with little interference to each other. Of course, the idea of the *Long Slanty-Rope Principle* is to see if you can organize all your practices, regardless of the type of skill, along the same conceptual lines. There are a couple of avenues for doing so. One way is to modify the equipment for the students. If in a batting practice drill, the students are not successfully hitting pitched balls, a switch to t-ball might be appropriate. If some were still experiencing difficulty, the conceptual rope could be slanted by assigning or allowing the students to select from jumbo or flat bats and larger balls. If the children are having difficulty with badminton striking activities, short-handled, large-faced racket variations might serve. If their volleyball skills are not ready for official volleyballs, what about balloons, beach balls, and lightweight vinyl balls.

Another means of individualization is to set different task criteria. There are many ways of doing this. Setting different target criteria: shooting at different size targets from different distances. Different time criteria can be set: when a teacher tells the students to attempt as many push-ups or skier-jumps as possible in a minute, he/she is using time in a slanted rope manner because the students are being encouraged to set the task difficulty suitable to their abilities. Different technique criteria can also be presented: doing the dribble with the opposite hand, doing the skill switching from forehand to backhand, doing the skill with the eyes up and with toes pointed, doing push-ups either from the knees or toes. Notice that the Figure 6.2 *Circuit Training* example employed a number of the above means of creating different challenges.

Before leaving the issue of having the children practice skills I would like to make the point about the kind of movement skills best practiced during school and outside of school. I have said over and over that most movement skills require a large amount of practice to be mastered. No matter how high of an On-task activity standard you are able to have in your class, the children's skill levels are likely going to be low unless they also practice beyond the lessons you have for them. And due to the great individual differences in learning rates, some of the slower learners can only be expected to make minimal progress in class. Because of this, it so important that we always remember to remind and encourage further practice outside of class or to make either formal or informal homework assignments. Individual movement skills are especially conducive to this. Most of the students can get good exercise outside of class as they practice individual skills you might have introduced to them: shooting baskets, dribbling a soccer ball, practicing jump rope or gymnastic stunts, etc. Skills that require partners and more teammates become more difficult for them to do at home because getting together with friends might not always be possible. If you can get the children to achieve some level of individual skill mastery as a result of outside of class practice, you will be able to focus on more cooperative skill learning. Encouraging the students to practice together during recess periods is another opportunity. I know of some good youth sport coaches who follow this concept of promoting individual skills beyond practice so that the actual time, when the team members are together, can be spent on developmental games using those skills. An excellent, easy to apply book addressing this issue, was written by Alan Lander.[1]

Feedback

As children are practicing skills you can play an important role in the learning process by providing feedback. Feedback can be divided into two basic kinds: *General Feedback* and *Specific Feedback*. *General feedback* is when the instructor projects encouragement or disapproval about the overall performance of the students. It can be verbal: "Great going today." "Nice job Mary." "Good swing, Jason." "I am disappointed with our behavior today." It can be non-verbal: smiling, head nods or shakes, yawns, folded arms, inattention, high fives. The function of this sort of feedback is to improve motivation either by rewarding good or punishing undesirable performance. Both verbal and non-verbal feedback are important but some believe that non-verbal messages carry the most weight because they often are perceived to be more accurate indicators of the teacher's true feelings. The teacher may say, "great going" or "you did wonderful" and not really mean it. It is less likely that the teacher's actions and gestures are disingenuous.

It is desirable to establish a warm learning environment in which the positive reinforcers outweigh the negative ones by a high ratio. Hopefully enthusiastic instructions/demonstrations and well-established class rules/procedures will minimize generally poor conduct and efforts. This should free the teacher to be supportive and praising.

It is also believed that for the *General Feedback* to be most effective it should be varied. The *Global Good* is a term used to represent an instructor's repeating of the same general feedback over and over, in this case, good. It is good this and good that, good job, good going, good try. Have you

---

[1] Lander, A.G. Play Practice: *The Games Approach to Teaching and Coaching Sports*, Human Kinetics, 2001.

heard something like this before? The repeated mantra may have been a different word or phrase than good but the repetition was unmistakable in its global presence. Overuse of the same words and actions lessens their motivational impact. It is an easy, almost normal trap into which teachers may fall. It is probably wise for every teacher to have a lesson or two video taped and then to look and listen for excessively common language and movement habits. Awareness is the first step. If you catch yourself guilty of some mannerisms don't despair. As already mentioned, it is expected and normal and it is easily corrected. Simply give thought to some ways that you might begin to increase your repertoire for reinforcers, both verbally and gesture-wise. Figure 6.3 offers a small list of suggestions. Perhaps you can think of some others you could progressively begin to add which might be more in vogue and hip with the culture of your students and which are best suited to your personality. I sometimes have had my preservice teachers teach a lesson in which they were going to be assessed entirely upon the variety of their feedback, you could think of it as their instructional *Learnable Piece*. It is impressive how quickly they acquire the skill, especially if they have given a priori thought to the movement and verbal possibilities. It is also striking how improvements in this one aspect of instruction invariably creates a noticeably more enthusiastic learning environment.

Specific Feedback is feedback that does more than identify if performance was good or bad. It qualifies or quantifies. It identifies what was good or bad. "You didn't follow-through." "Your knees weren't bent." "You watched the ball well." This kind of feedback will be critically important for some to learn skills correctly. Not only can it be motivational like *General Feedback,* it may convey the information needed to learn the skill and avoid the formation of bad habits. Research indicates that the best teachers give much more *Specific Feedback* than less skilled teachers. In fact, it is not uncommon for many teachers to give virtually no *Specific Feedback* at all.

When the students are practicing it is good procedure for the teacher to move about the area and at some point get close to every student. This better facilitates the ability to give personalized *Specific Feedback* to everyone. The *Specific Feedback* given should be kept simple, it is easy to try to correct and help too much. This excess of feedback often ends up confusing the student and results in the phenomenon of *Analysis Paralysis.* This means that the student is overloaded with so many suggestions he/she cannot incorporate any change. One way to keep your feedback simple is to remember the *Learnable Piece* and so focus your feedback. When our feedback is related to the *Learnable Piece* we are employing *Congruent Feedback.* Here is an example. The class is working on soccer dribbling skills and I have explained and demonstrated the *Learnable Piece* of "Happy feet." Happy feet is a label for remembering to keep your feet moving with quick, short steps. As I move about

---

Figure 6.3. Ideas for Varying General Positive Feedback

Verbal	Gestures
super	smiles
terrific	thumbs up
awesome	high fives or tens
stupendous	hand shakes (traditional & otherwise)
great	head nods
wonderful	raised arms

the practice area I am looking and commenting primarily on this aspect. "Mary, what are we working on?" "Amazingly happy footwork Jim." "Jan, you are moving those feet nicely!"

As stated before with regards to *General Feedback,* learning best occurs in a mostly positive environment. You might question how you can keep your *Specific Feedback* positive for students who are not performing the skill correctly. A helpful technique for these situations is the *Sandwich Principle.* This principle is where you surround your corrective feedback with positive comments about other aspects of performance. In a situation in which a child is not adhering to the *Learnable Piece* of swinging the bat level this feedback could be offered; "I like your ready position, remember you need to swing level rather than upwards, keep up the good effort." You can notice how these kinds of messages are more sensitive to potential discouragement than correction-only comments might be.

Thus far I have been exemplifying only verbal *Specific Feedback.* You will find that that will not always suffice. Telling the child he/she is not swinging level will not always remedy the situation. A useful feedback progression is first to tell, then show, and then provide *physical guidance.* If the swing is not leveled when you verbally commented on the noncompliance it is useful to take the bat and demonstrate the swing again. If they still have not gotten the idea, the final *physical guidance* step may be required. At this stage you attempt to give them the kinesthetic feel by guiding their bat and or limbs through the proper path. I have found that this final hands-on stage makes the critical difference for some learners and shows that you are truly interested and involved in the process. A cautionary note is worth mentioning here pertaining to physical touching students. We need to remind ourselves that everyone, regardless of age, has a right to their personal space and should not have others touching them if it makes them uncomfortable. Because of this right, we need to be absolutely sure that we do not touch students if it would be unwelcome, no matter how good and innocent our intentions. If you have the slightest doubt about their feelings, be sure to ask their permission before jumping in to help. A simple "Can I help you through a level swing?" would be wise. The issue of appropriate and inappropriate touching will be further covered in Chapter 10.

Review

When we think of review we normally think of the lesson's closure and summary statements by the teacher. Here I am taking a somewhat broader view of the review process. Review is not something that only occurs at the completion of practice, it must also be taking place throughout the introductory explanation-demonstration and during practice.

When a skill is being explained and demonstrated to students, they must not only pay attention to the salient points, they must also review or rehearse those concepts in their minds. If they do not repeat what they have seen or heard, that information will quickly fade from short-term memory and never enter long-term memory. It will go into one ear and come out the other. If this happens they likely will not have purposeful practice even it that practice occurs a fairly short time following the explanation/demonstration. Many teachers of the young have experienced this phenomenon. Research indicates that school children have just as good short-term memory mechanisms as adults and if they rehearse what has been presented to them, are as capable of moving information into long-term storage. However, children sometimes do not acquire concepts as readily because they use rehearsal strategies less effectively than mature learners do.

The instructor can do a couple of things to insure that presented information gets into useful long-term memory. We have already stressed the importance of keeping your message simple and directed at one *Learnable Piece.* The more different things you attempt to explain the less likely any one of those aspects is going to be thought over and repeatedly imaged. The second thing is to develop the habit of ending your presentation with a question such as, "What are we going to think about?" You need to know if what you introduced registered with them and this quizzing may force them to immediately rehearse. Also, the manner in which we ask questions has much to do with whether or not reviewing will be stimulated. *The Effective Questioning Strategy* is a good technique for promoting rehearsal of all the students. It consist of posing the question, waiting at least five seconds or more so everyone has time to mentally consider, and then randomly picking on a student to respond. If the students get used to you always asking questions in this manner they may learn that they must be thinking about what you say because they may be called upon to respond in front of the class. When you throw open questions to the class the same quicker, hand waving children will tend to dominate and the others may feel no pressure to mentally prepare. They may zone out on you.

During practice, the reviewing process continues if you are giving feedback. Instead of always immediately providing *Specific Feedback* you might ask the student to review for his/herself what it is that is to be remembered. Also, you might wish to provide another demonstration for that student, or to stop the whole class and give a repeat demonstration. Just because an excellent demonstration was provided at the beginning does not mean that it was totally grasped or retained. A good means of providing this review during practice is to employ the technique of *Spotlighting*. This is were you stop the class and have them watch a couple of students who are performing well. This provides the review you want for the class and may bolster their *self-efficacy*. It additionally gives those demonstrators a chance to show-off a little and receive some kudos. Having two or three simultaneous demonstrators works well because it allows you to have more children receive recognition and it takes some of the pressure off them as everyone watches.

At the end of the period the traditional summing up review is considered a sound teaching procedure. Final questioning will result in a terminal review and hopefully this will solidify the concept to be transferred into beyond class use. But even yet the review process should not be considered to be over. Reminding yourself to ask review questions at the beginning of next period and periodically throughout the remainder of the year might make a telling difference. If something was worth a lesson's instruction it is worth the students' recalling.

Laboratory Exercises

1. Create an *individual tumbling circuit* patterned after the one illustrated in Figure 6.2. (Remember you can accommodate ability levels by using different equipment, target sizes, score criteria, distances, and technique criteria.)

2. Create a *partner volleyball circuit* patterned after the one illustrated in Figure 6.2. (Remember you can accommodate ability levels by using different equipment, target sizes, score criteria, distances, and technique criteria.)

How You Can Make Games and Sports Fun and Educational

7

Making Games Fun and Educational
Introducing Games
SOS Principle Revisited
  Safety
  On-Task Activity
  Successful

Making Sports Fun and Educational
Changing the Rules
Matching Competitors
Changing the Equipment and Facilities
Adjusting the Contextual Aspects of Sports
Traditional vs. Games Approach to Teaching Sport Skills
Beyond Traditional Sports

"Happy hearts, and happy faces / Happy play in grassy places."

unknown poet

Description of sports: "Tumultuous merriment," and "animated relaxation."

Samuel Johnson

"It should be noted that children's games are not merely games; one should regard them as their most serious activities."

Michel de Montaigne

Most of the children in your classes will be incessantly clambering "Lets play a game!" "Let's play softball!" "Let's play basketball!" Games and sports can be gleeful fun for children and they can be a great avenue for developing motor skills, affective skills, and physical fitness. However, you may have some students who are not always keen to participate; some games and sports may not provide everyone with much activity for motor and fitness development; and sometimes the students can learn poor, rather than good, social-emotional behaviors.

In this chapter you will learn how to introduce, select, modify, design, and organize games and sports so that they can be enjoyable and profitable for all.

Making Games Fun and Educational

Introducing Games

In Chapter 6, we discussed how motor skills might be effectively introduced to learners by means of the concept of *Anticipatory set*. We said you might improve the students' interest in learning a skill by presenting some reasons how the skill would help them in the sports contest. This understanding should increase their motivation to learn. When you are introducing a game to the students it is also a good practice to create an *Anticipatory set* or desire to participate. Your manner of introduction can make a big difference. Imagine the dissimilar reactions you might get from second graders in these two scenarios. In scenario one you tell the children they will be playing a tag game. If you are tagged you will run over to a hula-hoop and jump in and out of it three times. This completed, you can re-enter the ongoing tag. In scenario two the teacher is wearing a false face and robe and is wielding something that is supposed to resemble a sword. In a stentorian voice she proclaims herself to be a samurai warrior of the highest order. Stirring music is playing. In "Samurai Warrior Tag" the tagged students run to her and she slams the sword on the ground and yells, "Samurai warrior will save you!" Then she swings the sword along the ground at the students feet and then over their heads, carefully of course. They jump and duck the sword three times and then can join the tag.

The above point being made is that names, themes, music and a little hamming by the instructor can have a major impact on how well games will be received. As another example, a mundane set of "grass drills" might become more exciting when it assumes the challenging name, "THE ONE MINUTE TORTURE TEST." With a little thought and creativity, a simple tag game can easily become Pac Man Tag, Star Wars Tag, Ninja Turtle Tag, Jurassic Park Tag, Power Ranger Tag, Pokemon Tag, or Good Wizard-Bad Wizard Tag. Notice these names illustrate how quickly some themes become hot or not so hot. If Napoleon was right when he said, "men are ruled by names," how much more true can that not be said for excitable elementary children.

Another useful concept to remember when introducing games is *The Three-Rule Rule.* This means that you can explain your game in three rules or less. If there are only three rules you will be able to explain the game quickly and move right into action. More rules necessitates that your explanation must be lengthier, and as a consequence, the children may become fidgety and in all probability not remember all those rules anyway. Once the game is in progress, you not uncommonly will have to stop the confusion and try to re-start the game. Here is an example of *The Three-Rule Rule*. You have the children positioned in a double circle. Each child is facing a partner so that outer circle child is looking towards the center and the other child outwards. You introduce the "Horse and Jockey" relay like this: the people facing outwards are the horses that will start racing by crawling between the spread legs of their partners (this is rule 1). The horses then make a left-hand turn to race a lap around the outside of the circle (rule 2). When they arrive home they straddle their partner who has assumed a hands and knees position (rule 3). Now maybe, just maybe, if all the children were attentive, and you demonstrated all the actions as you clearly explained them, the game will be understood and properly performed.[1] Of course you may have spiced up your introduction with some *anticipatory set* things like bugle calls, summons for horse to be at the gates, and race music and commentary. But can you not see that even three rules are pushing the information processing and retention capacities of at least some of the students?

The Three-Rule Rule does not mean that you cannot ever play more complex games with your classes. It just means that you probably will not be successful if you begin with more than three. Lets stay a bit longer with our example of the horse and jockey game. The next time the horses complete their laps they must give their partners high-tens before assuming the ending straddle position. The time after that they give the high-tens and then do five curl-ups. And so it goes with more and more rules and activities being added on. What we are doing here is employing *The Expansion Principle*. This means that once the game has been played a couple of times in a simple form, and those rules have been internalized, it now becomes feasible to add others. Once the fundamentals of a skill or game is learned you can then elaborate to a more advanced level.

SOS Principle Revisited

You remember what *The SOS principle* is, right? In Chapter 6 we said that as children begin to practice a skill you step back and ask yourself three questions in this order: are the children <u>S</u>afe? are they actively <u>O</u>n-task? are they being <u>S</u>uccessful in their performance? In this section we are advocating that you ask those same questions of games. Games will not be fun or educationally sound if they are unsafe, if there is not abundant activity, or if successful performances are not the norm.

Safety

Every game should be initially assessed as to both its physiological and psychological safety. As for physical safety, there is always an inherent risk in any movement game. Even if the game is basically safe, the environmental conditions are safe, and it is being played in an orderly fashion, there is no end to the minor, and even major, catastrophes that are possible. People can fall down, collide with others, get hit by implements or balls. These events can result in contusions, sprains, dislocations, cardiorespiratory problems, dismemberment's . . . Okay, Okay, now I am exaggerating, but you get the point. Even though inherent risks are a reality they do not prevent us from living active lives. Staying in bed is not the answer. But the games we offer our children must be reasonably safe and the hazards minimized to the lowest possible levels. If we, as *reasonably prudent* people, can foresee the likelihood of a game causing injuries we must not allow it to continue. It is not worth the risk. Furthermore, once we select a game as having an acceptably low level of risk, we must do whatever we feasibly can to make sure it is carried out in a safe manner.

There is no steadfast, always easily discernible dividing line between games that are safe enough and those that are not. Here are some red-flag activities that might serve as touchstones of

---

[1] Permit me to reiterate the point that if all the children are to understand a game you had better demonstrate it, not just explain it. Seeing someone actually going through the legs, seeing the direction of the lap, and seeing the finishing horse position are necessary. Taking the time to show will save you time. If you believe anything I say, believe this.

sensitivity. What about a "Battleball" type game where children are throwing playground or volleyballs at each other. We should be able to anticipate the real eventuality of someone getting hit in the head and being hurt. This would be true even if the instruction were to throw to hit below the waist because errant throws will happen. Teachers who have their classes play these kinds of games feel that they are not overly hazardous and say that only some stings and bruises might result. But detached retinas and damaged eardrums have also sometimes occurred and the courts have not ruled in favor of the teachers. *The American Alliance of Health, Physical Education, Recreation and Dance* does not endorse such games.

"Wheelbarrow walks" and "piggy-back carries" might be safe enough activities, but if they are used in a relay race they become much more dangerous. The courts and I can visualize the "wheelbarrow" being pushed onto his/her face by an overeager pusher, or the runner with someone on his/her back losing balance and awkwardly falling. What about having all your students racing up and down a narrow all-purpose area at full speed? If some children have a full head of steam are running towards others moving at full speed in the other direction, there is a real potential for a miscalculated dodge and a literal head-on collision. What about the game of "Red Rover" in which children attempt to run across an area while others attempt to catch and restrain them? This seems like it may be producing some pretty significant body contact for young people who do not have the benefit of training and protective equipment.

As mentioned earlier, once you have deemed the nature of a game to be reasonably safe, it must also be implemented in a safe manner. Safe games can become dangerous if the playing surface is slippery due to gravel, water, or littered with clothing, notebooks and papers. Protruding obstacles such as poles, bleachers, and waste cans need consideration. I am always surprised that some teachers will organize tag and relay type games in which boundary lines are placed within a couple of feet of walls. Have they not thought that some racing child will ineluctably not be able to stop quickly enough? In addition to the physical environment, the manner in which the children participate in the activity can negatively impact its safety. Unruly players can make tidily-winks dangerous. What if the children are not under control as they run and dodge? if they carelessly wield implements? if they are not abiding by the class and game rules? The key to remedying these conduct problems is twofold. Firstly, when the game is introduced it should always be understood that a major purpose of playing the game is to see if everyone can play by the rules and be respectful of other peoples' safety. This means that the teacher might often have to remind the students of this at the inception. Secondly, the feedback the teacher provides at the completion of the game should be congruent to this behavior. The primary purpose of these games is not to see who was the fastest or who won. Winning can be recognized and congratulated but it should not take precedence over enthusiastic praise of fair play and rule following. And of course, if the game is not being played in a safe fashion you need to exert your supervisory role and immediately stop it.

Thus far our discussion has been focused on physical safety, but we should be adhering to the stricter standard of psychological safety. Not only should the children be safe, they should not feel threatened. If some children feel fearful, even if it is an unwarranted fear, we are not accomplishing our enjoyment goal. We may sometimes become exasperated at those who will not venture something and show reasonable courage and resolve, but we should never force or coerce a child to do something he/she is truly afraid to do. Their fear could make participation counter-productive and maybe even physically dangerous. Our task should be more one of gently and persistently leading and assuring them.

A word of caution is in order here. We must be careful in assessing the stresses our games place upon the children. It is not uncommon for students to vociferously exclaim that they want to play "Battleball" or some rough game akin to it. But can you really be sure that the sentiments of the most skilled and vocal reflect those of everyone? Can you expect a boy or girl who might be apprehensive about this game to stand up and admittedly announce that he/she is frightened? I don't think so. Many may accede to the cries of the majority, and even lend their votes and voices of support to a game they fear. We need to be sensitive to these kinds of social dynamics and pressures.

On-Task Activity

One of the best and easiest ways to evaluate a game is to look at the quantity of activity it produces. High participation rates are needed to best develop fitness, motor, and affective skills. In the most enjoyable and educational games everyone plays an important part and will be actively involved throughout. Little time will be spent waiting for turns and no one is eliminated from participation. Many of the traditional games you learned in school may not meet this criterion. Let us analyze a few old stand-by games and see if they can be altered for the better. If we learn to critically analyze these games we should be able apply this skill to improve many others which we know or will encounter.

Do you remember "Duck, Duck, Goose?" That is a game in which the children are seated in a circle, facing inward. One child walks around the outside of the circle tapping everyone on the head and saying "Duck." When the tapper taps someone and says "Goose!" the chase is on. The person who has been tapped tries to catch the person before he/she makes it around the circle and into the vacated spot. Children have long enjoyed this game, probably because of the suspense as to whether or not they will be picked. However, it is not difficult to see that the amount of activity is low. Only one or two children are physically active at a time and the others wait and wait. If we measured the percentage of time any one child was active during the course of the game we would probably find it to be something like 5 percent or less. Some children might not get picked at all. What could be done to increase activity? In games like this one, in which many students are standing or sitting as they await their turn, it often is possible to have them *Actively Waiting*. In "Duck, Duck, Goose," everyone could be jogging in place or walking counterclockwise as the chooser walked in the opposite direction. Think how much healthful walking the children would experience throughout the game. Another basic means of increasing activity levels is to see if the format of the game can be changed from one single game to numerous, simultaneously played *Mini-Games*. I know a teacher who played "Duck, Duck, Goose" in a format in which the students formed two lines down the center of the area. Everyone was paired with a partner, one line of partners faced away from the others. Each pair played their own mini-game. They took turns being the tapper and chased or fled to one line or the other based on whether or not they were pronounced a duck or goose. The amount of activity the children got in five minutes far exceeded that of what would have been produced in a half-hour under the traditional organization. As an example of wise *Anticipatory Set* usage, this teacher said that even the upper elementary children enjoyed this high activity version of "Duck, Duck, Goose" when the name had been changed to "I'm it! You're it!"

"Steal-the-Bacon" is a game that has been played across the country for many generations. I recall playing it when I was in school and I taught it many years in my early teaching career. The normal set-up is one in which two teams of students are aligned at opposing ends of the court. Each team was numbered one through whatever the number of players. Then, for instance, when the number 10 was called the number 10s from each side would run out and attempt to get the bacon, usually a knotted towel, and carry it back across his/her goal line without being tagged by the other player. Here again we find a game with a lot of exciting anticipation but with little total activity. Notice how we might again use the concepts of *Active Waiting* and *Mini-Game* formats to increase the activity. We could create *Active Waiting* by everyone walking or jogging in a circle. When a number is called, those two individuals rush into the center for the bacon and attempt an exit in any direction to the perimeter. All the rest of the children keep right on walking or jogging. Figure 7.1 depicts a sample mini-game format with three players per team. The teacher's call of one, two or three would initiate a number of games. All the ones, twos, or threes would go at the same time resulting in a third of the class members being involved at any one time. If you did not want children always playing against the same opponent, everyone could be moved one position clockwise by a simple rotation system. Also, to add some variety, variations of the games could be offered at the different sites. Stealing and dribbling basketballs or soccer balls could be done in one game while hockey sticks and pucks were used at another.

Figure 7.1. Steal the Bacon: Mini-Game Format and Rotational System

```
----  (1)  (2)  (3)  --------  (1)  (2)  (3)  ---------  (1)  (2)  (3)  -----
       x    x    x              x    x    x               x    x    x

         * (bacon)               * (bacon)                 * (bacon)

       x    x    x              x    x    x               x    x    x
----  (1)  (2)  (3)  --------  (1)  (2)  (3)  ---------  (1)  (2)  (3)  -----
```

* When students rotate one position clockwise they must understand that they may have a new position number. Numbered poly-spots on the floor is a good idea.

Another simple way to insure more activity is to *Eliminate the Elimination* in elimination games. "Musical Chairs," as traditionally played, is a classic example of an elimination game. Everyone is circling around a double line of chairs which numbers one less than the number of children. When the music stops or the command is given everyone attempts to sit on a chair. The person left out is removed to spectator status. The game continues with one less chair each time until one winner remains. This game, and variants of it, can be great fun and still be played. Rather than eliminating those not finding a chair, why not simply assign them a point and allow all to continue. The excitement of the game will be still there as everyone strives to avoid points. I have played many successful variants of musical chairs where the children ran or dribbled basketballs and soccer balls around an area to music. When the music stopped everyone scrambled to get inside a hula-hoop or on a poly-spot. I found that having two or three less hoops or spots worked well because then no one was singled out as the sole person caught.

Finally, because many instructors commonly use relay games, a few words had best be said specifically about them. Activity rates in line relays will necessarily be low if the lines of children are long and only one team member at a time performs. The most obvious remedy, many times inexplicably overlooked, is to keep the lines short, four or less would seem wise. Another possibility is that of having more than one person going at a time. Could pairs of children be doing the activity together? Or what about the entire squads performing together in a cooperative manner? I have had children put hands on the waist of the person in front of them and race train fashion, or join hand in a circle with a team member inside so as to transport them in a "circle of friends" fashion (or maybe it was a spaceship to ride in). Not only do these types of cooperative relays promote greater activity, cooperation is demanded and the races tend to be closely contested.

As you might see, with a little imagination more activity can be added to most any game to make it better. In the exercises at the end of this chapter you will get a chance to practice your skills at altering games.

Successful

If you have been able to devise games where everyone is safely moving, that's terrific. But don't forget the second *S* in *SOS*. Is everyone generally experiencing success? Children will not enjoy a game if they are not experiencing success.

There are three different types of game structures: *individual, cooperative* and *competitive*. In *individual activities* the children are personally attempting to accomplish an activity according to a criterion. The key to ensuring high success rates in these individual games is the employment of the *Long Slanty Rope Principle* introduced in Chapter 6. The children are either given different criteria suited to their abilities or they are given different versions of the task. For example, if we were going to have the children do as many skiers' jumps back and forth across a line in one minute, we might wish to set different criterion levels. We could say that if you can do 145 you are "Simmering!" Doing 175 equals " Cooking!" and at 185 you are "Hot Stuff!" Or we could encourage them to set their own personal targets, maybe to exceed the previous days achievement. Different versions of this particular task could entail one-legged performance, wider lines, or even a slightly raised obstacle to clear. An example of yet another skill would be to give the children a number of jump rope skills and then have them select those they think they may be able to accomplish in a given time (see Figure 7.2 for an example of this kind of *Task Style Teaching*).

Figure 7.2. Partner and Three-Person Jump Rope Challenges

Each group of children is given a copy of one of the two diagrammed sheets. Challenge them to see how many of the stunts they can complete in a set time period. To master a stunt, each student must assume each position and 10 continuous jumps must be accomplished.

Partner Skills

Names_____ **and** _____

Place a check in the boxes you were able to complete.

In *cooperative activities* the children are attempting to accomplish a task either individually, in partners, small groups, or as an entire class. I think this approach to game organization can be especially conducive to feelings of success. This occurs because everyone tends to receive encouragement and help from his or her peers; everyone is on your side. Also, since the children are not being encouraged to compare their level of performance against other groups, they will be tending to work towards criteria appropriate for them. Of course, in cooperative games as with individual games, some thought may need to be given to making game variations to suit personal needs.

It is in *competitive activities* and games where we need to be especially vigilant about some students feeling unsuccessful. Competitive games can be great fun but competition can also be a set-up for failure; and a little failure can go a long way. If a child's skills are much below the skills of others, the competitive environment can become stressful and embarrassing. Suppose a relay race is being played in which the children are to crab walk down to a line and back. Imagine the feeling of children who cannot perform the skill well and flounder. Their ineptitude is displayed to all and their team is losing because of them. Because of this inherent problem in competitive games it is essential that we are sure that children possess the perquisite skill before we place them into these pressure, high profile game situations. In the following section we will address this issue of adjusting games to the children's skill levels and matching competitors.

Making Sports Fun and Educational

Some people are critical of including competitive games and sports in the regular school curriculum. They remember physical education class as placing too much emphasis on competition, especially competitive team sports. They believe that we should rather be offering cooperative experiences and life-long recreational activities. Such activities would be less stressful and, instead of focusing attention on comparing abilities and attempting to surpass others, the children would learn how to be satisfied with their own performances and how to get along with others. Some educators also feel that the larger than ever heterogeneity of today's classes are especially unsuited for the competitive approach; some children have had extensive training in youth sports while others have had precious little movement experiences; some children are gifted with many athletic abilities while others are not; the maturational levels of some children are far ahead or behind the age norms; and most classes typically include students with a range of disabilities. All these factors are thought to result in a sports experience in which the haves will dominate and the have-nots will be overrun or pushed to the sidelines. The less gifted, who might most benefit from learning to enjoy physical activity, are at risk of encountering failure and hence at risk to being turned off to the active lifestyle.

The above are legitimate concerns. I recognize the potential hazards of competitive sports and do not think they should dominate the physical experiences of children. All children would benefit from learning that movement experiences could be fun without competition. However, having said that, I do not agree that we should view competition as an evil to be always discouraged. Competition between sports performers can yield great excitement and joy. Your children will be beseeching you to play games and keep score. Many of us have had unforgettable, thrilling memories of competitive games and youthful sports involvement. If there are potential problems with competitive sports, as we have already established, the solution is to mend it, don't end it. Competitive games and sports can be a valuable part of children's education. They can be designed so that children of all ability levels and backgrounds can be successful and experience the fun and excitement of participation. They can be designed so they are an effective laboratory for teaching important affective skills such as: striving to do one's best, persevering, cooperating with teammates, respecting opponents, abiding by rules, winning gracefully, accepting defeat. In the following sections are ideas of how that might be achieved.

Changing the Rules

The rules of sports are generally written with the intent of establishing which of two skilled teams or players are the best, and worthy of being declared the winner. They are not written so as to accommodate players of lower abilities, nor are they written to maximize the activity levels and educational experiences of the participants.

Probably the most significant rule change we can make is the number of members on team sports. Activity is far from being maximized in ten-on-ten softball or kickball, eleven on eleven soccer or football, and six-on-six volleyball. And even less activity is present when you divide your class of 30 students into two teams and play fifteen-on-fifteen. When the ball-to-student ratio is low the amount of physical activity and skill development normally is low. Also, the better skilled of those groups will tend to monopolize a large share of the activity and the lesser skilled will be relatively inactive. In a typical mass-on-mass kickball game, each child will average only two or three kicks throughout a 40 minute game, average fielding experiences will be naturally low and they will be unequally distributed; the key positions of pitcher and shortstop will be more active at the expense of outfielders.

A *Mini-Game* format is educationally sound remedy. It should not be difficult to organize a number of simultaneous mini-games. A number of smaller hockey fields could be marked out by cones, basketball games could be run at each of the baskets, with a long net or rope strung across the gym or playing field multiple volleyball games could occur. A *Team-Size Rule of Thumb* is to keep the number of players on a team equivalent to or less than the grade level: first graders play one-on-one, second graders go two-on-two, third graders go three-on-three. The thinking here is that the younger children are not ready to understand the increased complexity that working with partners and teammates demands. For the older children it is still recommended that teams not normally increase beyond three per side. In three per side most strategy implications of the game remain intact, and activity levels are many times higher than normal.

In order to play mini-games other rule changes are necessary. Boundaries must be miniaturized. One goal, rather than two, might be used, and sizes of those goals might be reduced. Here are a couple of examples. A two-on-two volleyball game could be played in a small court space, the smaller the court space the more successful and longer the rallies would tend to be. The net or rope height might be adjusted. If the children could not consistently get their serve in and hence it was discouraging and holding up play, it could be dispensed with. Rather, an underhand throw-in or "courtesy toss" might work. Continuing to serve from a spot closer to the net will sometimes be effective.

For a game such as softball some major rule changes will be required. How, you are asking, can you play softball with only 2 or 3 per side? Instead of official softball I visualize playing games like "Over-the-line Softball" or "Bonkerball"[2] (see Figures 7.3 and 7.4). In these kinds of mini-games certain aspects of the official game may be lost ("Over-the line Softball" does not require throwing or base running), but the skills of batting and catching are hugely increased. "Bonkerball" is a similar game but it does contain some throwing, catching, and base running elements. After the ball is batted the player must run around the cones before the fielders retrieve the ball and throw it to the cones.

Another useful rule change is to miniaturize the length of the games. Shorter games tend to be more exciting and less lopsided. Five or ten minutes might be sufficient.

---

[2] Mills, B. D.; Riemer, P. C. & French, (1997). L. M. Bonkerball: maximize participation with an innovative game, *Strategies*, 10: (3), 24–26.

110

Figure 7.3. Over-the-Line Softball

O		O
	O	
(fielders)	(fielders)	(fielders)
O		
	O	
O	O	O O

X	X	X
(friendly pitcher)	(friendly pitcher)	(friendly pitcher)

X	X	X
(batter)	(batter)	(batter)
X	X	X
(on-deck player)	(on-deck player)	(on-deck player)

Figure 7.4. Bonkerball

(outfielder)	(outfielder)	(outfielder)
O	O	O
(base cone fielder)	(base cone fielder)	(base cone fielder)
O	O	O
(base cone)	(base cone)	(base cone)
(home cone)	(home cone)	(home cone)
batter *	batter *	batter *
(home cone fielder)	(home cone fielder)	(home cone fielder)
O	O	O

* The batting team member hits the ball from off the home cone in the tee-ball version (or from a friendly pitcher) and then attempts to run around the base cone and back to the home cone before the fielders have relayed the ball home and placed it on the cone.

Matching Competitors

One factor in helping to make competition enjoyable for all is the matching of competitors. Regardless of our degree of ability, competition can be an enjoyable experience when we are paired with and against people of our own level. Go to the tennis courts, golf courses or softball fields and observe some games in progress. You may notice that the courts and fields in which the people are unskillful are enjoying their contest just as much or more than the experienced performers. Excitement resides where reasonable challenges exist for all. However, when mis-matches exist, competition can easily become frustrating and threatening, boring or even physically dangerous.

There are a variety of ways individuals or teams can be ability matched. One is to allow the children to self-select: they can choose to play in the beginner's league, the experienced league, or the advanced league. I know one teacher who allows his volleyball students to choose between a "blood and guts" and a "hit and giggle" version. Or you might assign the children to teams. You could do this based on your estimates or perhaps on some try-out skill test. Another assignment method is to have student captains help equate the teams. I am not here advocating the *Slave-Market Approach* warned against in Chapter 5. Instead, a few skilled students privately help you divide the class into equal groups. They are not selecting people for their own squad but once that task is fulfilled you might assign them to a captain position.

Changing the Equipment and Facilities

Regulation sized equipment and facilities are not generally conducive to children's skill development or enjoyment. When confined to using official sized equipment and facilities, some weaker and less skilled students will learn incorrect techniques and will have frustratingly low success rates. I can still remember the initial dissatisfaction I held for basketball because of the size and weight of the ball and the height of the imposingly high rim. With some consideration given for equipment and facilities, virtually any child should be able to be successful. If a child cannot hit a pitched ball, a lighter, larger diameter bat may solve the problem; if that does not do it get a bigger ball; if not yet, a yet bigger ball or even beach ball; if not then, a batting tee could be used. A variety of equipment and facility modification ideas are offered in Figure 7.5.

Figure 7.5. Sample Equipment Modifications for Various Sports

Softball
> *Fat jumbo plastic bats*
> *Flat bats (one side is flat)*
> *Larger and softer balls*
> *Batting tees* (large cones can serve this purpose well, if they are not large enough they can be raised by being placed on cardboard box)

Volleyball
> *Balloons:* They can be used in the beginning to learn the basic skill of setting, bumping and digging (some people are leery of using balloons because of the danger of children putting them in their mouths and choking; check your school's policy and be vigilant if you use them).
> *Beach balls or other large light-weight plastic balls:* They are not expensive and are easy to successfully play with. Another important benefit is that it does not hurt to hit or be hit by them (preventing these kinds of things early in the learning process can make the difference as to whether or not a child likes or dislikes the sport).

Trainer volleyballs: These are bigger and lighter than regulation balls. They make a great progression between beach type balls and official volleyballs.

Ropes: When stung down the length of the gym (from basketball rim to rim works) they become a serviceable net. The height can be adjusted to suit the needs of the different teams. Usually having them fairly high works best because then the ball must be projected high and permits the opposite side a better chance to get into receiving position. Of course, the rope is too high if some are having difficulty getting the ball up and over it.

Basketball
Mini-basketballs
Waste cans: These can serve as targets when set on chairs or other things

Soccer
Soccer balls: Sometimes they are easier to dribble when slightly deflated. I have even had younger children dribbling crushed milk containers around (they do not bounce and fly as out of control).

Racquet Sports
Short handled wooden or plastic paddles: These are a must for most all elementary children because speed and control can be much more easily regulated.

Coat hangers with nylon stretched over them: This is a simple construction project to make a functional implement.

Shuttlecocks: These work well in the early stages of learning because of their slower flight characteristics.

To gain access to equipment or other such learning aids I would first suggest notifying the physical education specialist in your area. Most specialists would love to see your interest and would find a means of getting you what is needed. If that fails, many items can be readily found in local toy stores. Others can, with a little construction ingenuity, be made. Here are the addresses and 1-800 numbers of three of the larger companies specializing in physical education equipment. They would be delighted to send you their catalogs (SPORTIME, 1 Sportime Way, Atlanta, GA, USA 30340 (1-800-444-5700); WOLVERINE Sports, 745 State Circle, Box 1941, Ann Arbor, MI 48106 (1-800-521-2832); THINGS FROM BELL, P.O. Box 135, East Troy, WI 53120, (1-800-432-2842). Even if you didn't plan to purchase anything, leafing through the pages might give you some good ideas for teaching progressions and aids.

Perhaps the best of all possible sources of sports equipment might be had by getting on the web and contacting the various specific sports organizations. Whether it is the *U.S. Soccer Association, U.S. Skiing Association, U.S. Gymnastic Association,* or most any sport association you can think of, they will likely have something to help you. All these organizations are most desirous of promoting their sport and would love to have it introduced in the schools. Most have specific materials and programs developed for school grades K through 12. For example, if you contact the *U.S. Tennis Association (USTA)*, PO Box 5046, White Plains, NY 10602-5046, (914) 696-700, //www.usta .com/theusta /program.html#3 or the *U.S. Handball Association*, 2333 N. Tucson Blvd., Tucson, Arizona 85716, 1-800-345-2048, http://ushandball.org you would discover that they have excellent lesson and curriculum plans specifically designed for elementary schools and teachers like you. If you like, they will send representatives in to give demonstrations and/or in-service training. They will provide rackets and balls for all your students to keep. Everything is free.

Adjusting the Contextual Aspects of Sports

What is meant by the *contextual aspects of sports*? Here is a list of six primary features integral to sports. (1) Seasons: sports usually last for an extended period of time, perhaps a few months. (2) Affiliation: sports see a number of teammates working together throughout the season. Close, long-term friendships are often formed. (3) Formal competition: practice times, league play and tournaments are scheduled prior to the season so that teams and individuals can anticipate and prepare appropriately. (4) Record keeping: as competition occurs, records of all kinds are kept on individual and team performances. (5) Festivity: sport is replete with banners, announcers, cheerleaders, publicists, bands, team names, uniforms, etc. (6) Culminating events: sports tournaments and post-season events with trophies, speeches and awards are a common practice.

To make sports enjoyable and educational, what approach should we take toward these contextual aspects? Should we view them as irrelevant detractors from the educational process? Do they create excessive stress and *hyper-competition*? If so, we should eliminate or reduce these aspects. On the other hand, should we view these contextual aspects as desirable additions to the sports experience which give it more meaning and fun? If so, we might want to incorporate and foster their presence. Based upon the philosophy I have advanced in the previous chapters you might correctly assume that I would subscribe to the more commonly excepted first point of view; that downplaying these contextual aspects is normally a sound practice. My reasoning is that it might be fun and educational to give children some competitive sports experiences, but we do not want to excessively heighten the importance of winning. Why not have team memberships frequently rotated so that cliques do not form and so everyone learns to play with everyone else? Why keep score? When a game is completed and the children ask who won the best response might be, "Did you have a good time? Did you get some good exercise and learn some skills? If so, then you won; we all won." We don't need league schedules, records, and culminating tournaments. The idea is to teach the young people to focus on their own performance and to not worry about how they compare to others; winning per se is not important. George Shehan was an excellent runner who loved to compete, but he had this to say regarding the competitive process, "I am not diminished by those ahead of me nor am I enhanced by those behind. I have moved from an antagonistic relationship with other runners to an agonistic relationship with self."

But does my above stance mean that you might be wise to always diminish the *contextual aspects of sports*? Perhaps not. Maybe an effective approach for some teachers and classes would be to do the opposite and take advantage of the contextual aspects to increase interest and commitment to the sport. For example, let's say that you have, at one time or another, richly enjoyed participating on a basketball team. You feel confident that you know the sport well, that you learned many valuable skills and lessons from the experience, and that you would like to provide that beneficial experience to your 5th graders. So here is what you did. You divided the class into 3 teams equally matched according to skills in this sport (maybe you used the private captain selection process previously described). Let us say that you had 24 students and hence three teams of 8 players. You explained to them that following some pre-season practices, they were going to have a basketball season with a schedule of contests. You encouraged team esprit de corps by having them practice as units and come up with team names and some sort of uniforms. Then, on the first day of the league play, team one played team two. The games were of the two-on-two *mini-game* format. This meant that team one had 4, two-person teams, and so would team 2. The squads had ranked themselves in A, B, C, and D levels. The games lasted 10 minutes, with the As playing the As, the Bs playing the Bs, and so on. Time permitted another round to be played that period, with the As playing the Bs and the Cs playing the Ds. Throughout the games, the role of the third, non-playing team, was that of fulfilling a variety of sport contextual roles. For instance, four of them served as officials and the others as record keepers, managers and publicists. When the next day of competition arrived, the teams were rotated so that team 3 became one of the playing teams while either team 1 or 2 assumed the roles of officials, scorekeepers, etc. At the end of the season a special round-robin tournament was scheduled in which some significant people were invited to attend. Awards and recognition of various kinds where made.

Some of you might be thinking that trying to incorporate all these contextual elements would be difficult and more than what you might be willing or able to do. However, some of you might be emphatically saying "Yes! I see how I could organize something like this. I might not be able to do everything the first time, but I could start small and perhaps build off it in future years." And you might be thinking that the children could really get excited and motivated in such an environment. It contains many of the things you liked so much about sports. Furthermore, having the students playing the diverse roles of officiating, record keeping, and announcing, would be good learning experiences. The children would be learning to work together, take more responsibility for their own games, and might learn to better empathize with the work and difficulties of these jobs. Also, you might be able to integrate some of these duties into other academic areas: reporting and journalistic skills, record keeping and calculation skills, and more.

For a compete argument for the inclusion of the contextual aspects of sports, I would refer you to the text *Sports Education,* by Daryl Siedentop.[3] The book is not long but provides many excellent ideas and implemented examples for teaching a variety of sports at a variety of grade levels. Siedentop's sport education philosophy is that competition is the essence of sports. Competition is fun and exciting and can be a great learning experience under our tutelage. We should make sports developmentally appropriate by matching the competition and modifying the rules, but let us not take the fun out of sports. Teaching children to fully compete and strive to win is not to be avoided but encouraged.

Traditional vs Games Approach to Teaching Sport Skills

If you as the classroom teacher would simply provide the opportunity and encouragement for your students to participate in some sports, either during recesses or physical education sessions you could well be helping them to improve their fitness, motor, and social skills. This small amount of helpful initiation from you could make a difference as to whether or not some children will engage in any active play throughout the day. Research shows that during free playtime it is normal for some of the children to be quite active while others are not. Characteristically many of the less fit children will be engaged in rather passive games or will simply sit and talk with friends. Data also shows that girls will on average be less active than the boys.[4] The next time or two you observe children at recess make note of the action patterns to see if the research seems confirmed.

Although your fulfillment of the above recreational-supervisory role would be helpful, sports has the potential of teaching a great deal more if you are motivated enough to take a more active instructional role. Incorporating the ideas presented in the above sections (modifying rules and equipment, matching competitors, etc.) will better protect against some of the skilled students dominating play and the less adept being left out and feeling unsuccessful. However, there is another aspect that needs to be addressed if success is to be fully maximized. That aspect is skill instruction. Even with rule and equipment modifications many children will not possess adequate skills. They will adopt incorrect techniques and the games may sometimes break down because they cannot catch, throw, strike and so forth. Chapter 6 offered information of how to teach skills. What is covered in the following paragraphs is the question of whether sport skills are best taught in drills separate from the game, this being called the *Traditional Approach to Teaching Sports,* or whether sport skills are more enjoyably and effectively taught within the context of the game, this is known as the *Games Approach to Teaching Sports.*

---

[3] Siedentop, D. *Sport Education: Quality PE through positive sport experiences.* Human Kinetics, 1994.

[4] European-American elementary school boys engage in moderate-to-vigorous physical activity during 52 percent of their recess time. European-American and Mexican-American girls both engage in physical activity about 40 percent of the recess.

The *Traditional Approach to Teaching Sports* skills is to have the students participate in drills isolated from the game situation. In volleyball that would mean that we would have partners, or small circles of players, setting or bumping a ball to each other. They might also be divided up to serve the balls back and forth to each other; or they might be tossing or setting a ball for another to spike. The philosophy of the traditional approach is that many of the children will not have the prerequisite serving, setting, and bumping skills to successfully play the game unless the skills are first learned outside of the game. They reason that if those skills are not learned prior to the game, they will not be acquired in the game because the stress of competition is too great and the already skilled students will dominate.

In recent years some authorities have advanced the *Games Approach to Teaching Sports Skills.*[5] Proponents of this approach feel that the traditional approach has not been wholly effective for a couple of basic reasons. The first concern is that many students are not content with doing drills. They want to play the game and motivational levels are low until they can. The second concern is that students do not learn how to apply skills to the game when those skills have been practiced separate from it. They might get better at passing the balls around a circle but that does not mean they will correctly use that skill in the stress of specific game circumstances. The proper techniques acquired in practice may yield discouragingly little *transfer* to the game. I certainly can attest to having witnessed this phenomenon. In practice everyone is masterfully getting into good position to pass the ball around the circle or properly bumping the ball with their forearms, but when the same opportunity presents itself in the game, those positioning skills are not to be seen and the bumped balls are almost invariably struck with open hands in an illegal fashion.

According to the *Games Approach,* it is best to allow the children to immediately begin playing and have them learn the techniques and strategies within the context in which the skills will be performed. But they are not advocating that we just throw out the ball and hope for the best. Rather, they see the learning key to lie in the progressive structuring of the games. Let us use the volleyball example again. The earliest introduction of children to volleyball, or any net sport, might consist of a one-on-one game in which each child has a very small area to guard. They throw the ball back and forth over a net or rope and attempt to have it land in their opponent's court. The other player attempts to defend his/her area by catching the ball. All the children have the skills necessary to play this simple game and they are learning the beginning strategies and scoring rules that will form the foundation of future volleyball or other net sport games. The next progression is where the ball is hit over the net. Now the skills of overhand and underhand passing are required. For the children who use improper techniques, some on-the-spot tips and instructions are given and the game is permitted to continue. Instruction introduced in this way hopefully has great relevancy and can be immediately applied. Eventually games with expanded court sizes will be organized and serving or other more advanced skills will be integrated. When two-on-two games are introduced, passing to teammates and other cooperative strategies are required. Now timely instructions on passing strategies will be given as the need arises. Overall, the concept of the *Games Approach* is that the children will understand and appreciate the role and need for skills as they play, and they will therefore be more eager to gain them. All the while, they of course will be enjoying playing the sport. You can see how *the Games Approach* dovetails well with the concept introduced in the previous chapter in which it was recommended that you strongly encourage children to practice individual sport skills outside of class time. By doing so they might be more ready for the in-class games.

It is hoped that the outlining of the arguments of the above two approaches will help you formulate a philosophy that will serve you. Rather than taking sides on the issue I would conclude by saying that your decision does not need to be one of either or. Drills do not need to be abandoned,

[5] Werner, P.; Thorpe, R. & Bunker, D. (1996). Teach games for understanding: evolution of a model. *Journal of Health, Physical Education, Recreation and Dance*, 67: (1), 28-33.

but with wise progressions, some games could be initiated early in the learning process. Probably a useful concept to draw from this discussion would be that if we do use drills, we should make at least some of them as game-like as possible; by so doing, the children will better recognize how the skills integrate into the game. For instance, instead of only having the students pass a ball around a circle, a task that is not done in a game, it would be more realistic to organize a drill where the ball comes from over the net and the performer's task is to pass it to a front line position. In the questions at the end of this chapter we will test your skills at recognizing and creating game-like drills in some other sports.

Beyond Traditional Sports

I have previously made the point that there are advantages to having children learn a variety of games and sports. Children will have greatly different interests and aptitudes (remember the *Specificity of Motor Ability Hypothesis*). I also believe that if each year we continue to follow the pattern of repeatedly exposing children to the same limited range of traditional team sports experiences, we risk turning many of them off to adopting an active lifestyle. I call this the curriculum of *Overexposure*. It means that each year we reintroduce the same few sports for a week or two of rather superficial coverage. This is conducive to lowering interest and results in little in-depth learning.

Consider our most common traditional sports of football, softball, basketball, soccer and volleyball. They have much in common in that they favor a quite similar set of motor abilities. Those students who are bigger and who can sprint faster have a decided advantage. Also, all those sports favor similar psychological make-ups. If you like working in large social groups you will probably like them. But if you don't particularly care for the team atmosphere you could very well be unhappy. In Figure 7.6 I have provided a categorization of sports. Some of the placements are somewhat arbitrary but I think that they identify significant differences among the sports. In general the "invasion sports" have many similarities in games strategies, required physiological and motor abilities, and psychological propensities. Likewise, the other sports categories have their own unique set of basic strategies, ability requirements, and psychological demands.

An alternative to the *Overexposure* curriculum model would be a model in which, over the students' tenure in school, they would have a quality experience in at least a few of the sports categories. For example, third graders would have a unit of instruction in an "invasion sport" such as soccer. It would be rather thorough instruction replete with all the contextual elements of the *Sport Education Model*. The fourth graders might have an in-depth unit in a "net/wall sport" such as tennis. The fifth grade season might be devoted to a "form sport" such as gymnastics, and so on. You can see that the purpose of such a curriculum would be to provide the students with thorough training in some very different sports that would tap into a variety of different motor/physiological abilities and psychological interests. Those children who did not have the make-up to be very successful at soccer might discover that tennis or gymnastics was what they were better suited for. My preference would be that somewhere down the line, certainly by the high school grades, students could be given electives. The young people would be able to draw on their experiences and select those kinds of activities they most preferred.

Of course, all this macro curriculum planning is beyond your role as a classroom teacher. Nevertheless, I think it is important for you to recognize that your students will have different interest/abilities and you could play a part in introducing an activity that they may not be encountering in their physical education program or anywhere else. In wrapping up this chapter I offer some activities and unit plans for two sports that might not be normally covered. Whether or not you ever decide to use these specific lessons they should provide you some ideas for equipment modifications and lesson planning.

Figure 7.6. Categorization of Sports

Wall.Net Games

Strategies are very similar: making opponent move, attacking net to get angles, trying to find opponent weakness, returning to home base, clear to buy time, bisecting angle for best position, etc.

Techniques are moderately similar: striking and serving

Motor/physiological abilities very similar: quickness and fast reactions are essential

Psychological skills are similar: Except for volleyball, individual or partner

Badminton	Squash
Tennis	Handball
Racquetball	Table Tennis
Volleyball	

Invasion Games

Strategies are very similar: move with ball, give and go, feinting, move without ball, move to open space, signal, screen, fill lane to attack, stay between attacker, mark a man, mark a zone, use boundary lines, etc.

Techniques are only moderately similar: expect for Field Hockey and Ice Hockey and Rugby and Football

Motor/physiological abilities very similar: size and running speed, fast reactions

Psychological skills are very similar: body contact, aggressiveness, teamwork

Basketball	Field Hockey
Soccer	Ice Hockey
Rugby	Lacrosse
Football	

Striking/Fielding

Strategies are very similar: make contact, place ball in open spaces, learn when to hit long, short, positioning, fielding/where to throw, preventing, etc.

Techniques are very similar: most skills are almost identical (batting, throwing, fielding)

Motor/physiological abilities very similar: hand-eye coordination (tracking and catching)

Psychological skills are very similar: slower pace, suspenseful, strategic planning, teamwork

Baseball	Cricket
Softball	Kickball
Rounders	

Outdoor Recreational Activities

Strategies only moderately similar: careful planning and maintenance of equipment

Techniques not necessarily similar:

Motor/physiological abilities moderately similar: many athletic abilities not necessary, endurance and stamina, climbing and canoeing require strength

Psychological skills are very similar: enjoyment of nature, separating from crowds and engines, self-paced, reflective

Hiking	Canoeing
Camping	Sailing
Climbing	

Racing

Strategies moderately similar: pacing and achieving maximal effort
Techniques moderately similar: of course the running events are very similar
Motor/physiological abilities are very similar: muscular and cardiovascular endurance
Psychological skills are very similar: more individual, disciplined training

Bicycling	Triathloning
Track	Orienteering
Swimming	

Form Sports

Strategies are very similar: learning routines, mental focusing
Techniques are very similar: take-offs, spins, rotations, landings, balances
Motor/physiological abilities are very similar: muscular strength and flexibility, balance, body and spatial awareness, small size not a disadvantage
Psychological skills are very similar: appreciation of the aesthetic aspects of movement, courage to learn and perform dangerous movements, individual

Gymnastics
Dance
Diving

Target Sports

Strategies are very similar: focused concentration, control of anxiety and emotions
Techniques are not very similar:
Motor/physiological abilities are similar: fine motor control, hand steadiness
Psychological skills are very similar: individual, self-paced

Bowling
Golf
Archery

Skiing/Skating

Strategies are not very similar: this depends of whether the focus is on stunts or racing and leisure performance
Techniques are very similar: weight control, carving turns
Motor/physiological abilities are very similar: leg strength, dynamic balance
Psychological skills are very similar: courage to learn and perform dangerous movements, individual

Water-skiing	Skateboarding
Snow Skiing	Ice Skating
Snow Boarding	Inline Skating

Figure 7.7. Track and Field Unit

Track and Field Unit

Preface: the culminating activity of this unit is an *in-class track meet.* Every event is taught and practiced before the class track meet is held. Emphasize to the children that everyone's effort contributes to their team's performance so each child must do the best he/she can. If they encourage everyone on their team they improve their team's chances of doing the best they are capable of. No put downs are allowed. Only positive encouragement.

Skills taught:
1. Look Pass: distance relay
2. Shuttle Pass: shuttle relay
3. Hurdle form—i.e. lead leg & trail leg
4. High jump form:
   a. scissors method
   b. Fosbury flop method
5. Shot put form (intermediate grades only)
6. Team cooperation toward healthy team competition

EVENT # 1: SHUTTLE RELAY
Points of emphasis:
- use right hand only to pass and receive baton
- hold baton like a candle (i.e. at the bottom with the flame on the top)
- receive at the top of the baton (i.e. the candle flame)
- "Punch" the baton against the body to slide the hand down to the bottom of the baton
- always run past the next runner to the left of them (i.e. never cross the baton across your body)
- declare the number of passes you want the teams to make and then have the team members count them out loud as they make the passes
- first team to have every one sitting in line gets 4 pts, net gets 3 pts . . . etc. last gets 1 pt

***** _____ *****
the four teams are split with half the team on each end of the gym
***** _____ *****

***** _____ *****

***** _____ *****

EVENT # 2: DISTANCE RELAY
Points of emphasis:
  Look pass:
  Outgoing runner
- face shoulders toward inside of track and put left foot back
- put inside hand (i.e. left) back with palm facing up
- look over inside (i.e. left) shoulder
- start to jog slowly when "incoming" runner crosses the warning line
- when incoming runner has placed the baton into you hand immediately transfer the baton into your right hand as you pick up speed

Incoming runner
- baton should be in your right hand.
- place baton into outgoing runner's left hand

General considerations:
- outgoing runner is the key because he/she is the freshest
- outgoing runner must judge the speed of the incoming runner and not take off too fast
- outgoing runner must never run backward even though they look back
- intermediate grades run from 5–7 laps
- primary grades run from 3–5 laps each
- have next runner up and in the outgoing runner position immediately after preceding runner has started his/her last lap
- first team to be seated and in line gets 4 pts, next gets 3 pts and so on

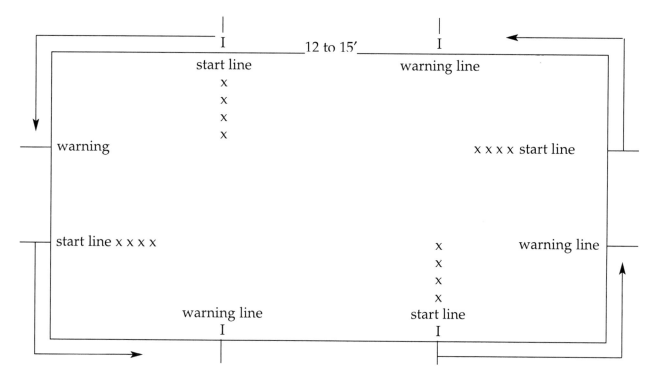

EVENT #3: HURDLES
Points of emphasis:
- "lead" leg is straight as possible
- "trail" leg is bent and toe is out to the side
- try to run over the hurdles and not to high jump over each one
- do the "layout" position hurdle stretch and imagine you are on top of the hurdle

General considerations:
- the hurdles (foam) can't hurt you
- don't slow down if you knock the hurdle over
- have two flights of hurdles going—one flight a bit higher than the other to allow for a challenge to those able to do it
- students must be able to go over the lower flight of hurdles without knocking over any of them before they are allowed to go over the higher flight

Continued on next page

121

- adjust the heights according to the grade level and by the legs being used in an upright or flat position
- have three hurdles in each flight and have a mat at the end to run into
- allow kids to time practice runs.
- always come back to the start along the outside of the hurdles and never between the hurdles

Start   Finish   Wall
                                                                                      Mats

EVENT # 4: HIGH JUMP

Points of emphasis for scissors style:
- start with scissors jump
- emphasize straight legs
- "near" leg goes up and over first
- land on feet
- try from both sides of bar to see which side is most comfortable to get the near leg up first

Transition to Fosbury flop:
- same near leg as scissors but it is bent
- instead of legs going over bar first, turn your back toward the bar and have your seat go over first
- land on your seat
- gradually try making your shoulders go over bar first by arching your back and landing on your back

General considerations:
- let everyone get over a low height
- give everyone a second chance at the lowest height to ensure a clearance and a team contribution
- have one team at a time line up at the start cone of their choice (having already been determined in practice sessions)
- once a person has missed in the competition they may go and practice over the hurdles while others are still participating in the high jump
- emphasize landing in the middle of the landing mat
- some can't help but do the straddle where the stomach faces the bar and the outside leg goes over the bar first
- during practice jumping the jumper may indicate to the event workers how high bar should be. This allows for appropriate comfort levels
- make sure the side safety mats are always up against the side of the landing mat

EVENT #5: SHOT PUT (FOR 4TH, 5TH, AND 6TH GRADES ONLY

Points of emphasis:

- **This is a put—not a throw!!!** This means that the shot must always precede the elbow in the direction of the put.
- start with the right foot facing the opposite direction of the put and the shot tucked under the right side of the chin. (these directions are for a right handed putter so reverse the hands and feet directions for a left hander)
- the left hand is pointing down toward the back of the putting area so that the putter is leaning over at the waist with the body weight over his/her right foot
- the shot is held in the fingers of the hand and not down in the palm
- the putter then rapidly and forcefully scribes an arc with his/her left hand upward at about a 45 degree angle as he/she shifts the body weight to the left foot. During this motion the shoulders are rotating toward the front of the putting area and the shot is put off the shoulder in the direction of the putting area. The shot must precede the elbow in order to save damage to the elbow joint.
- **Extreme care must be followed so that no student is in the putting area when the shots are being put!!!**
- four putters can put at the same time but they may not be released to go get their shot until the teachers says "Retrieve your shot." This will ensure that no student gets hit with a shot.
- all other putters on the team are behind a line that is behind the putting area.
- make sure all four putters are in the starting position at the same time so that they are ready to put at the same time
- the teacher's commands are: ("Putters ready" "Put" "Retrieve your shot")
- taped lines at 10, 15, 20, 25, and 30 feet are put on the floor and if the shot hits the line or beyond it the putter gets credit for that distance

30' _____	30'	_____	30'
25' _____	25'	_____	25'
20' _____	20'	_____	20'
15' _____	15'	_____	15'
10' _____	10'	_____	10'

Putting   _____   _____   _____   _____
Line   X   X   X   X

Safety line   X   X   X   X
              X   X   X   X
              X   X   X   X

Figure 7.8. Handball Unit (K-1)

Handball Unit (K–1)[1]

Lesson 1 (Grades K–1)
Activity: Eye/Hand Coordination Drills
Objective: (1) Develop eye/hand coordination. (2) Develop one-handed striking skills of smaller objects.
Equipment: Balloons, large Nerf (foam) balls
Facility: Any controlled area. Indoor area is better.
Drills: (1) Student taps (strikes) balloon 3 times with right hand. Same with left. (2) Student taps balloon once with right hand and once with left hand. (3) "See how many times you can tap with your right hand." Same with left. (4) RELAYS: Groups of 2 or 4. Student does tapping activity then passes balloon to next person. (5) "Tap the balloon to yourself with your right hand, then tap to your partner." (6) "How many times can you tap with your right hand in 10 seconds?" Same with left. (7) Student taps balloon within a limited space, such as a hula-hoop. As tapping in a controlled space is mastered, movement may be even more limited by having student kneel or sit within the hoop.

Lesson 2 (Grades K–1)
Activity: Eye/Hand Coordination Drills
Objective: (1) Develop eye/hand coordination. (2) Develop catching skills.
Equipment: Bean bags
Facility: Any controlled area
Drills: (1) Student tosses bean bag up (no more than 3 feet) with right hand and catches with right hand. Repeat several times. Same with left hand. (2) Student tosses bean bag up with right hand and catches with left hand. Repeat several times. Same, only left to right. "How many times can you toss and catch in 15 second?" (3) With partner about 6 feet away, student tosses to partner with right hand. Partner catches with right hand and tosses back. Repeat several times. Same with left. (4) Student performs previous drills within a limited space, such as a hula-hoop.

Lesson 3 (Grades K–1)
Activity: Eye/Hand Coordination Drills
Objective: (1) Develop eye/hand coordination. (2) Develop one-handed striking skills of smaller objects.
Equipment: Smaller Nerf balls, sponge balls or yarn balls
Facility: any controlled area. Indoor area is better.
Drills: Same as in Lesson 1
Comments: The same drills may be used, but, if possible, make them more challenging (more repetitions or for a longer time, or in a more limited space). Emphasize "Watch the ball," or "Watch your hand make contact with the ball."

Lesson 4 (Grades K–1)
Activity: Drop and "Push"
Objective: (1) Develop eye/hand coordination. (2) Develop striking skills
Equipment: 10-inch playground ball
Facility: Any area that is flat, wall space
Drills: (1) Student holds ball at waist (with two hands), drops and catches (with two hands). (2) Student is positioned approximately 5 feet from wall. Student drops and "pushed" the ball to wall and catches on rebound after first bounce. (3) Student continues same drill with increasing repetitions. (4) Repeat with one or two hands.
Comment: (1) Emphasize "watching" the ball. (2) Students who are able to perform drills with one hand should be encouraged to do so.

---

[1] Abstracted from *Teaching Handball in the Elementary Schools*, 4th Edition, United States Handball Association, 2000.

Lesson 5 (Grades K–1)

Activity: 2 Square (modified)

Objective: (1) Understand the concept of striking. (2) Participate in a partner activity.

Equipment: 10-inch playground ball

Facility: Any area that is flat and can be marked with line

Drills: (1) Partner A drops ball and hits to his/her partner (one or two hands). Partner B catches and repeats. This game is similar to Newcomb volleyball. (2) Student performs previous drill while hitting with dominant hand only. (3) Student performs previous drill while hitting with non-dominant hand.

Comments: (1) Regulation 2 Square size (6' × 12' or 9' × 18') will work, although a smaller size will probably work better. (2) Bouncing or dribbling is a good warm-up or lead-up. "Watch your hand hit the ball." (3) Make this a cooperative activity by having partners work together to see how many repetitions they can complete before the ball bounces twice or gets away. (4) Emphasize "watching the ball."

Lesson 6 (Grades K–1)

Activity: 2 Square (one hand without catch). This is regular 2 Square, but contact with the ball can be made with one hand at a time.

Objective: (1) Understand the concept of striking. (2) Participate in a partner activity.

Equipment: 10-inch playground ball

Facility: Any area that is flat and can be marked with line

Drills: (1) Partner A drops ball and hits (one hand) to his/her partner. Continue. (2) Student performs previous drill with specified hand.

Comments: (1) Emphasize cooperative theme. "You want your partner to hit the ball." (2) If the ball does not bounce in the correct area (on partner's die of line), student should catch the ball and start again.

Lesson 7 (Grades K–1)

Activity: 2 Square (one hand). This is regular 2 Square, but contact with the ball can be made with only one hand at a time.

Objective: (1) Develop one-hand striking ability. (2) Participate in a partner activity.

Equipment: 8 or 10 inch playground ball

Facility: Any area that is flat and can be marked with line

Drills: (1) Same as previous lesson. (2) Student performs previous drill while alternating hand (depending on the side of the body to which the ball rebounds).

Comments: (1) Some students may be able to work with 8 inch balls while others may need 10 inch balls. (2) Emphasize cooperative theme to avoid students striking the ball too hard. This can be done by using "time trials" (15 seconds—1 minute). Have students count how many times they and their partners make contact with one hand. (3) Begin to emphasize use of non-dominant hand. "If the ball goes to your left side, use your left hand."

Lesson 8 (Grades K–1)

Activity: Rebound Activities

Objective: (1) Understand the angles of rebound. (2) Intercept a rolled or thrown ball rebounding from a wall.

Equipment: 8-inch playground ball

Facility: Level area, wall space

Drills: (1) Student roils ball to wall and retrieves ball on rebound. (2) Partner A rolls ball to wall, Partner B retrieves. Alternate. (3) Student tosses ball to wall and catches after first bounce. (4) Partner A tosses ball to wall, Partner B catches after first bounce. Alternate.

Comments: (1) Tosses to wall should be tow-handed underhand or easy chest passes. (2) If possible, a line drawn on the wall about 2 feet from the ground will indicate how high tosses need to be. Emphasize cooperative theme. "You are working WITH your partner." (4) If possible, students need to start 5 feet away from wall. If students are extremely successful, you may want to back them further from the wall. (5) Students could work in groups of 4. Two partners would participate (for time or completion of a task) while the other two partners act as retrievers about 10 feet back. Alternate pairs.

Lesson 9 (Grades K–1)
Activity: Striking Drills (dominant hand)
Objective: (1) Develop striking skills. (2) Participate in partner or small group activity.
Equipment: 8-inch playground ball
Facility: Level area, wall space
Drills: (1) Warm up with Lesson 8 drills. (2) Student stands behind line 5 feet from wall and drop ball to floor. As ball bounce up, student hits it to wall. Student then catches rebounding ball after first bounce. (3) Partner A drops and hits ball to wall. Partner B catches after first bounce. Alternate. (Alternate pairs or rotate). (4) Relay activities—Use same drill as (3). Instead of 'partner,' use 'next person.'
Comments: (1) Emphasize cooperative theme. "You want your partner to be successful." (2) A hit ball should rebound from the wall and make contact with the ground in front of the 5-foot line. "If the ball bounces behind the 5 foot line, it is out of bounds." (3) Ideally, students should contact the ball about waist high. (4) Individual drills can be done singularly, or in small groups while taking turns. Partner drills work best with 4 students.

Lesson 10 (Grades K–1)
Activity: Striking Skills (non-dominant hand)
Objective: (1) Develop striking skills. (2) Participate in partner or small group activity.
Equipment: 8-inch playground ball
Facility: Level area, wall space
Drills: Same as previous lesson except done with non-dominant hand

Lesson 11 (Grades K–1)
Activity: Striking Skills (dominant hand)
Objective: (1) Develop striking skills. (2) Participate in partner or small group activity.
Equipment: 8-inch playground ball
Facility: Level area, wall space
Drills: (1) Warm-up with previous drills. (2) Student tosses ball to wall and strikes rebounding ball after first bounce. Partner acts as retriever about 10 feet back. Alternate. (3) Partner A tosses ball to wall. Partner B hits rebounding ball after first bounce. Alternate. Another pair acts as retrievers. Alternate pairs or rotate.
Comments: (1) Retrievers (partner or other pair) need to be about 10 feet back. (2) Begin to introduce "position." Ideally, student should have side to the wall when striking the ball (as in baseball), especially when striking the ball from a shoulder high or lower position. "Face the front wall more when striking from higher than shoulder high."

Lesson 12 (Grades K–1)
Activity: Striking Skills (non-dominant hand)
Objective: (1) Develop striking skills. (2) Participate in partner or small group activity.
Equipment: 8-inch playground ball
Facility: Level area, wall space
Drills: Same as previous lesson except done with non-dominant hand

Lessons 13,14,15 (Grades K–1)
Activity: One-Wall Handball
Objective: (1) Develop striking skills. (2) Develop eye/hand coordination. (3) Participate in partner activity. (4) Participate in a "lifetime sport." (5) Understand the concept of rebound.
Equipment: 8-inch playground ball, 6-inch playground ball for the more skilled students
Facility: Level area, wall space
Comments: Partner A starts rally from behind the 5-foot line. Partner B returns the ball, and partners attempt to rally (hit the ball to the wall before the ball bounces twice on the floor). Ball must rebound from wall and bounce in front of the 5-foot line or it is considered out. This game should be played in a cooperative way. "Try to hit the ball so your partner can hit it." Have students count how many times they can keep the ball in play. Alternate pairs or rotate. Retrievers should be encouraged to go after ball as quickly as possible.

Figure 7.9. Handball Unit (2-5)

Handball Unit (2–5)

Lesson 1 (Grades 2–5)
Activity: 2 Square (1 handed). Students play regular 2 Square, but contact must be made with one hand.
Objective: (1) Understand the basic concept of striking. (2) Participate in a partner activity.
Equipment: 8 inch playground ball (Grades 2,3), 6 inch playground ball (Grades 4,5)
Facility: Any area that is flat and can be marked with lines
Comments: (1) Emphasize "watching the ball." (2) Encourage students to use non-dominant hand, as well as dominant hand. (3) Make this a cooperative activity. Have partners work together to see how long they can keep the ball in play. "You want to make your partner successful"

Lesson 2 (Grades 2–5)
Activity: same as previous less
Objectives: Same as previous lesson
Equipment: Same as previous lesson
Facility: same as previous lesson
Comment: Especially with grades 4 and 5, challenge students to play with non-dominant hand only

Lesson 3 (Grades 2–5)
Activity: Eye/Hand Coordination Drills
Objective: (1) Develop skill of one-handed striking of small objects. (2) Develop eye/hand coordination.
Equipment: Balloons, large Nerf balls
Facility: Any controlled area. Indoor area is better.
Drills: (1) Student hits balloon (or Nerf ball) 5 times in a row with right hand. Same with left. (2) "how many times can you hit the balloon with your right hand in 30 seconds?" (3) "How many times can you alternate hitting with your right, then your left, then right, and so on?" (4) "How many times in a row can you and your partner hit with your right hands only?" Same with left. (5) RELAY Activities—Divide students into small groups. Have student perform same drills, then pass balloon to next person.
Comments: (1) Number of completed tasks (i.e. five in a row) or time (i.e. 30 seconds) will vary according to grade level. (2) Bouncing or dribbling 6-inch balls or racquetballs (grades 4 and 5) is a good warm-up activity. "Watch the ball hit your hand."

Lesson 4 (Grades 2–5)
Activity: Eye/Hand Coordination Drills
Objective: Same as previous lesson
Equipment: Yarn balls, balloons. Racquetballs (Grades 4 and 5).
Facility: Same as previous lesson
Drills: same as previous lesson
Comments: (1) Increase the number of times students need to hit in a row, or increase the time in which students attempt to make maximum successful contacts. (2) In grades 4 and 5, alternating hands while bouncing the racquetball is a good warm-up activity.

Lesson 5 (Grades 2–5)
Activity: Throwing—Sidearm and overhand (dominant hand)
Objective: (1) Develop sidearm throw with proper reciprocation. (2) Develop the overhand throw with proper reciprocation.
Equipment: Racquetballs
Facility: Wall space, level area
Drills: (1) Student throws ball to wall with overhand stroke and catches after first bounce on rebound. (2) Partner A throws ball to wall with overhand stroke. Partner B catches on first bounce

after rebound. Alternate. (3) Partner A throws ball with sidearm stroke. Partner B catches after first bounce on rebound. Alternate. (4) RELAY activities—Same drills as above except substitute 'next person' for 'partner.' Have students work in small groups.

Comments: If using racquetballs, have students (grade 2 and 3) start about 10 feet from wall when throwing ball. If 6-inch balls are used, the distance should be shorter. Grades 4 and 5 should start about 15 feet from wall when using racquetballs.

Lesson 6 (Grades 2–5)
Activity: Throwing—Sidearm and Overhead (non-dominant hand)
Objective: (1) Develop sidearm throw with proper reciprocation. (2) Develop the overhand throw with proper reciprocation.
Equipment: Racquetballs
Facility: Wall space, level area
Drills: Same as previous lesson except done with non-dominant hand.
Comments: (10) Student should attempt to imitate the throwing motion of dominant hand. (2) Pay particular attention to the footwork. "Step toward the wall as you throw."

Lesson 7 (Grades 2–5)
Activity: Drop and Hit (dominant hand)
Objective: (1) Develop striking skills. (2) Develop eye/hand coordination.
Equipment: 6-inch playground balls (grades 2,3), racquetballs (grades 4,5)
Facility: Wall space, level area
Drills: (1) Student drops the ball (bounces it) and hits it to the wall with a sidearm stroke. Student retrieves as next student moves to line to hit. This works well in groups of 4. Grades 2 and 3 should start about 8 feet from the wall and grades 4 and 5 should be about 15 feet from the wall. ALL grades should start with 6-inch playground balls. Grades 4 and 5 should progress to racquetballs. (2) Partner A drops and hits ball to wall with sidearm stroke. Partner B attempts to catch ball after first bounce.
Comments: (1) Remember, the hitting stroke should imitate the throwing stroke. (2) When students begin to hit the racquetball, encourage them to "cup your hands and relax your arms." (3) Students can work in groups of 4 in a rotation. The 3 back may serve as retrievers and boundaries (far enough back so that they are not in the way and they can prevent the ball from going past them). Students rotate one position counterclockwise after completed task.

Lesson 8 (Grades 2–5)
Activity: Drop and Hit (non-dominant hand)
Objective: (1) Develop striking skills. (2) Develop eye/hand coordination.
Equipment: 6-inch playground balls (grade 2,3), racquetballs (grades 4,5)
Facility: Wall space, level area
Drills: Same as previous lesson except done with non-dominant hand.
Comments: Make sure students drop ball far enough away from their body so that their elbow is slightly bent as the hand contacts the ball.

Lesson 9 (Grades 2–5)
Activity: Move and Hit (dominant hand)
Objective: Develop striking skill when contacting a thrown ball rebounding from a wall.
Equipment: 6-inch playground balls (grades 2,3), racquetballs (grades 4,5)
Facility: Wall space, level area
Drills: (1) Student stands behind line and tosses ball to wall so that it rebounds in front of line. Student attempts to hit ball to wall before ball bounces twice on floor. Grades 2 and 3 start 8 feet from the wall. Grades 4 and 5 start 15 feet from the wall. Student retrieves own hit as next student moves to line to toss (or 3 back can retrieve). (2) Partner A tosses ball to wall. Partner B moves and hits rebounding ball to wall. Other pair of partners may retrieve. Alternate. Alternate pairs or rotate.

Comments: (1) Always emphasize cooperative theme. Keep score (number of successful hits) of partners—NOT individuals. "You want to make your partner successful." (2) If a partner throws the ball to the wall, and it rebounds back toward himself, he/she should quickly move out of the way so as not to interfere with the partner's hit.

Lesson 10 (Grades 2–5)
Activity: Move and Hit (non-dominant hand)
Objective: Develop striking skill when contacting a thrown ball rebounding from a wall.
Equipment: 6-inch playground balls (grades 2,3), racquetballs (grades 4,5)
Facility: Wall space, level area
Drills: Same as previous lesson except drills done with non-dominant hand
Comments: Throws that begin drills should be with dominant hand.

Lesson 11 (Grades 2–5)
Activity: Rally
Objective: (1) Develop striking skills. (2) Participate in a partner activity.
Equipment: 6-inch playground balls (grades 2,3), racquetballs (grade 4,5)
Facility: Wall space, level area
Drills: (1) Student stands behind line (8 or 15 feet) and tosses ball to wall and attempts to hit the ball to the wall in succession as many times as possible. Ball must bounce in front of line after rebounding from wall. (2) Partner A stands behind line and tosses ball to wall. Partner B attempts to hit the ball back to the wall. Then Partner A attempts to return, and so on. Partner pairs alternate, or players rotate.
Comments: (1) If a continuous rally is too difficult, make the goal 2 hits or 3 hits. (2) Emphasize use of non-dominant hand. Perhaps require rally to start with a hit by non-dominant hand. (3) Player who hits ball must make every effort to get out of the way of the other player attempting to hit. Students must understand that this is a rule.

Lessons 12,13,14,15 (Grades 2–5)
Activity: One-Wall Handball
Objective (1) Participate in a partner activity. (2) Develop eye/hand coordination. (3) Develop striking skills with both hands. (4) Learn and participate in a "lifetime sport" activity.
Equipment: Wall space, level area
Comments: (1) Students begin rally by hitting ball to wall from behind line. Rally continues as long as: (a) Ball rebounds off wall in front of line. (b) Students return ball to wall before it bounces twice (rebounding ball does not have to bounce; it can be hit "on a fly"). (c) Ball goes directly to wall after leaving student's hand. (2) Instead of the winner of the rally serving the next ball, have one player serve for 3–5 rallies, and then the next player. (3) This is a good activity for the 4-person rotation set-up. The ball will get away many times, and the 3 back players may serve as retrievers.

How You Might Evaluate the Psychomotor Domain

8

"That which gets measured gets done."
Ralph Waldo Emerson

"Increasing a child's aerobic capacity or maximal strength should be a by-product of games and activity not the primary goal"
Charles Corbin

Evaluation can serve a number of functions. It can provide accountability to your instruction and offer insights regarding teaching methods that work and those that need reconsideration. But by far the most important role it can have is that of lifting the motivation of you and your students. What can be more rewarding than clear evidence that you indeed are having a positive effect on the knowledge and behavior of the children? No matter how hard your work may be, or how poor your financial gains, teaching is a joy when you know that you have made an impact. However, without this assuring verification, doubt, weariness and burnout can threaten. Also, like teachers, the children's enthusiasm can easily wane when there are no noticeable improvements. This discouragement can be countered when you provide them with data verifying that they are doing more curl-ups then earlier in the year or that they are making measurable improvements in their throwing skills. Learning is often a painfully slow process and we must miss no opportunities to help children appreciate learning whenever it occurs. Telling yourself or the children that progress is being made might be sufficient, but sometimes more tangible evidence is needed.

In this chapter you will be introduced to a variety of ideas concerning how you might evaluate your students' skills in the psychomotor domain. We will separately look at assessing physical activity, physical fitness and motor skills.

Evaluating Physical Activity

If you will recall from Chapter 2, one of our primary goals is to move children into an active lifestyle. More specifically we want children to adhere to *The Activity Pyramid*. At the basic level young people should be establishing lifestyle behaviors that that will result in at least 60 minutes of light/moderate activity everyday *(The Children's Lifetime Physical Activity Model C-LAM)*. And hopefully, in addition to that, they would be participating in both vigorous aerobic activities at least three times per week and muscular endurance/flexibility activities three or four times per week.

With this being a worthy, agreed upon goal, it is most strange to me that so little evaluation of physical activity has been done in the schools. You could easily begin evaluating movement in a simple informal manner. It does not have to be any more complex than asking for responses or a show of hands. You could ask how many felt like they got some good exercise in class. You might use *The Perceived Exertion Scale* to help them judge the intensity of their performance. Or you might get estimates of the physical activity engaged in outside of class, "Over the weekend, how many participated in at least 60 minutes of physical activity?" "How many remembered to do their curl-ups yesterday?" I know from experience that it can be hugely rewarding to get an indication that some students are being influenced by my instruction. And if I happen to receive an indication that many were not following through as I had hoped, that too was good for me to know.

To take the above informal assessment one small step further you might easily and profitably begin to record and track their movement behaviors. "Let's put up on the board the number of us who were able to get an hour of activity the previous day and we will see if we can do even better the rest of the week." Maybe you could begin recording the number of children participating in a walking program or the level of activity of some formally inactive students during recess. Another idea is to have the children begin tracking their own behaviors. Simple log keeping could be a good skill for them to learn and it could be made a part of their portfolios. Checking those logs could be a useful way to verify the effect of your instruction.

Assessment Instruments

In recent years, two technological instruments have begun to be used in the schools to measure physical activity: heart-rate monitors and pedometers. Also, researchers have been developing different types of questionnaires designed for the assessment of school children's activity selections during and outside of school.

Heart-Rate Monitors

Heart-rate monitors consist of a chest belt that detects a person's heart rate and a wristwatch that picks up that information for display. They can be effective in informing the student and teacher of exercise intensity and whether or not the performer is in his or her aerobic training zone. The devises are as of yet rather expensive and thus it is difficult to use them in large classes or for outside of class assignments. Nevertheless some teachers have found them educational by having students take turns wearing them and then discussing the findings with the rest of the class.

Pedometers

Pedometers are a small, inexpensive ($20–$35) devise that I believe has much potential for both assessing and motivating physical activity. It is worn on the belt and accurately measures how many steps a person takes. Some models will translate steps taken into distances and calories burned. I think they have good educational potential to teach students about accumulating activity not just during the school day but outside of class as well. They are effective at showing kids that *found activities* could make a valuable contribution to our health. There are many sources springing up for creative ways to use of pedometers for both children and adults. A couple good web sites you could start with would be http://www.creativewalking.com and www.exercisexpress.com. Below I have listed four implementation ideas.

* Classroom teachers and students can wear pedometers during the school day. At the end of the day, students check the number of steps they have accumulated. Physical activity goals are then discussed and set, and students try to meet their personal goal for two consecutive days.

* Students can be asked to monitor their parents or another significant adult for one day. They are given a handout explaining the rationale behind *The 10,000 Steps Criteria* for adults. The purpose of this assignment is to familiarize parents with the need for daily activity and to make them aware of their own and their children's activity levels. A brisk 30-minute walk usually requires approximately 3,800 to 4,000 steps. Research shows that the average sedentary classroom teacher takes around 3,000 to 7,000 steps per day. To be considered to have an active lifestyle and derive significant health benefits, adults should be achieving *The 10,000 Steps Criteria*.

* Students can wear a pedometer for a 24-hour period to see how much activity they accumulate during school and free time. These data can be compared to class goals or personal goals. Monitoring out-of-school activity is more important than monitoring in-school activity because students have greater control over the former.

* Students can be given a one-week log to complete in which they record the types of activities and the number of steps they accumulate each day. An average daily count can then be calculated to see whether they are accumulating adequate amounts of activity on a daily basis.

Physical Activity Questionnaires

Recently, a variety of reliable and valid activity assessments have been developed specifically for children. While most have been developed primarily for research purposes, you might be able to make practical use of them or variations of them. In Figure 8.1 I have included a reproducible copy of one of them (ACTIVITYGRAM Assessment).[1] To get reliable scores it is recommended that the questionnaire be administered on at least two or three different days. *The ACTIVITYGRAM Assessment* in Figure 8.1 is part of the *FITNESSGRAM Physical Fitness Test* that will be further discussed in the next section. It has computer software that allows the children to easily enter their own data with helpful prompting. For both the fitness scores and the physical activity information that is entered each student will get an individualized printout regarding what he/she is doing well, and what might need more attention.

Evaluating Physical Fitness

What about physical fitness testing? What does it tell us? How should we use them? Which test should we use?

What Does a Physical Fitness Test Tell You and the Child?

There are four basic factors that determine how well a child will do on a physical fitness test. Before reading further or referring to Figure 8.2, ask yourself what you think these factors may be and select which of those might have the most pronounced effect. Have you done so? Okay. The amount of "physical activity" the child is engaging in might have been the most obvious one and the first to come to your mind. After all, the more one is exercising the better they will be prepared for the test. The "lifestyle" factor is referring to things like sleep, nutrition, stress, and medical care. Inadequacies in any of these areas, singly or particularly in concert, can potentially impair vigorous performance. The "heredity" factor is simply the recognition that each individual is born with unique capabilities in the various components of physical fitness. Some people are going to be inherently many times stronger than others, while others may be far more flexible, or leaner, or have greater aerobic capacities. These large genetic variations are often known as *The Principle of Individual Differences*. Finally, "maturation" is recognition that children develop at different rates. I hope you did not forget this one. A child may naturally mature a year or even two years earlier or later than the norm of their age group. This means that even if your class contains children of all the same chronological age, it can be expected, due to early and later maturing, there will exist a developmental range potentially as large as four years. Obviously, those children who develop earlier will have a decided advantage on many components of fitness.

Of the above four factors, it is important to understand that the combination of the latter two, heredity and maturation, have much the dominant impact on children's fitness test scores. It is estimated that genetic abilities alone account for well over half the variances in performance. This is true for both children and adults. Also, the typical four-year spread in maturational levels can mightily impinge upon performance. Allow me to give an example of some research that dramatically accents this point. A number of years ago some physiological data was collected on ballplayers participating in the "Little League World Series" held in Williamsport, Pennsylvania. Teams were drawn from all across the United States and from many other nations. The young players were eleven and

---

[1] For a more comprehensive listing and description of procedures refer to *The Journal of Physical Education, Recreation and Dance*, Vol. 71, No. 1, January 2000.

Figure 8.1. ACTIVITYGRAM Assessment

ACTIVITYGRAM Logging Chart

Name_____ Age____ Teacher_____ Grade____

Record the *primary* activity you did during each 30-minute interval during the day using the list at the bottom of the page. Then select an intensity level that best describes how it felt (Light: "Easy"; Moderate: "Not too tiring"; Vigorous: "Very tiring"). *Note:* All time periods of rest should have Rest checked for intensity level.

Time	Activity	Rest	Light	Mod.	Vig.	Time	Activity	Rest	Light	Mod.	Vig.
7:00						3:00					
7:30						3:30					
8:00						4:00					
8:30						4:30					
9:00						5:00					
9:30						5:30					
10:00						6:00					
10:30						6:30					
11:00						7:00					
11:30						7:30					
12:00						8:00					
12:30						8:30					
1:00						9:00					
1:30						9:30					
2:00						10:00					
2:30						10:30					

Categories of Physical Activities

Lifestyle activity	Active aerobics	Active sports	Muscle fitness activities	Flexibility exercises	Rest and inactivity
"Activities that I do as part of my normal day"	"Activities that I do for aerobic fitness"	"Activities that I do for sports and recreation"	"Activities that I do for muscular fitness"	"Activities that I do for flexibility and fun"	"Things I do when I am not active"
1. Walking, bicycling, or skateboarding	11. Aerobic dance activity	21. Field sports (baseball, softball, football, soccer, etc. . .)	31. Gymnastics or cheer, dance or drill teams	41. Martial arts (Tai Chi)	51. Schoolwork, homework or reading
2. Housework or yardwork	12. Aerobic gym equipment (stairclimber, treadmill, etc. . .)	22. Court sports (basketball, volleyball, soccer, hockey, etc. . .)	32. Track and field sports (jumping, throwing, etc. . .)	42. Stretching	52. Computer games or TV/ videos
3. Playing active games or dancing	13. Aerobic activity (bicycling, running, skating, etc. . .)	23. Raquet sports (tennis, racquet-ball, etc. . .)	33. Weight lifting or calisthenics (pushups, situps, etc. . .)	43. Yoga	53. Eating or resting
4. Work– active job	14. Aerobic activity in physical educa-tion	24. Sports during physical education	34. Wrestling or Martial Arts (Karate, Aikido)	44. Ballet dancing	54. Sleeping
5. Other _____	15. Other _____	25. Other _____	35. Other _____	45. Other _____	55. Other _____

Source: FITNESSGRAM Test Administration Manual, Second Edition

(Cooper Institute for Aerobics Research, 1999)

Figure 8.2. Factors Affecting Children's Fitness Performance

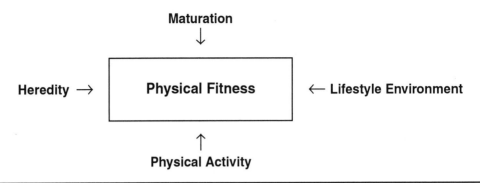

twelve years old. Measurements of bone density and pubic hair growth confirmed that the most dominant players (the clean-up hitters, pitchers) had an average maturational age comparable to fourteen-year-olds. Clearly early maturation was playing a major role in their successful performance.

We need also understand that exercise and lifestyle do not effect children's physical fitness scores nearly as much as they do for adults. This is true because children are not as *trainable* (remember this term from Chapter 4) or susceptible to physiological adaptations to exercise as are adults. Nor have the environmental factors of inactivity and poor lifestyle choices had years to accumulate and degrade fitness. How well adults do on a physical fitness test much better reflects lifestyle choices than tests of children, and as adults age this becomes even more the case. In youth we can abuse our bodies with much less immediate consequences than we can later on. This reminds me of a pertinent poetic passage, *"Oh for boyhood's painless play, / Sleep that wakes in laughing day, / Health that mocks the doctor's rules, / Knowledge never learned in school, . . . / Oh that thou couldst know thy joy, / Ere it passes, barefoot boy!"*

Now that we know what a physical fitness test might or, more to the point might not tell us the teacher, what may the results be telling the child? To them, what could be the implication of a low correlation existing between their fitness test performances and their health practices? Consider these two scenarios. Child A has been dutiful and conscientiously following your exercise and nutritional prescriptions throughout the year. But because he is maturing slower than most of the other children, and because he is not particularly genetically gifted or *trainable* in a number of fitness components, he still makes only modest gains and sees that his fitness test performance is far below most of his peers. Quite naturally that child may be despondent and discouraged. His conclusion could be "What's the use? Why try?" Clearly such a reaction would be a demonstration of *learned helplessness*. Research data has confirmed that poor performance on a fitness test has a tendency to reduce a child's motivation to engage in further physical activities.

In our second scenario, Child B has not been so carefully adhering to advisable exercise or eating practices; in fact, she may be wallowing in a foul sink of sloth and nutritional debauchery. But, because she happens to be maturing early and is relatively physically gifted, she scores near the top of the class on the fitness test. What does she think? She might erroneously feel reassured that her habits are just fine, even though they are leading her down the primrose road to some future health problems.

Okay, where does all this leave us? Are physical fitness tests archaic, not worthwhile or even counter productive? Should they be abandoned? I would say this might not be necessarily true. The manner in which we do the testing could determine whether the motivational effects are good or bad. Let us judge the merits of three possible approaches.

Three Approaches to Physical Fitness Testing

Traditional Approach

The *traditional approach* is where everyone is required to take the test. Test performance and scores are carefully evaluated and counted by judges to ensure accuracy. Also, the test results are distributed to everyone, with the better performers typically receiving special recognition in the form of patches, certificates or public displays of names. Some of these tests are *norm referenced* because a child's performance is compared to other children either within the school, the school district, or nationwide. To earn the special recognition of having passed the test, a percentile score of something like 50 or 80 percent must be achieved on all the test items. *Criterion reference tests* are those in which a cut-off level has been set for each component of fitness. The level is an arbitrary one, but it is hoped to represent a minimal level of fitness below which none of the children should fall. Under this system it is of course theoretically possible that everyone could be recognized for passing.

Possibly there is something to be gained from the schools accurately tracking the physical fitness status of its students. It may identify areas of strengths or weaknesses and might detect significant group trends. However, to fulfill this institutional role it is doubtful that yearly instructional and administrative time is justifiable. Perhaps a few spot checks throughout the school years would be sufficient (maybe once in upper elementary, once in middle school, and once during high school years). Whatever the schedule, because testing for these purposes is large scale and needs to be very accurately done, it should normally fall not to you but to the province of a physical education specialist of some sort.

Traditional testing is also justified on motivational grounds; namely, the existence of the tests will serve to make the children more diligent about their fitness. We need to be careful here. As discussed earlier, even if all the children do view it as an incentive to work determinedly on their fitness, some likely will still fail to perform well on the test because of maturational, genetic and trainability factors. These people could be very deflated by the results, particularly if they are normative evaluations. I would say that another danger is that many of the lower fitness students will not be motivated to do well on the test because they already know that it would be futile for them to try. They perceive they are low in fitness, and the approach of the testing process is only something to dread. They fear their ineptitude will be displayed in a highly public forum. Physical skills are highly valued in children; can you not empathize with the feelings of a child struggling, and failing to do a pull-up in front of a waiting line of peers? The net effect seems to be one in which those possessing above average fitness abilities are likely being motivated (although some of the very fittest may not be because the cut-off levels are too easy for them) while those of low fitness, who are most at risk and in need of encouragement, are being ill served.[2]

Personal Approach

The essence of the *personal approach* has the children less formally self-testing themselves and then setting individual goals. Suppose you thought it important for the children to do regular curl-ups so as to have firm abdominal muscles. Besides having them do curl-ups in class and encouraging them to continue outside of class, you add an evaluation component. Shortly after introducing

---

[2] At a recent meeting of *the American Alliance of Health, Physical Education, Recreation and Dance*, I remember a presentation point made by Dr. Robert Pangrazi (a renowned authority in elementary physical education). He said that public physical fitness tests could be an extremely stressful and unpleasant psychological experience and that . . . "Our fitness test results should be as private as our sex lives."

the concepts of how and why to do abdominal exercises you say, "Let's all give ourselves a test to see where we are. Following these procedures do as many curl-ups as you possibly can." After they have completed the task, you tell them to remember how they did and to be prepared for the same test latter in the term. You also encourage each to set a reasonable personal improvement goal.

To my mind, this personal approach to testing has some real pluses. Although the students' self-scoring may not be as accurate as under the traditional instructor scored system, it should tend to be motivational to all the students. Everyone should be capable of making some improvement toward his/her goal. The potential for embarrassment is minimal because everyone is simultaneously working and not likely to be standing about watching others. Also, their results and goals are private, maybe known only to themselves, the teacher, or to those friends with whom they wish to share.

The personal testing approach could take on more elaborate forms if you so chose. A battery of test items could be administered where the children either scored or worked with a partner. The goal setting process could involve you sitting down with each child and helping them set and write challenging, but reasonable goals. Practice plans and schedules could be designed. Short-term enabling objectives could be established and monitored. Incentives and recognition could be developed for all those who achieve their goals. Everything could be made a part of their portfolios. This sort of personal goal setting process could be a valuable learning experience for teaching perseverance.

Challenge Approach

Some of you might give credence to the potential problems of the traditional testing approach, and yet you are not comfortable in evaluating only on improvements and totally dispensing with fitness standards. Surely you are thinking, there can be some goodness in establishing a desirable fitness standard and recognizing those who can attain it. The *challenge approach* to physical fitness testing is the same as the *traditional approach* but with the exception that participation is voluntary. Using this system we might announce a physical fitness "challenge" test to be administered near the end of the term or year. It is to be an extra-class event scheduled during a lunch hour or after school. You explain what the test consists of and what standards must be achieved to pass the test. You make clear that passing the test may not be possible for everyone and that those planning on participating will most likely need to be training for it. A few special training practices may even be planned.

The *challenge approach* is much like that with which we take in sports and in many other disciplines. If a child shows good aptitude in the track or gymnastic activities introduced in class, we quite appropriately would encourage them to go out for a school or club team and thus maximize their talents. If a child were good in music or math we would attempt to integrate him/her into any programs, clubs or contests which might exist in these fields.

Selecting a Physical Fitness Test

I think that a good first step in deciding what to evaluate is to ask yourself what it is you believe in most strongly and what kind of instruction and experiences have you been giving the children. It makes little sense to give a physical fitness test, or any test for that matter, if you have not been seriously teaching for improvement. If you have been encouraging the students to engage in aerobic activities than you want to use a test that tests that component of fitness. If you have devoted attention to diet and calorie burning then assessment of body fat is in order. My view is that those components of physical fitness which are most related to long-term health are of central concern. In Chapter 4 it was pointed out that all the components of fitness can relate, in one way or another, to both our athletic performance and our long-term health. However, we saw that some components play a more significant role in health than others. Aerobic cardiovascular fitness and body fat control would certainly need to be listed as such because of their relationship to common disabilities. Tests that focus on these aspects of health are classified as *health related physical fitness tests*. Anaerobic fitness and muscular power play a big part in many sports activities but much less of a central one for health. Tests that include assessment of these aspects of fitness are classified as *performance related physical fitness tests*. Example items they would be testing would be a sprinting shuttle run, standing broad or vertical jump, or softball throw for distance. It can be seen that coaches in many different sports might be interested in testing some of these.

There are many different physical fitness tests from which you can select and possibly your school district may already have a policy for using one. The two most widely used national physical fitness tests are *The President's Challenge* developed by the President's Council on Physical Fitness and Sports (E-mail: preschal@indiana.edu, Website: http://www.indiana.edu/~preschal) and *FITNESSGRAM* developed by The Cooper Institute for Aerobics Research (E-mail: hkmank@hkusa.com, Website: www.humankinetics.com). I will describe the basics of each. You should be able to discern that the FITNESSGRAM fits my philosophy better. I also am impressed with its software designed for easy student use. But it is up to you to compared and decide what might work best for you.

The President's Challenge

The primary purpose of *The President's Challenge* has been to motivate children and youth age 6–17 to begin and continue an active lifestyle by providing awards for reaching appropriate fitness levels and engagement in an active lifestyle. Different attractive patches are awarded for each of the five awards. Suggested guidelines are included for accommodating special needs students.

The Presidential Active Lifestyle Award (PALA) rewards an active lifestyle. Students who are active for 60 minutes per day, five days per week, for six weeks are eligible for this awards. They are encouraged to repeat their participation throughout the year, earning a series of stickers placed on the certificate indicating the number of times the award has been won.

The Presidential Physical Fitness Award (PPFA) recognizes an outstanding level of physical fitness. Boys and girls who score at or above the 85th percentile on all five items of *The President's Challenge*: (curl-ups or partial curl-ups, shuttle run, endurance run/walk ¼ mile—6–7 year old, ½ mile—8–9 year old, 1 mile—10–17 year old, pull-ups or right angle push-ups, v-sit reach or sit and reach) are eligible to receive the award. Emblems are numbered to correspond with the total number of times the award is earned.

The National Physical Fitness Award (NPFA) recognizes the achievement of a basic yet challenging level of physical fitness. Boys and girls scoring at or above the 50th percentile on all five items on *The President's Challenge* are eligible to receive this award.

The Participant Physical Fitness Award (PA) recognizes boys and girls who attempt all five test items on *The President's Challenge* but whose scores fall below the 50th percentile on one or more of them.

The Health Fitness Award (HFA) recognizes students who achieve a healthy level of fitness. As with the physical fitness award, the HFA is given based on the results of a five item assessment: (partial curl-ups, one mile run/walk: ¼ mile 6–7 year old, 1.2 mile 8–9 year old, 1 mile 10–17 year old, V-sit: sit and reach, right angle push-ups or pull-ups and a measurement of body mass index). Body Mass Index is an easy way, based on height and weight, to estimate body composition without actually measuring body fat.

Figure 8.3. *The President's Challenge* Qualifying Standards

Please Note: Award standards were most recently validated in 1998 by means of comparison with a large nationwide sample collected in 1994.

The Presidential Physical Fitness Award

	AGE	CURL-UPS (# one minute)	PARTIAL* CURL-UPS (#)	SHUTTLE RUN (seconds)	V-SIT REACH (inches)	SIT AND REACH (centimeters)	ENDURANCE RUN (min:sec)		PULL-UPS (#)	RT. ANGLE* PUSH-UPS (#)
BOYS	6	33	22	12.1	+3.5	31	1:55	1/4 mile	2	9
	7	36	24	11.5	+3.5	30	1:48		4	14
	8	40	30	11.1	+3.0	31	3:30	1/2 mile	5	17
	9	41	37	10.9	+3.0	31	3:30		5	18
	10	45	35	10.3	+4.0	30	7:57		6	22
	11	47	43	10.0	+4.0	31	7:32		6	27
	12	50	64	9.8	+4.0	31	7:11		7	31
	13	53	59	9.5	+3.5	33	6:50	1 mile	7	39
	14	56	62	9.1	+4.5	36	6:26		10	40
	15	57	75	9.0	+5.0	37	6:20		11	42
	16	56	73	8.7	+6.0	38	6:08		11	44
	17	55	66	8.7	+7.0	41	6:06		13	53
GIRLS	6	32	22	12.4	+5.5	32	2:00	1/4 mile	2	9
	7	34	24	12.1	+5.0	32	1:55		2	14
	8	38	30	11.8	+4.5	33	3:58	1/2 mile	2	17
	9	39	37	11.1	+5.5	33	3:53		2	18
	10	40	33	10.8	+6.0	33	9:19		3	20
	11	42	43	10.5	+6.5	34	9:02		3	19
	12	45	50	10.4	+7.0	36	8:23		2	20
	13	46	59	10.2	+7.0	38	8:13	1 mile	2	21
	14	47	48	10.1	+8.0	40	7:59		2	20
	15	48	38	10.0	+8.0	43	8:08		2	20
	16	45	49	10.1	+9.0	42	8:23		1	24
	17	44	58	10.0	+8.0	42	8:15		1	25

The National Physical Fitness Award

	AGE	CURL-UPS (# one minute)	PARTIAL* CURL-UPS (#)	SHUTTLE RUN (seconds)	V-SIT REACH (inches)	SIT AND REACH (centimeters)	ENDURANCE RUN (min.:sec.)		PULL-UPS (#)	RT. ANGLE* PUSH-UPS (#)	FLEXED-ARM HANG (sec)
BOYS	6	22	10	13.3	+1.0	26	2:21	1/4 mile	1	7	6
	7	28	13	12.8	+1.0	25	2:10		1	8	8
	8	31	17	12.2	+0.5	25	4:22	1/2 mile	1	9	10
	9	32	20	11.9	+1.0	25	4:14		2	12	10
	10	35	24	11.5	+1.0	25	9:48		2	14	12
	11	37	26	11.1	+1.0	25	9:20		2	15	11
	12	40	32	10.6	+1.0	26	8:40		2	18	12
	13	42	39	10.2	+0.5	26	8:06	1 mile	3	24	14
	14	45	40	9.9	+1.0	28	7:44		5	24	20
	15	45	45	9.7	+2.0	30	7:30		6	30	30
	16	45	37	9.4	+3.0	30	7:10		7	30	28
	17	44	42	9.4	+3.0	34	7:04		8	37	30
GIRLS	6	23	10	13.8	+2.5	27	2:26	1/4 mile	1	6	5
	7	25	13	13.2	+2.0	22	2:21		1	8	6
	8	29	17	12.9	+2.0	28	4:56	1/2 mile	1	9	8
	9	30	20	12.5	+2.0	28	4:50		1	12	8
	10	30	24	12.1	+3.0	28	11:22		1	13	8
	11	32	27	11.5	+3.0	29	11:17		1	11	7
	12	35	30	11.3	+3.5	30	11:05		1	10	7
	13	37	40	11.1	+3.5	31	10:23	1 mile	1	11	8
	14	37	30	11.2	+4.5	33	10:06		1	10	9
	15	36	26	11.0	+5.0	36	9:58		1	15	7
	16	35	26	10.9	+5.5	34	10:31		1	12	7
	17	34	40	11.0	+4.5	35	10:22		1	16	7

The Participant Physical Fitness Award

Boys and girls who attempt all five items, but whose scores fall below the 50th percentile on one or more of them are eligible to receive the Participant Award.

*Norms from Canada Fitness Award Program, Health Canada, Government of Canada with permission.

Note: 1/4 and 1/2 mile norms from Amateur Athletic Union Physical Fitness Program with permission.

Figure 8.4. *The President's Challenge* Instructions for the Health Fitness Program

For the sixth year in a row The President's Challenge is providing interested teachers and youth leaders with a health criterion-referenced award as an alternative to the traditional Physical Fitness Awards. This Health Fitness Award (HFA) can be earned by youngsters whose test scores meet or exceed the specified health criteria on each of the five items comprising The President's Challenge Health Fitness Test listed below. Award standards are based upon health-related criteria adapted from several sources as indicated in the table below.

While teachers may choose to administer both The President's Challenge Physical Fitness Test **and** The President's Challenge Health Fitness Test to their students, it is not intended that students should receive awards from both tests. Although if a teacher so chooses, both awards can be ordered. The PALA may be earned in conjunction with either the President's Challenge Physical Fitness or Health Fitness Award.

Health Fitness Test Items:

For use when qualifying students for the Health Fitness Award.

Use criterion referenced standards listed on this page.

1. Partial Curl-ups
   See page 9

2. Endurance Run/Walk with distance option
   See page 10

3. V-Sit Reach or Sit and Reach option
   See page 12

4. Right Angle Push-ups or Pull-ups option
   See page 11

5. Body Mass Index (BMI)

Objective:	To estimate body composition
Testing:	Determine total body weight (kilograms) and height (meters). Use Table to convert to BMI (page 18), or use formula:

Wt (kg)/Ht (m)²

Wt [2.2 lbs = 1 kg)   Ht [1 inch = 0.0254 m]

Example:	A 16 year old boy weighing 154 pounds (70 kg), and 68 inches tall (1.727 meters) has a BMI of:

$$\frac{70 \text{ kg}}{(1.727\text{m})^2} = \frac{70}{2.98} \approx 23.5 \text{ kg/m}^2$$

Based on the BMI range for a 16 year old boy listed in the table below; a BMI index of 23.5 puts this boy in the desirable range. Use the BMI chart (next page) for quick calculation.

Rationale:	Body composition is an important component of physical fitness. Body mass index is one method to estimate this fitness component.

The Health Fitness Award

	AGE	PARTIAL CURL-UPS (#)	ENDURANCE RUN (min:sec)		V-SIT REACH (inches)	SIT AND REACH (centimeters)	RT. ANGLE PUSH-UPS (#)	PULL-UPS (#)	BMI (range)
BOYS	6	12	2:30	1/4 mile	1	21	3	1	13.3-19.5
	7	12	2:20		1	21	4	1	13.3-19.5
	8	15	4:45	1/2 mile	1	21	5	1	13.4-20.5
	9	15	4:35		1	21	6	1	13.7-21.4
	10	20	9:30		1	21	7	1	14.0-22.5
	11	20	9:00		1	21	8	2	14.0-23.7
	12	20	9:00		1	21	9	2	14.8-24.1
	13	25	8:00	1 mile	1	21	10	2	15.4-24.7
	14	25	8:00		1	21	12	3	16.1-25.4
	15	30	7:30		1	21	14	4	16.6-26.4
	16	30	7:30		1	21	16	5	17.2-26.8
	17	30	7:30		1	21	18	6	17.7-27.5
GIRLS	6	12	2:50	1/4 mile	2	23	3	1	13.1-19.6
	7	12	2:40		2	23	4	1	13.1-19.6
	8	15	5:35	1/2 mile	2	23	5	1	13.2-20.7
	9	15	5:25		2	23	6	1	13.5-21.4
	10	20	10:00		2	23	7	1	13.8-22.5
	11	20	10:00		2	23	7	1	14.1-23.2
	12	20	10:30		2	23	8	1	14.7-24.2
	13	25	10:30	1 mile	3	25	7	1	15.5-25.3
	14	25	10:30		3	25	7	1	16.2-25.3
	15	30	10:00		3	25	7	1	16.6-26.5
	16	30	10:00		3	25	7	1	16.8-26.5
	17	30	10:00		3	25	7	1	17.1-26.9

Criterion standards listed above adapted from Amateur Athletic Union Physical Fitness Program; AAHPERD Physical Best; Cooper Institute for Aerobic Research, Fitnessgram; Corbin, C. & Lindsey, R., *Fitness for Life*, 4th edition; and YMCA Youth Fitness Test.

Figure 8.5. *The President's Challenge* Body Mass Index

Directions: Use a ruler to connect the height column to the weight column and read the BMI number in the middle.

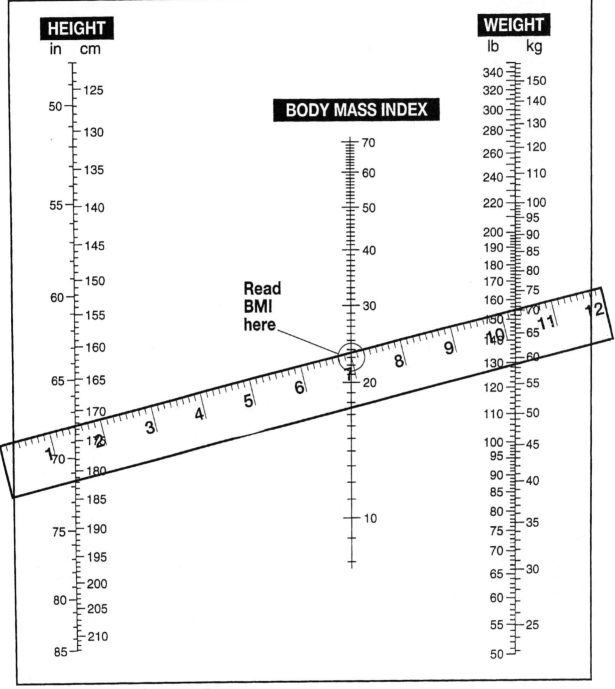

Example: Use same example as shown on page 17.
Modified with permission from David C. Nieman, *Fitness and Sports Medicine; A Health-Related Approach,* (3rd edition), Bull Publishing Co., Palo Alto, CA, 1995.

Figure 8.6. *The President's Challenge Active Lifestyle Award*

What is the Presidential Active Lifestyle Award?

The **Presidential Active Lifestyle Award** is an award you can earn by keeping track of any physical activity that you do. By earning this award you can learn the good habit of keeping active every day. Being physically active makes you healthy, gives you energy, and is just plain fun. Here's how to do it!

How to Earn this Award

(Follow these steps . . .)

There are two ways to keep track of physical activity for this award. One way is to accumulate a minimum of 60 minutes of physical activity. This activity can be done at one time for 60 minutes or the minutes of activity can be accumulated in shorter segments throughout the day. Another way to measure your activity is to use a pedometer. The pedometer measures the number of steps taken during the day. The number of pedometer steps that must be reached anytime throughout the day is 11,000 for girls and boys.

★

You may do many different types of activity, but you must gather 60 minutes of activity or enough pedometer steps at least 5 days per week.

★

Record your activity or steps every day for six weeks (see example).

★

At the end of each week verify your log by signing your name.

★

When you have completed all six weeks, fill out and have supervising adult sign the verification on this page.

★

Congratulations! You have earned the **Presidential Active Lifestyle Award**.

Directions for Recording Physical Activities

Example

Week 1	Activities	# Minutes or Pedometer Steps
Monday	Rode Bicycle, Skate Board	70
Tuesday	Pedometer	12,050
Wednesday	Dance Lessons, Walk the Dog	75
Thursday	Pedometer	11,177
Friday	Roller Blading, Street Hockey	65
Saturday	Scooter Riding, Soccer	75
Sunday	Went to Park w/family, Karate Lessons	60
	Participant Signature	

Other activities that count might include any teams that you play on, active games with your friends or any other activity that takes effort.

For more information about the
Presidential Active Lifestyle Award
visit our website at:
www.indiana.edu/~preschal

Verification

I would like to submit my form for the **Presidential Active Lifestyle Award**. I have completed the following requirements to earn this award.

_____ I have performed at least 60 minutes of activity or 11,000 pedometer steps for at least five days each week.

_____ I have performed my physical activities for at least 6 weeks.

I certify that I have accomplished the requirements necessary for the **Presidential Active Lifestyle Award**.

_____
Participant Signature

_____
Supervising Adult's Signature

FITNESSGRAM

FITNESSGRAM is a comprehensive health-related fitness and activity assessment and computerized reporting system. All elements within *FITNESSGRAM* are designed to assist teachers in accomplishing the primary objective of youth fitness programs, which is to help students establish physical activity as a part of their daily lives. Criterion-referenced standards are used to evaluate fitness performance. These standards have been established to represent a level of fitness that offers some degree of protection against diseases that result from sedentary living. Performance is classified in two general areas: "Needs Improvement" and "Healthy Fitness Zone" (HFZ). In Figure 8.7 are the test items and Figures 8.8 and 8.9 provide a list of standards for the HFZ. All students are expected to strive to achieve a score that places them inside the HFZ. *FITNESSGRAM* acknowledges performance above the HFZ but does not recommend this level of performance as an appropriate goal level for all students.

Research findings were used as the basis for establishing the *FITNESSGRAM* health fitness standards. With regard to aerobic fitness level, studies have shown that a significant decrease in risk of mortality results from getting out of the lower 20% of the population. Aerobic capacity standards for the HFZ have been established so that the lower end of the zone corresponds to getting out of the lower 20 percent of the population. The upper end of the Healthy Fitness Zone corresponds to a fitness level that would include up to 60 percent of the population.

The higher end of the body composition HFZ corresponds with 25 percent body fat for boys and 32 percent for girls. This is based on research showing that boys and girls with body composition readings above these figures are much more likely to have elevated cholesterol levels and hypertension. The lower end of the HFZ corresponds with 8 percent body fat for boys and 13 percent for girls. Some students may be healthy at lower levels of percent body fat but it is good to detect those that are this lean so that they know that they could encounter health problems. Also, it could be a tip-off of those who might be suffering from an eating disorder. It is important to understand that the interpretation of body composition from both skinfold measurements and the body mass index are only estimates. Even if you have good experience using skinfold methods measurement error of 3 to 5 percent are expected. The body mass index, because it is based on height and weight measures, also has a degree of inaccuracy in that it tends to overestimate the amount of body fat in the heavier boned and muscular students, and underestimate the amount of body fat in the smaller boned and less muscular.

There are four other positive aspects of the *FITNESSGRAM* that deserve mention. The first is the *ACTIVITYGRAM*, which was discussed, in the first part of this chapter. It is very useful in reliably measuring physical activity and of course can be used in conjunction with or separately from the fitness test. It is designed to fit nicely in with *The Activity Pyramid* guidelines.

The *PACER* test is the recommended test of aerobic performance (perhaps you recall it from Figure 3.3). The students are paced by music as they run back and forth between cones that are placed 20 meters apart. The music gradually becomes faster and the children try to keep up with it as long as they can. Their score is based on how many laps they are able to do. It is easy to administer, valid and reliable, and kids generally really like it.[3]

Third, a great feature of the *FITNESSGRAM* is its software. It is so easy to use and the outcome printouts are very complete (see Figure 8.10). The data is easy to enter and best of all, it is possible for the students to do the entering themselves. They can enter both their test scores and also their physical activity logs for the *ACTIVITYGRAM*. As the students enter data there are useful helping prompts.

Finally, there are some useful testing items and procedures for students with special needs.

---

[3] K–3 grades enjoy doing *the PACER* test but it is not recommended that any scores be recorded at this stage. Just let them do it as long as they are having fun. It usually will only take a few minutes before they are tired.

Figure 8.7. FITNESSGRAM Test Items

Aerobic Capacity

Teachers select one of the following:
* The PACER
One-mile run
The walk test (secondary students)

Body Composition

Teachers select one of the following:
* Skinfold measurements
Body mass index

Muscle Strength, Endurance, and Flexibility

Teachers will select as indicated

Abdominal Strength & Endurance

Must select.
* Curl-up

Trunk Extensor Strength & Flexibility

Must select.
* Trunk lift

Upper Body Strength

Must select.
* Push-up
Modified pull-up
Pull-up
Flexed arm hang

Flexibility

Must select.
Back-saver sit and reach
Shoulder stretch

* Recommended test.

Evaluating Motor Skills

In Chapter 2, we stated that our overriding goals were to get children (1) active and eating healthily and (2) to exhibit good affective behaviors. Although the acquisition of motor skills was not given this central status, it should be apparent that the possession of good motor skills is supportively important. As noted earlier, children who are more confident of motor skills are on average more likely to assume an active adult lifestyle.

Motor skills can be broken into two kinds: *fundamental* and *sport specific. Fundamental motor skills* are skills such as walking, running, skipping, throwing and kicking (see Figure 8.11 for a listing). There are two reasons it is hoped that children will acquire these skills during the primary grades. Firstly, these skills form the underlying basis of all future sports performance. Possession of these basic movement skills is said to have a positive *transfer* effect on the learning of sport skills. For instance, if a child has never learned the step-hop sequence involved in skipping, it likely will be difficult for him/her to later learn to perform a sport specific basketball lay-up which involves this skipping action. If he/she has not first learned to make a lateral slide step, later difficulties will be encountered when having to move quickly to the side when guarding a soccer player or covering a badminton court. It is obvious how the fundamental skills of running, throwing, catching and striking are prerequisite to sports that demand specific versions of those movements.

The second reason it is desirable for young children to master these fundamental skills is the terrific significance they have at this developmental stage. These motor skills tend to be valued more highly than all other aspects of a child's life. If a child cannot run or catch nearly as well as his/her peer group, it can be a bitter dose to a young and forming self-concept. We adults, who have come to place greater value on many other intellectual and affective aspects of our lives, sometimes

Figure 8.8. FITNESSGRAM Standards for Healthy Fitness Zone (Girls)

Girls

Age	One-mile Run (min:sec)		PACER (# laps)		Walk Test & $\dot{V}O_{2max}$ (ml/kg/min)		Percent Fat		Body Mass Index		Curl-up (# completed)	
5	Completion of		Participate in				32	17	21	16.2	2	10
6	distance. Time		run. Lap count				32	17	21	16.2	2	10
7	standards not		standards not				32	17	22	16.2	4	14
8	recommended.		recommended.				32	17	22	16.2	6	20
9							32	17	23	16.2	9	22
10	12:30	9.30	15	41	40	48	32	17	23.5	16.6	12	26
11	12:00	9:00	15	41	39	47	32	17	24	16.9	15	29
12	12:00	9:00	23	41	38	46	32	17	24.5	16.9	18	32
13	11:30	9:00	23	51	37	45	32	17	24.5	17.5	18	32
14	11:00	8:30	23	51	36	44	32	17	25	17.5	18	32
15	10:30	8:00	23	51	35	43	32	17	25	17.5	18	35
16	10:00	8:00	32	61	35	43	32	17	25	17.5	18	35
17	10:00	8:00	41	61	35	43	32	17	26	17.5	18	35
17+	10:00	8:00	41	61	35	43	32	17	27.3	18.0	18	35

Age	Trunk Lift (inches)		Push-up (# completed)		Modified Pull-up (# completed)		Pull-up (# completed)		Flexed Arm Hang (seconds)		Back-saver Sit & Reach** (inches)	Shoulder Stretch
5	6	12	3	8	2	7	1	2	2	8	9	
6	6	12	3	8	2	7	1	2	2	8	9	
7	6	12	4	10	3	9	1	2	3	8	9	
8	6	12	5	13	4	11	1	2	3	10	9	
9	6	12	6	15	4	11	1	2	4	10	9	
10	9	12	7	15	4	13	1	2	4	10	9	
11	9	12	7	15	4	13	1	2	6	12	10	
12	9	12	7	15	4	13	1	2	7	12	10	
13	9	12	7	15	4	13	1	2	8	12	10	
14	9	12	7	15	4	13	1	2	8	12	10	
15	9	12	7	15	4	13	1	2	8	12	12	
16	9	12	7	15	4	13	1	2	8	12	12	
17	9	12	7	15	4	13	1	2	8	12	12	
17+	9	12	7	15	4	13	1	2	8	12	12	

*Number on left is lower end of HFZ; number on right is upper end of HFZ

**Test scored Pass/Fail; must reach this distance to pass.

© 1992, 1999, The Copper Institue for Aerobics Research, Dallas, Texas.

Figure 8.9. FITNESSGRAM Standards for Healthy Fitness Zone (Boys)

Boys

Age	One-mile Run (min:sec)		PACER (# laps)		Walk Test & VO$_{2max}$ (ml/kg/min)		Percent Fat		Body Mass Index		Curl-up (# completed)	
5	Completion of distance. Time standards not recommended.		Participate in run. Lap count standards not recommended.				25	10	20	14.7	2	10
6							25	10	20	14.7	2	10
7							25	10	20	14.9	4	14
8							25	10	20	15.1	6	20
9							25	10	20	15.2	9	24
10	11:30	9.00	23	61	42	52	25	10	21	15.3	12	24
11	11:00	8:30	23	72	42	52	25	10	21	15.8	15	28
12	10:30	8:00	32	72	42	52	25	10	22	16.0	18	36
13	10:00	7:30	41	72	42	52	25	10	23	16.6	21	40
14	9:30	7:00	41	83	42	52	25	10	24.5	17.5	24	45
15	9:00	7:00	51	94	42	52	25	10	25	18.1	24	47
16	8:30	7:00	61	94	42	52	25	10	26.5	18.5	24	47
17	8:30	7:00	61	94	42	52	25	10	27	18.8	24	47
17+	8:30	7:00	61	94	42	52	25	10	27.8	19.0	24	47

Age	Trunk Lift (inches)		Push-up (# completed)		Modified Pull-up (# completed)		Pull-up (# completed)		Flexed Arm Hang (seconds)		Back-saver Sit & Reach** (inches)	Shoulder Stretch
5	6	12	3	8	2	7	1	2	2	8	8	
6	6	12	3	8	2	7	1	2	2	8	8	
7	6	12	4	10	3	9	1	2	3	8	8	
8	6	12	5	13	4	11	1	2	3	8	8	
9	6	12	6	15	5	11	1	2	4	10	8	
10	9	12	7	20	5	15	1	2	4	10	8	
11	9	12	8	20	6	17	1	3	6	13	8	
12	9	12	10	20	7	20	1	3	6	13	8	
13	9	12	12	25	8	22	1	4	12	17	8	
14	9	12	14	30	9	25	2	5	15	20	8	
15	9	12	16	35	10	27	3	7	15	20	8	
16	9	12	18	35	12	30	5	8	15	20	8	Passing = touching fingertips together behind the back
17	9	12	18	35	14	30	5	8	15	20	8	
17+	9	12	18	35	14	30	5	8	15	20	8	

*Number on left is lower end of HFZ; number on right is upper end of HFZ

**Test scored Pass/Fail; must reach this distance to pass.

© 1992, 1999, The Copper Institute for Aerobics Research, Dallas, Texas.

Figure 8.10. FITNESSGRAM Printout

FITNESSGRAM®

Charlie Brown
Grade: 5   Age: 11
Madison County Elementary School
Instructor: Kathy Read

	Test Date	Height	Weight
Current	07/15/99	5'01"	105
Past	07/13/99	5'3"	122

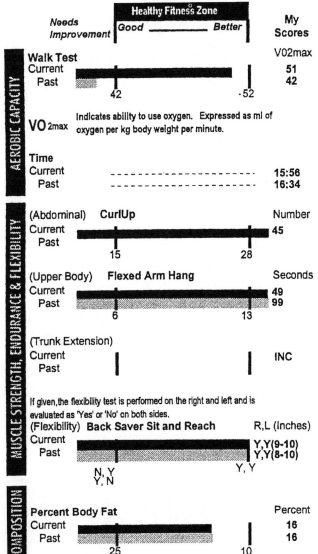

AEROBIC CAPACITY

Healthy Fitness Zone
Needs Improvement | Good ———— Better

My Scores

Walk Test
Current
Past
42   -52
VO2max
51
42

VO2max Indicates ability to use oxygen. Expressed as ml of oxygen per kg body weight per minute.

Time
Current
Past
15:56
16:34

MUSCLE STRENGTH, ENDURANCE & FLEXIBILITY

(Abdominal) CurlUp
Current
Past
15   28
Number
45

(Upper Body) Flexed Arm Hang
Current
Past
6   13
Seconds
49
99

(Trunk Extension)
Current
Past
INC

If given, the flexibility test is performed on the right and left and is evaluated as 'Yes' or 'No' on both sides.
(Flexibility) Back Saver Sit and Reach
Current
Past
N, Y
Y, N
Y, Y
R,L (Inches)
Y,Y(9-10)
Y,Y(8-10)

BODY COMPOSITION

Percent Body Fat
Current
Past
25   10
Percent
16
16

Lower numbers are better scores on body composition measurement.

ACTIVITY

Number of Days

On how many of the past 7 days did you participate in physical activity for a total of 30-60 minutes, or more, over the course of a day? — 4

On how many of the past 7 days did you do exercises to strengthen or tone your muscles? — 3

On how many of the past 7 days did you do stretching exercises to loosen up or relax your muscles? — 2

MESSAGES

Charlie, your scores on all test items were in or above the Healthy Fitness Zone. You are also doing strength and flexibility exercises. However, you need to play active games, sports or other activities at least 5 days each week.

Although your aerobic capacity score is in the Healthy Fitness Zone now, you are not doing enough physical activity. You should try to play very actively at least 60 minutes at least five days each week to look and feel good.

Your abdominal strength was very good. To maintain your fitness level be sure that your strength activities include curl-ups 3 to 5 days each week. Remember to keep your knees bent. Avoid having someone hold your feet.

Your upper body strength was very good, Charlie. To maintain your fitness level be sure that your strength activities include arm exercises such as push-ups, modified push-ups or climbing activities 2 to 3 days each week.

Charlie, your flexibility is in the Healthy Fitness Zone. To maintain your fitness, stretch slowly 3 or 4 days each week, holding the stretch 20 - 30 seconds. Don't forget that you need to stretch all areas of the body.

Charlie, your body composition is in the Healthy Fitness Zone. If you will be active most days each week, it may help to maintain your level of body composition.

To be healthy and fit it is important to do some physical activity almost every day. Aerobic exercise is good for your heart and body composition. Strength and flexibilty exercises are good for your muscles and joints.

Good job, you are doing enough physical activity for your health. Additional vigorous activity would help to promote higher levels of fitness.

©The Cooper Institute for Aerobics Research

Figure 8.11. Common Fundamental Motor Skills

Fundamental Locomotor Skills

Run
1. Brief period in which both feet are off the ground
2. Arms in opposition to legs, elbows bent
3. Foot placement near or on line (not flat footed)
4. Non support leg bent approximately 90 degrees (close to buttocks)

Gallop
1. A step forward with the lead foot followed by a step with trailing foot to a position adjacent to or behind the lead foot
2. A brief period in which both feet are off the ground
3. Arms bent and lifted to waist level
4. Able to lead with the right and left foot

Hop
1. Foot of the nonsupport leg is bent and carried in back of body
2. Nonsupport leg swings in pendular fashion to produce force
3. Arms bent at elbows and swing forward on take-off
4. Able to hop on the right and left foot

Leap
1. Take off on one foot and land on the opposite foot
2. A period in which both feet are off the ground (longer than running)
3. Forward reach with arm opposite the lead foot

Horizontal Jump
1. Preparatory movement includes flexing of both knees with arms extended behind the body
2. Arms extend forcefully forward and upward reaching full extension above the head
3. Take off and land on both feet simultaneously
4. Arms are brought downward during landing

Skip
1. A rhythmical repetition of the step-hop on alternate feet
2. Foot of nonsupport leg carried near surface during hop phase
3. Arms alternately moving in opposition to legs at about waist level

Slide
1. Body turned sideways to desired direction of travel
2. A step sideways followed by a slide of the trailing foot to a point next to the lead foot
3. A short period in which both feet are off the floor
4. Able to slide to the right and to the left

(continued)

Figure 8.11. Common Fundamental Motor Skills, continued

Fundamental Object Control Skills:

Two-Hand Strike
1. Dominant hand grips bat above non dominant hand
2. Non dominant side of body faces an imaginary tosser (feet parallel to batting tee)
3. Hip and spine rotation
4. Weight is transferred by stepping with the front foot

Stationary Bounce
1. Contact ball with one hand at about hip height
2. Push ball with fingers (not a slap)
3. Ball contacts floor in front of (or outside of) foot the side of hand being used

Catch
1. Preparation phase in which elbows are flexed and hands are in front of the body
2. Arms extended in preparation for ball contact
3. Ball is caught and controlled by hands only
4. Elbows bent to absorb force

Kick
1. A rapid continuous approach to the ball
2. The trunks is inclined backward during ball contact
3. Forward swing of the arm opposite the kicking foot
4. Follow-through by hopping on the non kicking foot

Overhand Throw
1. A downward arc of the throwing arm initiates the windup
2. Rotation of hip and spine to a point at which the non dominant side faces an imaginary target
3. Weight is transferred by stepping with the foot opposite the throwing hand
4. Follow-through beyond ball release diagonally across body toward side opposite the throwing hand

forget the once paramount significance of showing parents and playmates that you were good at jumping rope, hitting a ball, or that we at least could keep up with others and participate in the common cultural games.

Of course, it is ultimately desirable that children learn not only the fundamental motor skills but that they also then apply those skills to achieving some more advanced skills in specific sports. The larger one's repertoire of *specific sport skills* the greater the likelihood of adoption of an active lifestyle. Those who own these movement tools will be more successful at an expanded array of activities and will be less prone to injuries.

Before beginning to discuss the particulars of evaluating fundamental and sport specific skills, permit me to make a couple more points concerning the need of these skills being taught in the schools. Many people mistakenly assume that *fundamental skills* are acquired as a natural part of the maturation process. Although these skills are basic movement patterns, they are by no means instinctual and must therefore be practiced just as is any other skill. Granting that basic motor skills must be learned, others will say that young children are inherently active and learn these skills as a result of their own volition; witness them racing about, you literally cannot stop them from exuberant running, hopping, and bouncing. While there is truth in granting high energy levels to young children, we need understand that in today's society not all children are getting a wealth of movement experiences. In our introductory chapter we mentioned a number of environmental factors which were causing less activity in young people: the multifarious media attractions, reduction of safe play areas, greater reliance on motorized transportation, more unsupervised latch-key situations, etc. Not only does less activity mean demonstrably lower physical fitness levels, it also brings lower movement skills. Because of the more movement-restricting environment that many of today's children face, we are seeing a greater share of children exhibiting deficient fundamental skills. Also, it is worth noting that the early grades are considered a *critical period* for learning these skills; this is when most children are gaining these skills and if a child falls behind, it is generally the case that they will fall further behind rather than catch-up in later grades. Remedial programs for adults are commonly not effective because of the stigma of spending time working on skills which have long ago been mastered by our peers. Also, some recent research is suggesting that lack of motor skill experiences prior to around 12 or 13 years of age might have a permanent effect on brain development. If skills are not learned during the early years it may never be possible to achieve a high level of performance.

Finally, a point about the need for teaching sport specific skills during the school day. There is growing evidence that more and more school-aged children are deficient in a variety of sport skills. Why is this the case? Although many young people participate in youth sports programs, there still are those who are not involved, and many more that do so for only a limited length of time. A majority drops out of sports programs as early as elementary and junior high school ages and the trend towards earlier dropout has been occurring. Furthermore, even the more athletically advanced children who remain in youth sports are tending to acquire a narrower range of sport specific skills. This is because of a dramatic trend toward earlier and earlier specialization in single sports. A *sports arms race* to have the best team has been developing at the university and high school levels. This pressure is reverberating all the way to the youth sports level. The competition is tough and the coaches, parents and children are affected by it. The less talented are weeded out sooner and the more talented are channeled into year round devotion to one sport. This *sports specialization* undoubtedly results in higher skill attainment in the selected sport, but it also means they may be less prepared to diversify and enjoy other sporting activities later in life. If all one has done is focus on basketball, football, or soccer throughout school, will he/she not have missed out on some other athletic experiences? Will he/she easily be able to join a softball team, a master's swim club, a tennis league?

Formal vs. Informal Evaluation

Suppose you are convinced of the importance of motor skills and would like all your students to have adequate levels of them. But you foresee a couple of problems. For one thing, you may not have had an athletic background and hence do not feel sufficiently qualified to teach and evaluate in this area. The second problem is that even though you may have enjoyed sports and feel competent, you are afraid that evaluation of your student's motor skills will necessitate the addition of too great a burden on your other already heavy teaching responsibilities; as much as you might wish to, you simply cannot visualize yourself having time to be judging and recording everyone's performances.

Both of these doubts about sufficient knowledge and feasibility are legitimate practical concerns in need of being addressed. In response to competency concerns I would only say this, if your background skills are not great, you obviously must bow to your limitations and not expect to instruct and evaluate many skills. That is okay. However, surely you have knowledge of some basic movement patterns and can recognize major flaws. This might be particularly true with regards to the most fundamental elements of walking, running, or hopping, etc. As for your fear that motor skill evaluation will be too time demanding let me begin by giving you two examples of motor skills being assessed. Teacher A will represent a very complete and formal approach to evaluation, teacher B will be highly informal.

Teacher A desires that all her third graders have good fundamental motor skills. Early in the year she teaches her students a circuit training system in which they move from station to station while being paced by music. Twice each week she positions herself at one of the stations. Armed with a fundamental motor skill test (such as the one illustrated in Figure 8.4) and a checklist, she evaluates groups of four or five children as they rotate by. On the first day she might be able to assess the entire class on the criteria associated with each of the skills of running, skipping, and sliding (each criterion is scored as mastered, partially mastered, un-met). The next day, as she has the children throwing and catching balls, she measures the criteria related to those skills. After approximately four or five testing sessions everyone has been evaluated. The test results are then used in a variety of ways: she uses them as a guide to insure that she provides instructional help where deficiency have been identified, she files the results for future accountability sessions with administrators, and she has the outcomes sent home to the children's homes with a cover letter. The letter informs the parent(s) why it is important for their child to be mastering these basic skills at this developmental time. It also solicits their helping at home and tells them to anticipate another set of test results towards the end of the year.

Teacher B also is aware that it is beneficial for children to have sound motor skills. He does not have an extensive background in sports but he has played softball and can recognize a fundamentally good throw from a bad one. He knows for instance that it is essential to step forward with the foot opposite the throwing hand and that a good follow-through is one in which the arm finishes down across the body. One day he takes his second grade class out to play a game called "messy backyard." The game's arrangement has the class divided so that half the children are on one side of the play space and the others on the other. These areas are known as their "backyards." A number of yarn and nerf-balls have been equally distributed to both areas. When he shouts, "go," both sides are to clean up their yard as quickly as possible by throwing the cluttering balls from their yard to the other sides. Constant throwing ensues by everyone until the stop command is given. While the game is in progress our teacher B monitors the action and also looks to see if there is anyone throwing with poor technique. If anyone is noticed, he makes a mental note of finding an opportunity to give him/her a corrective tip or two.

It is apparent that Teachers A and B are at opposite ends of a formality in evaluation continuum. Teacher A's formal system is to be admired and it likely would yield more thorough results than teacher B. However, the methods used by Teacher A are much more demanding of time and preparation, maybe more demanding than can be generally expected of most classroom teachers. Certainly, in this dawning age of outcome based education, all physical education specialists will be required to implement this sort of in-depth evaluation. Instead of making independent decisions about which if any skills to assess, they will be held accountable for specific learning standards developed by state or professional organizations. And of course, if a school does not have a physical education specialist, or only minimal access to one, the mandated standards will still need to be met, and guess who might be ultimately asked to see that it is done?

To give you an idea of the kinds of skills children may be expected to demonstrate, refer to Figures 8.12, 8.13, and 8.14. The Figures give grade-specific benchmarks (K–4) established by *The National Association for Sport and Physical Education (NASPE)*. Those states mandating outcome-based education will probably be developing their guidelines around a template much like these.

Although the advent of greater documentation of student learning can seem worrisome and daunting to both physical education specialist and classroom teachers, I do not feel we should conclude that these are totally unrealistic expectations. Rather, we must face the facts and learn to do it; it can be done. I know a number of teachers who are now very successfully finding ways of regularly integrating evaluation into their lessons and who feel that their teaching has been enriched as a consequence. Computer technology has been a savior for some. A good example is the use of hand held computers (palm pilots) for entering student behaviors and skill criteria data. These allow information gathered in the field to be directly downloaded on to a computer for storage and organization.

To conclude this section, it is clear that you will have to weigh a number of factors in making your decisions regarding the degree of formality of your evaluation practices. Your unique situation might favor your following the less systematic model of Teacher B. Hopefully, as did he, you will be on the lookout for opportunities to help some children over rough spots in their attainment of motor skills. Opportune aid to one or two could be so important. And on the other hand, if circumstances permit, perhaps it will be possible for you to year by year meet the challenge of developing a more elaborate, but workable, system of motor skill evaluation. It would be no small thing indeed if along with what you were teaching the children in the classroom you could play a significant role in insuring all your children become effective movers.

Process vs. Product Evaluation

Earlier in this Chapter you were encouraged to consider evaluating whether or not the students were in the process of being physically active. That is what is important for health in the long run, and it is a realizable goal for everyone. We saw that measuring physical fitness outcomes was not as much under the students' control. Genetics and maturation rates skewed fitness scores.

When evaluating motor skills it is also useful to consider the difference between process and product outcome evaluations. *Process evaluation* of motor skills is where the focus is on how much the skill is being practiced and/or on the technique being used by the performer. If you or the child keeps a record of how much batting practice is occurring over a few week's time, that is evaluating the process. If you are judging the goodness of your students' dribbling technique or their volleyball service technique, that is also evaluating the process. The motor development test in Figure 8.11 would be considered process oriented, as are the *NASPE grade-specific benchmarks* of Figures 8.12 through 8.14. Although the dividing line between process and product evaluation is not always perfectly clear, *product evaluation* is when the emphasis is on the outcome rather than how the skill is done. It is a product test when the measurement pertains to how fast someone runs a given distance or how far he/she throws a ball.

The arguments in favor of using *process evaluation* as opposed to *product evaluation* of motor skills are similar to those presented for physical fitness. The product outcome level a child is able to achieve on a motor skill, as with physical fitness, is going to be effected by not only the amount

Figure 8.12. National Association for Sport and Physical Education (NASPE): Benchmarks for Kindergarten

The student is able to:

____ Travel in different ways, in a large group without bumping into others or falling.

    ____ *Walk*   ____ *Skip*   ____ *Slide*   ____ *Gallop*

    ____ *Run*   ____ *Hop*   ____ *Jump*

____ Travel in a forward and sideways direction, and change direction quickly in response to a signal.

    ____ Forwards

    ____ Sideways

    ____ Change direction in response to a signal

____ Distinguish between straight, curved, and zig-zag pathways while traveling in various ways.

    ____ Straight

        ____ *Walk*   ____ *Skip*   ____ *Slide*   ____ *Gallop*

        ____ *Run*   ____ *Hop*   ____ *Jump*

    ____ Curved

        ____ *Walk*   ____ *Skip*   ____ *Slide*   ____ *Gallop*

        ____ *Run*   ____ *Hop*   ____ *Jump*

    ____ Zig-zag

        ____ *Walk*   ____ *Skip*   ____ *Slide*   ____ *Gallop*

        ____ *Run*   ____ *Hop*   ____ *Jump*

____ Make both small and large body shapes while traveling.

    ____ Small shapes while traveling

    ____ Large shapes while traveling

____ Travel demonstrating a variety of relationships with objects.

    ____ Under while moving

    ____ Over while moving

    ____ Behind while moving

    ____ Alongside while moving

    ____ Through while moving

____ Place a variety of body parts in high, middle, and low levels.

    ____ Body parts: head, shoulder, elbow, hand, fingers, chest, thigh, knee, ankle, foot, toe, etc.

        ____ *High*

        ____ *Medium*

        ____ *Low*

____ Without falling, walk forward and sideways the length of a bench.

    ____ Forward the length of a bench

    ____ Sideways the length of a bench

____ Roll sideways (right and left) without hesitating or stopping.

    ____ Roll sideways to the right

    ____ Roll sideways to the left

____ Toss a ball and catch it before it bounces.

____ Demonstrate the difference between an overhand and underhand throw.

    ____ Overhand

    ____ Underhand

____ Kick a stationary ball using a running approach without hesitating or stopping.

____ Continuously jump a swinging rope held by others.

____ Form wide, narrow, or twisted bodies alone and with a partner.

    ____ Wide

        ____ *Alone*

        ____ *With a partner*

    ____ Narrow

        ____ *Alone*

        ____ *With a partner*

    ____ Twisted

        ____ *Alone*

        ____ *With a partner*

____ Sustain moderate physical activity.

Figure 8.13. National Association for Sport and Physical Education (NASPE): Benchmarks for First and Second Graders

The student is able to:

____ Travel in a backward direction and change direction quickly and safely without falls.

    ____ Travel backward

    ____ Change direction quickly

    ____ Does not fall

____ Change speed and direction in response to various rhythms.

    ____ Change speeds: slow-fast, fast-slow

    ____ Change directions

        ____ Forward-backward

        ____ Backward-forward

        ____ Backward-sideways

        ____ Sideways-forward

        ____ Sideways-backward

    ____ Use a variety of rhythms

        ____ Four-counts

        ____ Eight-counts

____ Combine traveling patterns in time to music

    ____ Walk with music   ____ Hop with music

    ____ Run with music   ____ Slide with music

    ____ Skip with music   ____ Jump with music

____ Jump and land using a combination of one and two foot take-offs and landings.

    ____ One foot take-off   ____ Two foot take-off

    ____ One foot landing   ____ Two foot landing

____ Demonstrate skills of chasing, fleeing, and dodging to avoid or catch others.

    ____ Chases   ____ Dodges

    ____ Flees   ____ Avoids or catches others

____ Roll smoothly in a forward direction without hesitating or stopping.

____ Balance: Demonstrate momentary stillness in symmetrical and asymmetrical shapes on different body parts.

    ____ Right foot   ____ Right knee

    ____ Left foot   ____ Left knee

    ____ Both feet   ____ Both knees

_____ Move the feet in a high level by placing weight on hands and landing in control.

    _____ Handstand against wall

_____ Use the inside of the foot or instep of the foot to kick a slowly rolling ball into the air or along the ground.

    _____ Uses the inside of the foot to kick a slow rolling ball.

    _____ Kicks ball into the air

    _____ Kicks the ball along the ground

_____ Throw a ball hard while demonstrating a correct throwing technique.

_____ Catch using properly positioned hands.

    _____ Fingers pointed up for ball caught above waist

    _____ Fingers pointed down for ball caught below waist

_____ Consistently dribble a ball using hands without losing control.

_____ Use at least three different body parts to strike a ball.

    _____ Hand to strike a ball to a target

    _____ Foot to strike a ball to a target

    _____ Forearm to strike a ball to a target

_____ Continuously dribble the ball using feet without losing control.

_____ Strike a ball repeatedly with a paddle to a wall or partner.

_____ Repeatedly jump a self-turned rope.

_____ Consistently strike a ball with a bat from a tee or cone, using the correct grip and side to target.

    _____ Can consistently strike a ball with a bat from a tee.

    _____ Uses correct grip

    _____ Side is facing target

_____ Skip, hop, gallop, and slide using age level motor skill.

    _____ Skip

    _____ Hop

    _____ Gallop

    _____ Slide

_____ Demonstrate safety when participating in physical activity.

_____ Identify appropriate behaviors when playing with others.

Figure 8.14. National Association for Sport and Physical Education (NASPE): Benchmarks for Third and Fourth Graders

The student is able to:

_____ While traveling, avoid or catch an individual or object.

    _____ Avoids individuals

    _____ Avoids objects

    _____ Catches individuals

    _____ Catches objects

_____ Leap, leading with either foot.

    _____ Right foot

    _____ Left foot

_____ Jump and land for height or jump and land for distance, using correct motor pattern.

    _____ Jump and land for height

    _____ Jump and land for distance

_____ Roll in a backward direction without hesitating or stopping.

_____ Transfer weight from feet to hands at fast and slow speeds, using large group extensions.

    _____ Transfers weight from feet to hands

    _____ Transfers fast from feet to hands

    _____ Transfers slow from feet to hands

_____ Hand dribble and foot dribble a ball

    _____ Hand dribble

    _____ Foot dribble

_____ Strike a softly thrown lightweight ball back to a partner using a variety of body parts and combinations of body parts.

    _____ Can strike a thrown lightweight ball with thigh (as in soccer) back to a partner.

    _____ Can strike a thrown lightweight ball with the forearms (like a bump in volleyball) back to a partner.

    _____ Can use a combination of body parts—forearm, foot, etc.

_____ Strike a softly thrown ball with a bat or paddle while demonstrating correct grip, side to target, and level swing.

    _____ Can strike a thrown ball with a bat or paddle

    _____ Can demonstrate correct grip

    _____ Side is to target

    _____ Swing is level

_____ Develop patterns and combination of movement into repeatable sequences. (Grapevine)

_____ Without hesitating, travel into and out of a rope turned by others.

    _____ Into

    _____ Out of

_____ Balance, with control, on a variety of moving objects.

    _____ Balance boards

_____ Throw, catch, and kick using correct motor patterns.

    _____ Can throw with correct motor patterns

    _____ Can catch with correct motor patterns

    _____ Can kick with correct motor patterns

_____ Demonstrate competence in basic swimming stroke and water survival skills.

    _____ Competence in basic swimming stroke

    _____ Competence in survival skills

        _____ In water

        _____ On water

        _____ Around water

_____ Maintain continuous aerobic activity for a specific time.

_____ Maintain proper body alignment during activity.

    _____ Can lift correctly

    _____ Can carry correctly

    _____ Can push correctly

    _____ Can pull correctly

_____ Can support, lift, and control body weight in a variety of activities.

    _____ Can support body weight

    _____ Can lift body weight

    _____ Can control body movement

_____ Regularly participate in physical activity for the purpose of improving skillful performance and physical fitness.

    _____ Regularly participate in physical activity

    _____ Purpose of activity is to improve skill

    _____ Purpose of activity is to improve fitness

_____ Analyze potential risks associated with physical activity.

_____ Identify activities that contribute to personal feeling of joy.

_____ Enjoy feelings resulting from involvement in physical activity.

of practice but also by genetics and maturational status. If you test running speed or batting distance outcomes, your results might not always tell you who has been practicing the most or even who has best developed the proper running or swinging technique which will best serve them in the long term. Someone could be batting cross-handed and not correctly transferring his/her weight forward into the swing and yet, because of more advanced inherent development, is still hitting the balls further than all others. Conversely, another child could be employing an essentially sound technique and still have less than mediocre outcome success.

Because a child's motor outcomes are determined in large part by genetics and maturation, outcome achievements are to only a minor degree under the students' control; this is not true regarding the process of doing the skills. With the exception of some children with physical disabilities, everyone will have sufficient physical capabilities to permit the use of proper technique in all the fundamental and sport specific skills. As a consequence it follows that, given sound instruction, you should generally be able to successfully develop, in a relatively short period of time, measurable improvements in everybody's technique.

In conclusion, although our ultimate motor development wish is to help our students produce good motor outcomes, i.e. running faster and batting balls farther, it would appear that our instructional goal is best directed at the acquisition of proper technique. Accordingly we should be generally selecting or developing motor skill assessments of process. If we can help the children to perform correctly and avoid developing initially bad movement habits, and we should be able to readily accomplish this, we have done what is most important for the long run. Once we have them on the right technique track, we can be assured that they will then be in a position to achieve their full potential. The final realization of that potential will be a function of their genetics and how much they continue to practice.

Figure 8.15 is an example of a test of a tennis groundstroke. Obviously you will not normally be this detailed in your evaluation of a sport specific skill, but the test is a good example of *process*

Figure 8.15. Process Evaluation of a Tennis Ground Stroke

5 - Excellent	Proper grip, good balance, footwork, and near perfect form. Consistently demonstrates correct stroke mechanics. Shots are hit with power and consistently placed appropriately.
4 - Good	Proper grip, good balance, adequate footwork, and acceptable, but not perfect form. Demonstrates above average consistency of stroke mechanics. Moderate power and consistent placement within court area.
3 - Satisfactory	Proper grip, acceptable balance, but footwork is poor. Form is somewhat erratic and inefficient, resulting in inconsistent shot placement. Style of stroke is more defensive in nature, but can sustain a short rally.
2 - Fair	Uses improper grip at times, poor footwork and basically incorrect form. Inconsistent stroke mechanics. Defensive style of play, merely trying to get the ball over the net. Unable to sustain a rally.
1 - Poor	Incorrect grip, off-balance, with poor footwork. Form is very poor and erratic. Virtually no control of ball placement. Experiences difficulty in getting ball over net.

evaluation. With much practice I have learned to quickly evaluate these criteria; seeing two or three swings is usually sufficient. If you were going to assess your students on this skill, you could simplify your task by paring the criteria to one or two aspects that you thought to be most important. There is no reason you could not establish your own *rubrics* for other sport skills with which you are familiar.

Authentic Evaluation

Your evaluating of motor skills can be done in drill situations isolated from the game or while the student is actually participating in game competition. The advantage of evaluating during drills is that you can organize the environment to get a good look at every person's skill under the exact same conditions. For example, you could have a circuit training situation set up so that you would be sure to have a good minute or two for each student to demonstrate his/her ability to execute an underhand volleyball pass or tennis groundstroke under controlled conditions. They might have the ball tossed to them or could be hitting off of a wall. I have done a good deal of testing like this to see if the students can demonstrate the correct technique.

Evaluating skills while they are being performed in a game situation is called *authentic evaluation*. There are two advantages of this type of evaluation. One is that it can be easily done while the children enjoy playing the game. No special circuit training or testing stations is required. The other advantage is that how the skill is applied in the game situation is the real test of whether or not the student has learned to use the skill; that is why it is called *authentic evaluation*. I mentioned in an earlier chapter that it is not unusual to see a deterioration of skill technique when the transition must be made from practice drills to the game. According to the exponents of *authentic evaluation* it makes sense for us to be judging the real thing, the ultimate objective.

One point needs to be made if *authentic evaluation* is going to be feasible. It is essential that the *mini-games* concept is being employed. Otherwise, it will be a long time before you will see players perform the game skills you are wishing to assess. As they wait and wait for a turn, you will also wait. But get them involved in games where they are on their own or with a partner or two and you will know what they can do very quickly.

Holistic Evaluation

In the Figures and examples provided thus far we have been zeroing in on evaluating specific process skills used within a sport. Is their groundstroke form correct? Is their underhand passing technique as it should be? In *holistic evaluation* you are making a more general assessment of the student's performance. You are not just evaluating a person's specific serving technique but are making a more generic assessment of all his/her overall tennis techniques, strategies and knowledge of rules and etiquette. Figure 8.16 provides an example of *holistic evaluation*. Notice that we are lumping all their techniques together to make a general judgement of goodness of technique, and they we do the same with their strategic decisions, knowledge of the game rules and affective behaviors.

With little or no adaptation you could easily apply the Figure 8.16 rubric to most any team sport. Holistic evaluation is only an estimate of sorts but it does give the instructor some objective guidelines. When small-sides games are in progress it is possible to completely evaluate everyone in a period or two. And certainly *holistic assessment* has the virtue of being authentic.

Figure 8.16. Holistic Assessment of Sport Skills

5 - Excellent	Demonstrates mastery of sport specific skills and ability to consistently perform with little or no conscious effort resulting in few errors. Extensive knowledge base and understanding of sport or activity. Employs effective strategy specific to the task or situation.
4 - Good	Demonstrates competency and ability to perform basic skills without making many errors. Complete understanding of rules and strategies of the specific sport or activity. Usually selects appropriate strategy and skill for situations and generally displays consistent performance.
3 - Satisfactory	Displays basic knowledge of sport or activity and ability to perform fundamental skills adequately to be able to play game. Performance is frequently inconsistent, resulting in numerous errors being made. Understands basic strategies, but lacks ability to effectively employ.
2 - Fair	Demonstrate inability to perform more than the basic skills. Has difficulty in executing even the basic skills, making frequent errors, some critical, during performance. Generally inconsistent performance with only a minimal understanding of strategies and rules.
1 - Poor	Rarely, if ever, performs skills well enough to be able to play a meaningful game. Demonstrates little understanding of sport or activity and inability to execute skills without making significant and frequent errors. Makes little attempt to adjust performance.

9

Changing Exercise/Health Habits

Changing Habits in the Affective Domain

"Education does not mean teaching people to know what they do not know; it means teaching them to behave as they do not behave."

John Ruskin

"The great aim of education is not knowledge, but action."

George Herbert

This chapter will be broken into to main sections: changing exercise/health habits and changing habits in the affective domain.

Changing Exercise/Health Habits

Teaching Self-Responsibility

Taking the children out to exercise and play games is good for their physical fitness and motor skill development. If they enjoy those games, and appreciate their improved fitness and motor skills, we can be sure that they will continue to regularly participate outside of school. Telling your students that they should adopt the lifestyle that incorporates the food and activity pyramids will be sufficient for them to do so. Okay, we can stop right there and get real. We know that if we wish to make major habit changes, and that is our long-range goal, we will need to do much more than expose students to activities and/or tell them what they should do. They will need to be fully convinced of the benefits of the new practices and they will require guidance and sustained encouragement in initiating those changes beyond school. Ultimately they must realize that they alone must be accountable for these exercise/health behaviors and then take that responsibility.

What must we do to establish this self-responsibility in young people so that they will independently adopt and maintain good exercise/health practices? Let us look at four important instructional considerations: (1) selecting the behavior, (2) recognizing the benefits of the behavior, (3) doing the behavior in school, (4) and tracking/reinforcing the behavior beyond school.

Selecting the Behavior

Although you may see many exercise/health behaviors in need of alteration, and for which you would love to affect a change, it will be best if you, at least initially, narrowed the field of possibilities to a few and then focus on one at a time. Perhaps with experience you will become more skilled and can accomplish more ambitious goals, but keep in mind the truth that habits are not easy to change, and changing just one habit can demand a lot of time and effort. Mark Twain said, "Habit is habit, and not to be flung out the window by any man, but coaxed downstairs a step at a time."

It also is probably a good idea to begin working on habits that are "relatively" easy to change, that is, ones not necessitating major lifestyle changes. Consider these examples: drinking more water, stretching daily, doing curl-ups, buckling your seat belt, flossing your teeth, drinking less soda. Notice that none of these demand a major time commitment, they are not particularly onerous, if at all. Nor do they require any equipment or items that should not be readily and inexpensively available.

From a list of these simpler kinds of habits, it is suggested that you select those that are particularly relevant to you. They should be ones which you either have already established in your

Figure 9.1. Stages of Change Exercise Model

STAGES OF CHANGE EXERCISE MODEL

This model classifies exercise habit formation into five distinct stages. What stage would you assign to yourself? Can you think of friends, family members or acquaintances to place in each stage? I know I am not totally convinced that someone truly has the exercise habit until he/she has continued all the way through the winter months. Then I know they might be more than Sunday patriots and sunshine warriors.

Using this model to understand where a friend or student is can be useful. It could help you better see what might be the best approach to help him/her move toward the next stage.

Stage 1: Pre-Contemplation: the person is not even thinking of exercising.

Stage 2: Contemplation: the person is thinking of exercising. He/she might say things like he/she should or might begin to exercise sometime.

Stage 3: Preparation: the person is making plans to begin exercising. Maybe some shoes or clothing was bought, a membership bought, or a specific beginning exercise date has been set.

Stage 4: Practicing: the person has been engaged in regular exercise for less than 6 months.

Stage 5: Maintaining: the person has been engaged in regular exercise for more than 6 months.

---

life and benefited from, or ones for which you are determined to begin following along with the children. Be sure you are beyond a mere contemplation stage and are resolved. With this level of commitment, your enthusiasm is bound to show and make you a more convincing teacher to be emulated.

Of course your selection decision should also take into consideration which habits you suspect the children are following and not following. Giving a simple survey of their practices might be usefully enlightening. The list of children's health practices introduced at the end of chapter 1 (Figure 1.5) might serve as a starting point from which to prioritize, select, or make additions.

Recognizing the Benefits of the Behavior

Although usually not sufficient, recognizing the benefits is a *sine qua non* for behavior change. No one is going to be disposed to endure the effort of behavioral change unless he/she is totally convinced of benefits to be derived. Therefore, it is our duty to make sure the children appreciate what is to be gained. Good exercise and health practices are going to yield their most pronounced pay-off years down the road and particularly late in life. While we should be informing our youngsters of these delayed consequences, and encouraging them to adopt a more long-term perspective toward their wellbeing, we need to be mindful of the limitations of children's life perspectives. They tend to be most influenced by more immediate consequences. As a result, as much as possible we need to be also showing them the short-term payoffs that they might value. Here are a couple of examples.

Suppose you have selected the behavior of "doing abdominal exercises three times a week." You begin by explaining why having strong abdominal muscles are good for them. To make the to-be-derived benefits as applicable to the children's present day interests as possible, you might stress how strong abdominals play an important role in their favorite sport skills and in an attractive postural appearance. You could show them the active and stabilizing function those muscles play in activities such as throwing, serving, and various gymnastic and dance skills. As for posture, you could contrast the attractiveness of a proudly erect posture to that of a slouching, sagging one. In addition to these immediate effects, maintaining abdominal strength will have long-term consequences. Neglect of the stomach muscles might see adults suffering from permanent structural problems and low bad pain. While it might be worth while to inform the children that 50 percent of adults will experience low back pain, you can see that this later-in-life disability may be too remote and a less powerful motivator than images of today's successful sports performances and better personal appearance.

A second exercise/health behavior example is "doing three or four aerobic workouts per week" as prescribed by *The Activity Pyramid.* In Chapter 1, an impressive list of benefits was shown to be produced by aerobic fitness. Remember the powerful long-term effects on heart attacks, strokes, cancers, diabetes, bone density, *compressed morbidity*, etc. Our explanations of why we should aerobically exercise should include these reasons. But what were all the various attributes which children might be able to gain now or in the not so misty future? Recall the quality of life factors such as having more endurance for sports, feeling better, sleeping more soundly, having more energy, losing weight, being more alert and thinking better, effectively coping with stress. And what about learning to appreciate the vigorous moving experience for its own sake. We would be wise to comprehensively stress all these salient kinds of things. Who knows what justification might become the motivator for some child?

There is final point that might be worth making regarding the recognition of the benefits of good health/exercises practices. Thus far the discussion has focused on what information the teacher should put together to argue the case. Another approach would be to have the students do their own research. Undoubtedly you will regularly be having your students engaged in reading and writing in content areas. My point is that you not forget the content area of health and fitness. This would be a great way to have children learn more about the benefits of sound health and exercise habits. I am sure their research would find a great amount of information that would interesting and relevant to them.

Doing the Behavior in School

Some of the behaviors you have earmarked for change can be easily begun in school while others may not. It should be apparent that it is a good idea to begin doing the activity in school if possible. If you can develop the skill through actual doing, and can perhaps even develop it into a routine or habit in school, you will be one step closer to moving it to your final goal of extra-school continuance. For best understanding of the manner in which we might do this, we will continue with our example of, "doing abdominal exercises three times per week."

For this particular habit you need not only know reasons for doing it, but you also need to know a number of things about how to do it (This is true for most behaviors, but not always to as significant a degree; consider the less technical skills of using seat belts, wearing bike helmets, washing hands.). Before having the students begin abdominal exercises, you would begin with a good demonstration. When demonstrating curl-ups you might point out errors such as failing to have your knees bent or coming up too fast in a jerking motion. You might also show them any good alternate ways of exercising the abdominals; putting your feet on a chair or bench and doing crunches would be a possibility. Showing a variety of ways of doing the activity should increase the likelihood they will find the one best suited for them. You might discuss not only the technical quality of the curl-up but also the issue of quantity of exercise. Here you would need to be communicating your exercise physiology knowledge, namely *the F.I.T. Principle* and how it relates to overloading the muscles on a regular basis (to near exhaustion, two or three times per week).

As they began exercising, you could check for proper technique and give encouragement. If possible, it would not be a bad idea to have them perform on a soft surface to avoid any unneeded discomfort during their beginning exposure. You hope their initial experience will not be "Ouch! That was uncomfortable and painful." Rather, you should be striving for a general class feeling that the activity was not hard, or at a minimum, not too unpleasant. It would be desirable to reach a class consensus that the effort involved was reasonable and well spent?

Having done the activity in class once, twice, or sporadically is good, but continuing to do the activity on a regular basis carries much merit. Actually doing curl-ups and/or crunches three times per week would solidify a routine mentality. It would do two other things as well. It would make clear the seriousness you attached to this activity by giving you repeated opportunities to make your argument. Furthermore, with practice the students' performance might progressively become more comfortable and improved. When they incur some gains they will have a greater vested interest. You could tell them they should be proud of the steady work done and the stomach fitness achieved.

Tracking/Reinforcing the Behavior beyond School

Great! We now know why and how to do the activity and we have even practiced and improved upon it in school. This is in many instances where instruction ends. The assumption is that now the children will integrate this behavior into their lifestyle and live happily ever after. In fact, we are stopping one difficult and most crucial step short of what is needed. We cannot expect that consistently doing an activity under a teacher's tutelage will invariably translate into the same self-directed behavior in the home and community environment. Far from it, the stage may have been set for the child to begin incorporating abdominal exercises into his/her life, but we are a long way from winning the war of establishing a self-initiated, self-sustained habit. This reminds me of a clever response Winston Churchill made following an early World War II battle victory. He gave this tempering admonition to those who were excitedly optimistic. "Now this is not the end. It is not even the beginning of the end. But it is, perhaps, the end of the beginning."

After we have established an in-class routine for say, curl-ups, it is nearly imperative to incrementally get the children doing it on their own outside of school. I see it as a weaning process moving from teacher-led to self-directed behavior. You must unequivocally convey the message that if they wish to remain fit they will have to begin to take responsibility for it. They must comprehend that you will not always be around to dictate when it is time for them to do curl-ups. Tell them the only way they will be fit in the long run is if they are self-motivated. They must know that over the holidays and during the summer months the *reversibility principle* will operate to nullify any hard won gains; and what do they expect will happen next year and beyond when you will no longer be there is lead them.

A specific *behavioral weaning procedure* regarding curl-ups would be to inform the class that, because of many other things demanding attention, there will only be time enough to do in-school curl-ups once or twice a week instead of thrice-weekly. The ramification is that either they lose the fitness gains made or they agree to start supplementary exercises outside of school. Perhaps you could begin by asking and getting everyone to agree that they will do a set of curl-ups over the weekend. They understand you think this is an important assignment and they know you will not be forgetting to check with a show of hands on Monday to see how many remembered.

When you are counting hands on Monday you might decide to record and post the percentage of students in compliance with the weekend assignment. Next you might decide to set a goal of more of the class achieving it next time. Maybe you could get peer pressure working for you by developing an *esprit de corp* in the class where everyone is reminding and encouraging each other. This would also be a good time to address the barriers, psychological or physical, which may have accounted for some of the non-compliance. For instance, some may have simply forgotten. This being the case, you could lead a discussion about things to help remembrance. One suggestion would be establishing a regular time for the exercise, another would be when you first get up or as soon as you get home from school.[1] This discussion session might also be a good time for you to *personalize behavioral practices*. Do you not think it might be influential if you could say that you successfully remembered to do your curl-ups by always doing them in conjunction with some other established routine, or that you do yours as a cool-down to your regular jog, etc.?

The ideal *behavioral weaning process* will progress until the students have eventually assumed complete self-responsibility. This does not mean that your task will ever be completely done (see Figure 9.1 for the *Stages of Change Exercise Model*). You would be continuing to track the students' performances during periodic check-up activities and/or discussions throughout the year. Adherence rates to behavioral changes are bound to drop-off over time and reminders and encouragement spread out over as long a period of time as possible is helpful. The last day of class would be a good wrap-up time for congratulations and wishing them well with all the exercise/health behaviors initiated during the year. In a laboratory exercise at the end of this chapter you will be challenged to plan your summer. You will see that I have personalized my behavioral intentions and provided different categories of activities for you to consider. The intent is to provide you with a model to use with your students.

I recently heard of an even further extension of this concept. A teacher was explaining how she always has had her third graders write essays about their life goals, and then, nine years later, mailed them their papers. Over the years, many of her students have given splendid testimonials of how fun it was to receive those letters. Additionally they were impressed by the teacher's continued concern for their wellbeing. Anyway, I thought her practice was an admirable one and wondered if her procedure could also be employed as a truly long-range check-up. Image the letter including the message, "I sincerely hope you, like I am, are still finding time to do those health habits we worked on."

As indicated before, the curl-up example we have been following is a behavioral change that, while by no means easy, might be easier to make than would be some others. Doing aerobic exercises would require a much greater lifestyle change because it requires more time, it is more physically demanding, and it might require more attention to facilities and equipment. Many dietary behavior changes would pose special problems because certain kinds of foods would need to be procured. If we wished children in eat *Five a Day* (fruits and/or vegetables) or drink a milk of lower fat content, it would be essential to involve parents in the process. The parents must understand why these changes are desirable if they are going to be supportive in purchasing and making the foods available.

In Figures 9.2 and 9.3 you will find homework assignments which attempt to inform and involve families in behavior change. They also exemplify an incentive system. Taking the extra simple step of designing an assignment of this kind could be well worth the effort. In the next section of this chapter we will be going into more detail regarding how to involve of parents and others for a variety of purposes.

Before leaving this topic of developing self-responsibility, one more suggestion is in order. We explained in this chapter, and in the chapter on evaluation (Chapter 8), how the teacher might record and track student behaviors. Would it not possibly be a worthwhile idea to teach children to document their own exercise/health accomplishments? The concept of journal keeping and portfolios is probably not a new one to you; you know that they can serve many valuable educational purposes and you may already have many ideas about how you intend to use them. What I am proposing is the idea that you could have your fourth, fifth, and sixth graders assume responsibility

---

[1] I am always bothered by well-meaning suggestions to squeeze in exercises, or other desirable activities, while they are watching television. I have strong feelings that regular television watching should not be a regular habit for anyone and we should not accept it as an expectation.

Figure 9.2. Family Homework Assignment (A)

Aerobic Exercise—Action Plan

This week you can earn TWO POINTS in this section by exercising 3 times.

✶   Choose an activity where you will frequently be near a 5 intensity level or higher (remember the 1-10 *Perceived Exertion Scale* we learned in class).

✶   Exercise for 20 minutes. Go slowly the first 5 minutes to warm up, then go faster.

✶   You can do the same exercise 3 times in the week, or a different exercise each time.

Write down the days you will exercise and what you will do (running, swimming, biking, etc.). It's best to make it every other day, not three days in a row.

Which day _____   What I'll do _____

Which day _____   What I'll do _____

Which day _____   What I'll do _____

Signed: _____   Date: _____

You can earn TWO BONUS POINTS if you get an adult to exercise three times this week too.

✶   Remind the adult to exercise at about a 5 on the 1-10 exertion scale.

✶   If the adult is not used to exercise, he/she might not be able to keep up with you. They shouldn't force themselves to go too fast. Tell your adult that it's best to start slowly and build up speed gradually.

Name of adult: _____

Your Score

Now add up your "Exercise" score, and ask a parent to sign this sheet for you.

I certify that _____ has earned _____ points in the "Race to Health".

Signed: _____

Figure 9.3. Family Homework Assignment (B)

Lowering Fat In-Take—Action Plan

You can earn FOUR POINTS in this section. You get two points if you make a change for a week. And you earn two bonus points if you can get an adult in the family to make a change too.

Your job will be to try drinking less fat in milk:

-----------Good News-----------

If you already drink nonfat milk you have just earned two points without even trying.

WRITE A BIG "2" HERE for your fast and easy points.

Everyone else should get their points the old-fashioned way, and earn them:

FOR TWO POINTS promise you will drink milk with less fat in it for one week. You may find you want to change forever.

 ❋   If you drink regular, switch to low fat.

 ❋   If you drink low fat, switch to nonfat.

Sign up: I promise to drink _____ milk for one week.

Signed: _____   Date:_____

Don't make the change this minute. Take a few days to get used to the new milk. Use a big pitcher, and mix your old milk with the new milk, half and half. Drink that mixture for a few days, then drink the new milk on its own. You'll like it!

Now, for your TWO BONUS POINTS in the "Race for Health," get an adult in the family to promise to drink milk with less fat in it for a week.

Name of adult: _____

If everyone in the family already drinks nonfat milk, you get your two bonus points anyway.

Your Score

Now add up your FAT score in the "Race to Health," and ask a parent to sign this sheet for you.

I certify that _____ has earned _____ points in the "Race to Health."

Signed: _____

for managing their own personal fitness education portfolios. These initially would not have to be elaborate compilations but they could grow and include such things as daily logs, individually designed exercise and health practices programs, family homework assignments like those discussed above, contracts (see Figures 9.4, 9.5 & 9.6), graphs, and personal fitness scores.

Going Multidisciplinary

We have already dwelt on how difficult it is to change habits; not only must the students be convinced tangible benefits will follow, they are likely to encounter many barriers to establishing and maintaining a self-directed routine. This can really seem like an daunting task when you realize that you are just one force out of the many influential forces shaping the children's lives; and often those others can be giving very powerful counter messages. Many children may be coming from homes in which the parent(s) does not value, model, or encourage good exercise/health practices. The students' close peers, with whom they so passionately wish to fit in, may be living inactive lifestyles supported by a diet mainly of "big gulps" and french fries. They may even be getting mixed messages from school personnel and policies. You have been laboring to have them eat according to the food pyramid while other teachers are constantly providing them with snacks and treats that are loaded with empty calories. They are being recruited for school fund-raising campaigns to sell candy and cookies for band trips or sports equipment. More and more machines are glowing in the hallways displaying enticing candy and soft drinks. Students are regularly being

---

Figure 9.4. Family Fitness Contract

Family Fitness Contract

We, the _____ family, promise that today
_____ (date) we will adopt an active lifestyle and become more physically active.

We acknowledge that general physical activity is very important to the health of all family members. We promise to devote _____ minutes on Mon., Tues., Wed., Thurs., Fri., Sat., Sun. (circle at least three days) toward making positive changes in our physical activity levels. The best time of day for us to work on this change is _____ A.M./P.M.

We will try our best to fulfill this one-month contract as we develop our family fitness goals. We understand that by fulfilling this contract, we will receive YMCA passes or frozen yogurt certificates from the school physical education program.

Family members: _____

_____

_____

_____

This promise was witnessed by _____

Figure 9.5. Open-Ended Student Choice Contract

Name _____ Date _____

Class _____ Level _____

Physical Fitness Contract

I, _____, would like to improve _____ (fitness area). I understand I need additional work in this area of fitness. My long-term goal is _____ _____.

I understand that I will be given class time to achieve this goal. I also promise to work on my goal outside of school at least two days per week. (Select two days: M Tu W Th F Sat Sun)

This contract will begin on _____ and will end on _____. I agree to inform my teacher each week about my progress and the specific activities used to achieve my goal.

If I achieve my goal, I will reward myself by _____.

Sign _____
                    student

Sign _____
                    teacher

Sign _____
              parent or guardian

served school lunches that contain high amounts of sodium, fat, and sugar. Also, the school may be providing a number of subtle messages that physical education is not really something to be taken seriously and to be done everyday: it is treated as a frill being scheduled only once or twice a week, it is taken away for misbehavior or failure to complete other academic assignments, it is commonly the preempted activity of choice when special events are planned. Would these things be done if in our heart of hearts we believed exercise/health was an integral element of the educated person.

So what do we conclude? Do we despair of swimming against a sea of opposition? Do we continue climbing the climbing wave alone? No. If we honestly want to make a difference in the health of our children we cannot give up, and fighting the fight alone might be noble but is not apt to be fully effective. There is some truth in the African proverb, "It takes a village to raise a child." To be

Figure 9.6. Contract for Drinking Water

Water Drinking Contract

Being well hydrated is good for your body in many ways:

(a) it helps sport performance

(b) all your body's organs will function better

(c) the risk of getting painful kidney stones is greatly reduced

(d) it is even a means of burning some additional calories (it requires 114 calories to raise 64 ounces of ice water to body temperature. That means, 30 days of 64 ounces/day would equal 3,500 calories, and that means one pound of body fat.

The minimal daily recommended intake of water is 64 ounces/day, that is eight, 8 ounce glasses. Most people are not achieving this. Will you agree to work to develop this habit? Here is a log to put in your journal. I will be collecting these on Monday. Anyone who has met the goal will earn a POWERBAR from me.

Hint: plan on having some times to remind yourself or you may forget. Other drinks do not count. Realize that drinks with caffeine in them dehydrate rather than hydrate the body.

Week's log
*Friday	_____	(practice)
*Saturday	_____	(practice)
*Sunday	_____	(practice)
Monday	_____	
Tuesday	_____	
Wednesday	_____	
Thursday	_____	
Friday	_____	
Saturday	_____	
Sunday	_____	

I can honestly say that I achieved this goal each day, Monday through Sunday.

Signed: _____

effective we need help, and be assured that help can be found if we seek it. You are not the only person in your school and community who is worried about children's health. There are citizens, parents, fellow classroom teachers, physical education specialists, administrators, health care workers, school lunch personnel, university faculty, and others who are already convinced of how critical an issue this is, and if asked, would be eagerly willing to work with you for this cause.[2] Beyond them, there are many more who would be readily receptive to this viewpoint if provided some information and leadership. After all, everyone wants to do what is best for children.

The question is how do we recruit all this aid which will permit us to employ a *multidisciplinary team approach* to behavioral change? The beginning step would be the formation of something like a wellness committee in your school. It might consist of such people as another classroom teacher or two, a physical education specialist, someone in the administration, the school nurse, a few interested parents or community members, a representative from health services, and a school lunch representative. Meetings might be scheduled every two weeks or once a month. The purpose of the committee would be the general promotion of the health of the children.

At the initial meeting you probably would have to do little more than explain some of your concerns and then ask for comments and ideas. It is hard to forecast what directions ensuing discussions may take, and what suggested courses of action planned. The possibilities are endless. For example, the school lunch director may think of an idea for coordinating some lunch offerings with an instructional topic you are planning; the physical education specialist might see how he/she could include a lesson or two reinforcing a certain topic the group feels to be important. Maybe the group could plan a special event like a health fair; the administrator would agree to organize some short, school-wide exercise stretching breaks at certain times during the day. Possibly the group might come up with some acceptable alternate treats which the other teachers could agree to (frozen yogurt certificates, jello-fruits, juices, low-fat cookies, etc.). A parent or community member might know or contact a guest monthly guest speaker for your class or the school. These speakers might represent both genders and a variety of ethnic groups; they could be fitness instructors, marathon runners, triathletes, bicycle club representatives, hiking club representatives, health care professionals, physical education professors. Sometimes it can be useful to have fitness conscious middle school or high school students/athletes visit you class; the testimonials of these near peers can have an influential modeling effect.

Another potentially useful avenue for some members of the committee is to research and contact national organizations that are interested in promoting health. Here are some example organizations with programs designed to help elementary schools:

* *U.S.Department of Health and Human Service*: Their Centers for Disease Control and Prevention (CDC) has great materials for how to start and run a "Kids Walk-to-School Program" (www.cdc .gov/nccdphp/dnpa/kidswalk.htm).

* *The Dairy Council* (www.eatsmart.org): This organization sponsors "The Nutrition Education People." Not only do they have free and low cost materials, they have trained regional workers who will visit your school to provide sample lessons and in-service training. Their materials and lessons are designed to satisfy state academic learning requirements.

* *The American Alliance of Health, Physical Education, Recreation and Dance (AAHPERD)*. (www.aahperd .org). This is a big organization with an extensive web site. Here you will have a wealth of information in such areas as coaching, recreation, health, physical education, adaptive physical education. This is where you will find all the particulars of the *Fitnessgram* and *Activitygram*. From AAHPERD you will find linkage to the state organizations who might be able to have people come to your schools. They could help with events such as "Jump Rope for Heart" and "Hoops for Heart."

---

[2] In a recent Louis Harris survey 6 in 10 parents said that they themselves would be willing to volunteer to supervise school and after school activity programs for children. Three-quarters of students said they would be willing to volunteer to supervise educational and recreational programs at their school when they reached an appropriate age. Ninety-five percent were willing to teach a skill to other students.

The *multidisciplinary team approach* could also be instrumental in establishing lines of communication between you and the parents. Parents are a critical link and some partnership must be formed to join home and school. If you adopt some of the homework and portfolio ideas presented earlier, you will be starting in this direction. However, more can be done. Parent/teacher conferences and PTA presentations are of course one approach to pursue and they should be taken advantage of to there fullest. Another approach is a newsletter. Although writing a newsletter requires significant time and effort, the returns can also be significant. It would be great if they could be published as much as three or four times a year, that at least could be a goal. Remember, you do not have to do it all yourself, you have a team and hopefully that team can be delegating responsibilities to others. The newsletter, just like your committee projects, could take many forms. It certainly could explain some of the concepts you and the school are attempting to teach the children. It might contain listings of student accomplishments. Fitness facts could be a regular section: articles in magazines and newspapers might be good material sources for this. Furthermore, the newsletter might be a means of getting information from home; it could be surveying the parents regarding their health practices and it could be a venue for soliciting their ideas and volunteered assistance. Finally about the newsletter, I would not think of it solely as a communication to the parents, I would hope it was suitable for the children to read, and you would be sending it to faculty, staff, administrators and other professionals.

The above discussion has taken the perspective that you, with the aid of a wellness committee, might write a separate newsletter devoted entirely to exercise/health issues. The possibly exists that you already have been planning to communicate with parents via a regular comprehensive report on all your academic goals and projects. If that is the case, your exercise/health newsletter could be conveniently attached and integrated with the overall report.

Changing Habits in the Affective Domain

Being concerned about the social and emotional behaviors of children is not new. Consider this statement, "Children today are tyrants. They contradict their parents, gobble their food and tyrannize their teachers." It may sound contemporary but Socrates made it over 2000 years ago. Nevertheless, many educators and people in society strongly feel that teaching these behaviors is needed today, more than ever. Many feel we are seeing a surge of social pathology because of more families becoming dysfunctional. In Chapter 2 we identified the teaching of good social & emotional values as a major goal; and we offered Hellison's *Personal and Social Responsibility Model (PSRM)* as a tool for quantifying these behaviors into six levels (Figure 2.5). In this section we will look at some ideas on how to use that model to instill desirable personal and social behaviors in our children. But before we consider two specific instructional practices, *awareness talks and reflection time*, it is worth reminding the reader that the physical activity instructional setting is a uniquely excellent environment for potentially teaching affective skills. Let us divide physical activities into three basic types (individual, cooperative, and competitive) and identify the unique contributions each can make in this realm.

Individual activities are activities where everyone works independently and non-competitively on his/her own. Maybe everyone is given a ball and practices dribbling skills; everyone has a hula-hoop and practices different spins; or everyone independently works on some self-determined physical fitness skills. This type of environment is ideally suited for learning motor skills. Everyone can practice at the same time and learn at his/her own rate. Also, performing in this manner is relatively stress free, their classmates are busy with their tasks and hence are not scrutinizing and making judgments. As for affective domain development, independently working on motor skills and physical fitness can teach valuable lessons about perseverance and self-responsibility. And if tangible progress can be made in skill development, as it more quickly can be made in many physical skills than in reading and writing and other academic skills, we should be able to anticipate improvements in self-esteem. It is questionable if unconditionally telling children to think better of themselves is effective or even always right to do, but I have witnessed many instances of children deservedly thinking of themselves far more positively after working and learning to juggle some balls or do a handspring.

Cooperative activities are where partners, small groups, or the entire class attempt to work together to accomplish a physical goal. These kinds of activities are also good for learning physical skills and hence self-concepts. This is because their partners are encouraging and often helping support their performance. Of course, encouragement and teamwork are just the kind of higher level affective interactions we want. I have seen it to be so strong, and spontaneous in physical settings. While you may be able to get the children to praise each other's art work or science project, I bet I have witnessed more vociferous, genuine congratulations and high-fiving when a group of children succeed in carrying a giant earth ball from one end of the gym to the other, or when a team can complete a circuit course in ten whole second less then the pervious day.

Competitive games and sports are eminently attractive and exciting to most children. These experiences result in emotionally charged and highly interactive situations which are filled with opportunities for teaching social responsibilities such as leadership, teamwork, fair play, emotional control and physical and verbal conflict resolution. Think how much cooperation can be learned in volleyball where the bump, set, hit sequence is so integral to the sport. Think of sports that are sometimes associated with violence, where trash talking and in your face attitudes have become common (i.e. basketball, football); would not experiences in these kinds of sports provide opportunities to confront and discuss these values. Think of two students playing a racquet sport in which they are responsible for making the line calls and other infractions on their side of the court. If an opponent made what was thought to be a bad call, what should be done? Complain? Retaliate? Abide by the call and never show any resentment? While this sort of ethical dilemma could be posed in the classroom for discussion, think how much more real and difficult the actual game behavior would be. To make appropriate affective decisions in win-loose situations of perceived importance is not easy, and is a true test of ethical advancement.

We see that each of the three types of physical activities can be an invaluable teaching tool for affective growth. However, we cannot expect that mere participation in them will always automatically produce the desired behaviors. We have already made the point that, even after long periods of participation, children still might not have learned the affective skill of self-responsibility. All that has happened is that they have become accustomed to the instructor making all the decisions regarding when and how to exercise. I have known extremely fit young and old students and athletes, who, when their instructor or coach was no longer standing over them to command physical training, ceased exercise thereafter. Those individuals had not internalized the self-actualizing discipline to continue on their own. Nor can we expect games and sports experiences to automatically yield better social-emotional behaviors. In fact, there exist troubling sport psychology research data that shows that in certain youth sports programs, some children have become more egocentric and developed a greater acceptance of violence and rule violating behavior.[3] Surely we all are aware of instances of poor ethical displays in competitive games and sports. Because of the glamorization of professional sports, it sometimes seems that winning at all cost has become the prevailing ethos and that emotional control and playing by the rules is not the norm (see Figure 9.7 for consideration of *Five Philosophies of Competitive Sports*).

---

[3] There exist a number of sport psychology studies which have found that boys involved in organized youth sports such as football, hockey, and wrestling tend to have more egocentric and less altruistic outlooks; and these philosophical viewpoints to some degree generalize beyond sport specific situations to everyday decision making. However, these philosophical shifts have not normally been found in boys and girls involved in other sports, and sometimes the trend is in the opposite direction. Most authorities believe that regardless of the sport or gender, the code of conduct followed by the coach is the chief factor in determining what affective lessons the children will learn.

Figure 9.7. Five Philosophies of Competitive Sports

Five Philosophies of Competitive Sports

very altruistic
perspective

↑

Philosophy 1: concern for the success of opponent
>*implications:* might entail intentionally loosing in some situations

Philosophy 2: sport as a physical challenge (purpose is to see who is physically best)
>*implications:* playing one's best to win, but playing by the rules, calling own infractions, and even helping competitors with advise and encouragement

Philosophy 3: sport as a physical & mental challenge (purpose is to see who is both physically and mentally toughest)
>*implications:* playing one's best to win, playing by the rules, calling own infractions, but not helping competitors with advice and encouragement, psyching out strategies are acceptable

Philosophy 4: winning is paramount
>*implications:* bending rules and doing most anything to win is acceptable, but you do not intentionally cause physical harm

↓

very egocentric
perspective

Philosophy 5: winning & aggression paramount
>*implications:* it is a battle, survival of the fittest

People hold different views of the purpose of sports. The philosophy which a person subscribes to dictates whether or not he/she will find certain practices acceptable and good. When people have different philosophies they naturally will disagree on which specific behaviors should be taught or condoned. The spectrum of philosophies presented above can be thought of representing a continuum moving from a extreme altruism (looking out for others) to extreme egocentrism (looking out for yourself).

One of the first tasks of teachers and coaches should be to determine which of the five they accept, making sure they have sound justification for their selection being in the best interest of the children. Once you know which philosophy you believe in, it will make it much easier to be consistent in your feedback and to know how to respond to the many dilemmas which will arise.

Whether or not children learn better or poorer affective behaviors is going to be mainly determined by the instruction they receive in conjunction with their physical participation. If we wish these physical activities to be a positive affective experience we need to talk to the children beforehand about what constitutes good and poor behavior. And then, during and following activity we must help them reflect on what happened. Let us look at these two strategies for moving the children up the personal-social responsibility levels.

Awareness Talks

An *awareness talk* occurs before physical activities are begun. It is where you explain your affective behavior expectations. In the model we are following, that would mean we would be describing Hellison's levels of personal and social responsibility. For the children to comprehend and visualize the model, it would be good to have a posted chart to which you could refer. The chart should be kept simple, but you might wish it to contain examples (see Figure 9.8 as one possibility). Make sure you go over a couple of examples that will be applicable to the present situation and the immediately ensuing activities or game. For instance, you might start by a congratulation of everyone for being good quiet listeners as you have been explaining the levels; can they see that they are all exhibiting a level one behavior? Or you might say that the game to be played today will require the finding of new partners in a rapid fashion; what level would you be exhibiting if you avoided someone and were unwilling to work with anyone in class? Can they see why that is a level four behavior?

Certainly all levels do not need to be introduced at once. For first and second graders it may be appropriate to focus on only the first two levels. With more mature students you could begin to focus more on levels three and four. My feeling is that it is never too early to start with *awareness talks* as long as they are brief and in language children can understand. Also, be careful about think-

Figure 9.8. "What's Your Level" Wall Chart

Level 0: Irresponsibility
    Home: Blaming brothers or sisters for problems
    Playground: Calling other students names
    Classroom: Talking to friends when teacher is giving instructions
    Physical education: Pushing and shoving others when selecting equipment

Level I: Self-Control
    Home: Keeping self from hitting brother even though really mad at him
    Playground: Standing and watching others play
    Classroom: Waiting until appropriate time to talk with friends
    Physical Education: Practicing but not all the time

Level II: Involvement
    Home: Helping to clean up supper dishes when asked
    Playground: Playing with others
    Classroom: Listening and doing class work
    Physical education: Trying new things without complaining and saying I can't

Level III: Self-Responsibility
    Home: Cleaning room without being asked
    Playground: Returning equipment during recess
    Classroom: Doing a science project not a part of any assignment
    Physical education: Undertaking to learn a new skill through resources outside the physical education class

Level IV: Caring
    Home: Helping take care of a pet or younger child
    Playground: Asking others (not just friends) to join them in play
    Classroom: Helping another student with a math problem
    Physical education: Willingly working with anyone in the class

ing the children are not yet mature enough to deal with the higher levels and are not ready to take much decision making responsibility. It may be true that they are not, but on the other hand, they never will get to higher levels until we give them some of those opportunities and communicate those expectations to them.

One last comment about *awareness talks*. You may be thinking that you could talk to the children about these affective issues without the concept of levels and the bother of the chart. This is certainly true, but I strongly recommend using the levels in some modified form to best suit your situation. I think you will find that the levels give you a vocabulary and an explicit progression for talking with students about taking responsibility for themselves and for their sensitivity to others. Next we will look at how you could usefully tie the model into your feedback and the students' self-assessments of how they behaved.

Reflection Time

Reflection time is time when you get the children to think about the affective behaviors displayed in class. Sometimes it is appropriate to stop everyone in the course of activity to focus their attention on some affective behavior, good or bad, which has just occurred. Although you are creating a small disruption in the physical activity, an opportunity may offer too much relevancy to pass up. Imagine this happening in your class. A child attempts to do a cartwheel and crashes awkwardly over on his/her back. A couple of students laugh at him/her, but another goes over and offers to get behind and spot the next attempt. You might say right then, what behavior did the spotting child display? What about the laughing students?

I knew a teacher who felt it was well worth the time to occasionally stop everyone so as to point out some affective behavior. Just as we sometimes might *spotlight* some students to demonstrate good motor skill performance, he would halt all activity to briefly recognize some person(s) who were modeling commendable socially responsible behavior. He also had instituted a time-out hand-signal which, if anyone was especially troubled by someone's behavior, he/she could use it to stop the action. Obviously the students needed to realize making these time-outs must be used judiciously so that activity would not be constantly interrupted. He believed that the students learned to use this responsibility appropriately and that it did get the class to analyze their behavior as soon as a problem was developing.

During the cool-down period at the end of class is probably the best opportunity to regularly reflect on and reinforce what has taken place. Having the students sitting in a circle is conducive for such a discussion. This gives you an opportunity to make some brief comments and to ask questions. You might have the students say the number that best represents their level that day. Or you could have them hold up fingers to show their level. I heard it reported of one teacher that she had a very simple system for using the levels concept. She had her levels chart located right at the entrance to the gym. When the children came in they tapped the level at which they intended to function that day. Then, they tapped it again on their exit. She reported that normally the system ran by itself and simply served as a means of the children being reminded and then self-monitoring themselves. But the teacher did say that she would often notice how they were scoring themselves. If she saw any zeros or ones on the way in, it might warn of somebody having a bad today and to watch out for him/her. Also, if discrepancies existed between the student's exiting self-score and what the teacher thought the score should have been, she would call these students aside for a brief discussion.

One more note. *Refection time* does not have to be entirely limited to the class. If you have been making use of logs and journals to record amounts and feeling about physical activity, perhaps journal assignments could also be made relative to affective experiences. Figure 9.9 is a form that could be used in the journal for self-evaluation purposes.

Figure 9.9. An Affective Levels Self-Evaluation Form

Level	Description
Zero:	I did not respect the rights and feelings of others
I:	I did not participate in all the activities today (but I did respect everyone's rights)
II:	I participated in all the activities today (and respected everyone's rights)
III:	I participated in everything and worked on my own (and respected everyone's rights)
IV:	Besides doing all the other Levels, I helped someone (or more than one person)
V:	I did Level IV, and I intend to try some things from the Levels outside of class

Questions for Reflection/Discussion

Name _____ Section _____

1. If you wished to get children exercising or following other health habits outside of school, what key instructional ingredient is missing from this list?

    a. giving reasons

    b. showing how it is done

    c. practicing in school

    d. _____

2. Suppose you wanted your class to develop the habit of drinking more water (say at least 32 ounces daily, half the adult recommendation). Explain what arguments you would use to convince them of the importance of the practice. Remember, it is probably a good idea to provide a number of reasons, and it is good to have, and stress, some reasons at are immediately relevant to them.

    a. _____

    b. _____

    c. _____

3. What is meant by the advocacy of a *behavioral weaning procedure*?

    a. the exercises and practices in class should become progressively more difficult

    b. the exercises and practices in class should become progressively easier

    c. the exercise and practices might be done regularly in class, but should gradually be faded to behaviors beyond school

    d. more and more reason for doing the exercise or practice should be introduced along the way

4. What is meant by a *personalize behavioral practice*? _____

    _____

    _____

5. What are the 5 stages of the *Stages of Change Exercise Model*?

    a. _____

    b. _____

    c. _____

    d. _____

6. I have taken a rather hard line against (1) allowing children to watch television, (2) rewarding them with unhealthy snacks, and (3) recruiting them to sell candies and cookies. Do you tend to agree or disagree? Be prepared to discuss this in class.

7. I advocated a *multidisciplinary approach* to creating habit change. List at least one thing you could do to gain support for improving the children's exercise/health habits.

   _____

   _____

8. List the three basic types of physical activities and list a unique contribution each has for potential development in the affective domain.

   a. _____

      _____

   b. _____

      _____

   c. _____

      _____

9. a. If you were having the children involved in competitive sports (either in class or a coaching situation), which of *the Five Philosophies of Competitive Sports* would you follow?

      _____

   b. Although it was not introduced in the chapter, can you give two distinct reasons someone might give in support of following philosophy IV—winning is paramount?

      a. _____

      b. _____

10. Here are a number of things that might occur in fifth and sixth grade youth sports. Identify which of them would you, as coach, condone. Be prepared to discuss why.

    a. _____ One of your softball player pretends the pitched ball hits him and runs down to first base.

    b. _____ You argue loudly with a clearly incorrect official call.

    c. _____ One of your players corrects an official error that gave her an unfair advantage (volunteered that she touched the ball last and it should be the other team's).

    d. _____ Your players begin to "ride" the other team.

    e. _____ Your supporters hold up large signs to the opposing team "Go Home" and "Score and Die."

    f. _____ Your players engage in a wild display of joy and dance crazily after a play or score.

    g. _____ Your tennis player retaliates with a bad line call after his opponent has made many bad calls.

    h. _____ Your player has been intentionally struck by an opponent and responds by striking back.

i. _____ An opponent has lost her racket through no fault of her own. Your player has an extra racket which she refuses to lend. The rules say that she will win by forfeit.

j. _____ It is a last inning win or lose situation. Your player swings (strike three) at a pitch which would be ball four and victory. The junior umpire was probably the only person on the field who did not notice the swing. He calls ball four. When you are approached by the other coach do you maintain that you did not notice the swing and claim victory or do you ask the umpire to correct his mis-call?

11. List Hellison's six levels of the *Personal-and Social Responsibility Model* (you learned this in chapter 2, can you do it without looking?).

Level 0: _____

Level I: _____

Level II: _____

Level III: _____

Level IV: _____

Level V: _____

12. What is the concept of awareness talks?_____

_____

13. What is the concept of *reflection time*? _____

_____

Laboratory Exercises

1. Imagine that it is at the end of the school year. Perhaps you have some reading suggestions and other pursuits you are encouraging the students to continue. Since you have been working with the children's health habits would it not be a good idea to help them plan for the coming vacation time. Research data shows that most children watch much more television and get less activity in the summertime. Here is an example of a summertime physical activity challenge you might help them fill out. It lists four categories of activity. For example I have personalized my plan in italics. I think it is a good teaching practice to personalize. What is your plan?

SUMMERTIME PHYSICAL ACTIVITY CHALLENGE

Found activities: *always taking stairs if less than five flights; bike or walk to store whenever possible; park away from destinations; etc.*

_____

_____

_____

Physical work: *wash own car; mow the yard with reel mower when possible; do house cleaning every 2 or 3 weeks, etc.*

_____

_____

_____

Sports and recreational activities: *hike with the backpacking club at least once per month, participate in two triathlons, plan a vacation which will include some biking, hiking or canoeing.*

_____

_____

_____

Exercises: *daily aerobic exercise of at least 45 minutes (run, bicycle, swim), weight training and stretching 3 times per week*

_____

_____

_____

Questions Often Asked by Classroom Teachers about Teaching Physical Activities

10

What Is and Isn't Appropriate Physical Touching in the Activity Environment?

How Can I Accommodate the Special Student?

How Do I Teach Movement Activities in the Classroom or Limited Space?

What Do I Need to Know about Safety and Legal Liability?

What Equipment Will I Need and How Might I Acquire It?

When Should and Shouldn't Boys and Girls Play Together?

I Have Been Urgently Asked to Coach Youth Sports. What Do I Do?

What Are Appropriate Physical Activities and Teaching Methods for the Pre-School Child?

"I had six honest serving men—They taught me all I knew: Their names were Where and What and When—and Why and How and Who"

Rudyard Kipling

"It is a shameful thing to be weary of inquiry when what we search for is excellent."

Cicero

"Seize the moment of excited curiosity on any subject, to solve your doubts; for if you let it pass, the desire may never return, and you may remain in ignorance."

W. Wirt

What Is and Isn't Appropriate Physical Touching in the Activity Environment?

If all questions are good, this qualifies as an extra good question. When teaching physical activities, many situations arise in which touching might occur either between the teacher and the student or among the students. Teacher-student contact might happen for a variety of reasons. Firstly, when physical skills are being learned it may be appropriate for the instructor to want to provide manual guidance. As related in Chapter 6, when children still do not perform a skill properly following instructor verbalizations and demonstrations, manual guiding might be in order. For instance, you might tell a child to swipe his leg and keep his toe more pointed when making a soccer kick. If that does not satisfactorily convey the message you might then demonstrate it. If the student continues to lack an understanding, it may be time to provide the proprioceptive sensation of the movement by actually grasping the lower leg and foot and moving him/her through the desired pattern. The hope is to give the idea of what the skill should feel like when gone properly.

A second situation that calls for teacher/student contact is that of spotting. This is where the teacher gives physical assistance to help in actual completion of a task. An example might be where a child is tentative about trying a forward roll. Both performance success and safety could be contingent on the teacher laying on hands to give some uplifting support under the shoulders and a bit of rotation impetus to the legs.

The sexual harassment authorities and guidelines I have consulted unanimously felt that it was appropriate for teachers to provide physical guidance and spotting for skills like those described above. However, they all were agreed that such help should not be applied if it would make the student feel uncomfortable. They recommended that rather than immediately jumping in and providing unsolicited physical assistance, it would be better to preface your action with a statement such as . . . "May I physically assist you through this?" or "Is it OK if I help you?" In most cases there will not be a problem and you may come to know where there is no possibility of any difficulty. But in that rare event when a child might have reason to not wish to be touched, we would know to refrain.

Besides lending guidance and spotting assistance, teachers are also frequently touching students to console, congratulate and minister to injuries. Here again contact may be inappropriate if it is perceived discomforting to the student. Probably the action of congratulating with handshakes, high 10's, and pats on the back will be acceptable to all. But what about embracing, arms around the shoulders, and pats on the butt? No, today's society considers these more intimate behaviors as potentially dangerous and therefore inappropriate between teacher and student. As for treating injuries, certainly it is our duty to attempt to respond to them with application of appropriate first aid.

But for the everyday bruises and scrapes, we are being asked to exhibit some restraint in our handling and condolences; wipe the tears away without hugs and kisses.

I know that there are you who will feel some resistance to adopting this level of aloofness, I do. I fondly remember having three or four first graders hanging on each of my legs because they are glad to see me; and I remember hugging crying children who had failed at a task or hurt themselves. But I think we cannot blithely dismiss these new restrictions as totally uncaring foolishness and legal absurdities. We must remind ourselves that everyone, young and old, has a right to a degree of personal space and privacy, and that there are always going to be a few people, in every profession, who will either knowingly or unknowingly overstep those borders (I would imagine that most of us, at some point in our lives, have experienced such a violation, great or small). If we do not accept any limitations to close contacts with children, some children will be abused who would not be otherwise. Surely we can compromise a little, we do not have to have completely unfettered liberties to still show warmly sincere, affectionate behaviors.

What about the physical contacts among the children? Physical contact is an integral part of many games and activities: bumping, pushing, pulling, holding, supporting, guiding, lifting, etc. Generally, I think it is a good experience for children to work closely together in these ways. It can break down barriers and produce an accepting, inclusive environment. Also, if we expect students to display caring behaviors, they will sometimes need to model your physically assisting, spotting, praising and consoling of others.

Having said this, we must be cognizant of the potential for bad touches as well as good. Perhaps a first step to reduce problems is to educate all children that they have a right to some personal space. If they feel uncomfortable with any too-close contact with another student, they should be able to say so. And we should teach everyone to be respectful of the privacy rights of others.

We, as teachers, can show our sensitivity to privacy rights by making it known that anyone can opt out of an activity that would be threatening to personal space. As much as we might believe a game to be beneficial, and as much as we might be disappointed by non-participation, forced involvement will likely be counter-productive. Perhaps a more fruitful approach in dealing with such problems is to consider modifications that would decrease the frightening features of an activity without eliminating the cooperative spirit. Instead of holding hands, arms around shoulders, or closed dance positions, maybe elbow touching or simple hand contact would sometimes be serviceable substitutes. Or in some instances equipment can be used to provide a level of separation. An example that comes to my mind here is a levitation activity I once had the children play. The children lay down in a circle with their heads close together. They then put their arms up to support a child which I laid backwards onto the surface of hands. This done they then were to rotate the rigid suspendee. While this was a good and enjoyable game I did find that some did not wish to have this many hands up and down their backside, and there were one or two situations in which I sensed bad touches might be occurring. A solution to the game was found in having the levitated person rest of a small tumbling mat.

How Can I Accommodate the Special Student?

It is so important we design our physical activities to enable successful participation of those children with mental and physical disabilities. They have the same desires, interests, and expectations to belong and achieve as their peers. With good encouragement and instruction, children with mental impairments can sometimes find more success and enjoyment in physical activities than what may be found in more intellectually demanding realms. And children with physical limitations are frequently in greatest need of establishing active lifestyle patterns because restricted movement opportunities are often leading them down a road to pathologically low fitness levels. It is wrong to think a physical disability precludes a lifestyle rich in exercise and sports (see Figure 10.1).

Figure 10.1. Activities for Those with Impairments

Physical impairments need not consign people to a life of inactivity. Listed below are some sports and recreational pursuits which would require no, or minimal adaptations. Can you think of a few more?

Major impairment of the visual system:
Step aerobics
Bicycling (exercise bicycle, tandem and "Spinning" classes)
Swimming (lane lines and a gutter beeper might be needed)
Water aerobics
Stair steppers
Running (treadmills and partner running—using the elbow as a guide)
Walking
Weight training, lifting and body building
Stretching and Yoga
Wrestling
Track (throwing events)
Dance

Major impairment to the lower musculoskeletal system:
Archery
Darts
Horseshoes
Swimming
Wheelchair racing
Wheelchair sports (basketball, tennis, etc.)
Weight training and lifting
Kayaking, canoeing and sailing

Major impairment to the upper musculoskeletal system:
Walking and hiking
Running
Soccer
Dance
Step Aerobics
Stair steppers
Bicycling (exercise bicycle, tandem and "Spinning" classes)

Finally, it is critical that the children without disabilities participate with those who do; such experiences can teach them how to accept the strengths and limitations of everyone.

The first idea I would offer regarding the inclusion of special needs students is that you consider the three types of activity structures that were presented in chapter 7: individual, *cooperative, and competitive.* In that chapter the point was made that it is easier to accommodate differences in ability when activities are designed as individual or cooperative. In *individual activities* everyone is working independently and hence not holding up or being held up by others. For example, those with impairments can be happily working on simpler ball or movement skills while the more gifted, without conflict, can simultaneously be experimenting with more advance tasks. In *cooperative activities,* group goals generally require everyone to help each other. The more advanced students will be forced not to disregard those who are slower, but rather to give them assistance. The cooperative structure will tend to elicit more caring behaviors. *Competitive activities* pose greater difficulties for inclusion of diverse abilities because mis-matches in abilities can result in the spotlighting of those differences. The performance of lesser-skilled individuals will be more evident if they are causing their team to fare poorly relative to others. This, of course, can result in embarrassment and frustration.

The point to be drawn from the above paragraph is that ways to achieve inclusion will be easier to find if all your activities are not socially competitive. However, it should not be concluded that competition cannot also be designed to yield successful performance for all, it just may require a bit more careful thought. Below are listed some elements of activities and games that can be altered regardless of the activity type. Throughout the text I have stressed the need to individualize tasks to match the disparate ability levels which exist in every class. Remember the *Long Slanty Rope Principle*? Including children with disabilities simply means that we must extend the long slanty rope a bit further.[1]

1. Equipment: Change the weight and size of objects and implements, target size, and ball resiliency. Bigger is usually better. Bigger balls are generally easier to bat and catch. Bigger and lighter bats are easier to use. Bigger targets are easier to hit. Softer, less resilient balls move slower and are easier to control; partially deflated soccer balls are easier to dribble, deader balls will rebound less erratically from rackets. Rigid paddles provide more controlled rebounds than tautly strung ones.
2. Space: Change the space involved in the activity, such as the distance from the target, the height of the target, or the number of yards between bases. Lower the nets and shrink the court sizes and areas to be defended.
3. Time: Vary the time it takes to complete an activity or the number of repetitions. Repeat dance steps before moving to the next.
4. Environmental dynamics: Motor skills can be classified as *environmentally closed* or *environmentally open*. *Environmentally closed* refers to situations in which the performer is dealing with fairly static surroundings. Hitting a ball from a batting tee is a more closed skill than contending with the dynamics of a thrown pitch. *Environmentally open* skills are those in which a performer must adjust to a quickly changing environment. A further example would be catching a ball while on a run or throwing to a moving teammate. It should be obvious that closed skills tend to place less processing demands on the performer and thus should be considered as a means of adapting activities to lower skill levels. In ball sports, low skilled individuals may be able to more easily fill the roles of serving, foul attempts, throw-ins.

How Do I Teach Movement Activities in the Classroom or Limited Space?

I believe it is important to continue activities even when the weather prohibits outdoor activities and when there is no available gym or large multipurpose room. Stretching and exercise breaks are good health practices to instill, and children need to learn that regular exercise is something you

---

[1] A good book for establishing an inclusive environment is *Strategies for Inclusion: A Handbook for Physical Educators* by L. Lieberman and C. Houston-Wilson, Human Kinetics, 2002 (www.humankinetics.com). Phone 1-800-747-4457. Also, the www.pecentral.org and www.aahperd.org web site have many adapted physical education ideas.

find time to do everyday, regardless of the weather or circumstance. You have taught them the *Reversibility Principle,* now you must take the even more important step of modeling behaviors to counter it.

It is hard to make specific activity recommendations without knowing the specifics of your facilities but there are a few general ideas that can be given. You can always make some space if your desks and chairs are moveable. Moving everything to one side of the room should provide a small space sufficient for many activities and games (a few small circuit training stations could be formed; poly spot and carpet squares could be arranged so each child would have a personal space for individual exercises and stunts; games like "No Touch," "Daytona Speedway," or "Walking / Beanbag Tag" could be played; aerobic activities to music; etc.).[2] Moving furniture to the center of the room can result in a perimeter area adequate for various circle formation games and activities ("Creative circles", folk dancing, "Around-the-clock" games, "Astronaut drills," etc.). When the desks can not be moved out of the way activity space is more constrained but there is still much that can be done. Students can do calisthenics, in-place jogging, stretches and isometric exercises beside their desks; they can do manipulative activities with lummi sticks, balls, and other objects; or they can follow each other up and down the aisles doing some of the same activities as those mentioned above.

When exercising in the classroom there is a need to keep the exuberance under control. Too much noise will frequently be disrupting to neighboring classrooms. Also, because the play space will be limited, extra care must be taken to avoid collisions with surrounding obstacles and each other. Rather than attempting to play with regular sports balls and bats, consider using less abrasive objects such as balloons, yard balls, beanbags, and foam balls.

What Do I Need to Know about Safety and Legal Liability?

More than 50 percent of all accidents in the school setting occur on the playground and in the gymnasium. It therefore is essential that you know how to make your activities as safe as possible. Also, it is important for you to understand a few basic facts regarding your legal obligations.

Teachers must offer a standard of care that any reasonable and prudent professional with similar training would apply under the given circumstances. They are expected to anticipate foreseeable dangers and take necessary precautions to prevent such problems. Below are three basic duties that must be met.

1. *Supervision:* Supervision can be classified as general or specific. *General supervision* means that the actions of all the children can be regularly monitored. The teacher is responsible for always maintaining this level of supervision. You should never leave your class unattended nor have some of your students participating in activity areas which you cannot watch. Even when dealing with emergency situations you must be able to maintain a degree of awareness of the rest of the class. For instance, if a child experienced a significant injury in class, the teacher should not leave to get help; rather, a student or two should be sent to get help or to find a responsible adult to monitor the class in your absence. *With-it-ness* is a term for the teaching skill of being able to attend to more than one thing at a time. Can you talk to someone or administer to a "boo boo" and still have an idea of the whereabouts and the behaviors of your class? With experience you will likely find your *with-it-ness* developing. One way to increase *with-it-ness* is to normally position yourself on the perimeter of the group so that your back will not be turned if a dangerous situation should arise (remember the *Back-to-the wall Principle*?).

---

[2] Descriptions of the activities in this paragraph can be found listed either under management games in chapter 5 or in the activities provided in chapter 11.

Specific supervision is when the teacher is directly present at the site of an activity and can quickly regulate or stop the action if necessary. This level of supervision is required when a child is performing a dangerous movement. Obvious examples would be when a child was high up on the climbing ropes or beginning to learn a gymnastic flip. Another kind of dangerous situation would exist if the students where in route to a playing field which required the crossing of a busy highway. To safely cross the street the teacher would have to be at the site of the crossing so as to be able to signal traffic and stop the children. It would not be sufficient for the teacher to have warned the children as to the proper manner of crossing the street and then to have trustfully followed at a distance.

2. *Safe activities:* All the activities you introduce must be reasonably safe. If a *reasonably prudent* person could foresee the eventual likelihood of an injury, the activity should be stopped immediately and then modified or terminated.

We should be able to see some activities as apparently dangerous. Football, "red-rover" and tag games in which tackling was occurring would be examples. "Battle Ball" games where playground and volleyballs are thrown at each other would be another. Having rules specifying that "Battle Ball" and kickball players must be hit below the waist would not satisfactorily solve the problem; we are still making children targets of potentially injurious balls and misdirected throws will inevitably occur.

The safety of most activities and games depends upon whether or not the children possess sufficient skill to handle the conditions demanded of them. If your class has not practiced rolling progressions, some of the students may not be fit or skilled enough to safely perform unassisted forward rolls. Even though the children may be able to execute a wheelbarrow walk, putting it into a relay race might exceed the ability of someone who could subsequently be pushed onto his/her face. It might be fine to match the children according to size and strength and progressively teach a skill like the fire person's carry, but piggyback relay races would make the activity much more hazardous.[3]

Skill levels become increasingly important to safety as the activities and sports involve more interaction and physical contact. For example, having low and high skilled students competing together in unmodified soccer, softball and basketball games could easily become unacceptably dangerous; those who are twice as big, and can move their bodies three times as fast as some other children, can pose a foreseeable risk to others. Visualize yourself on the fields and courts of powerful professional athletes—would you be safe? The best suggestion I can give to reduce large skill miss-matches in sports is to utilize the *mini-game* format suggested in chapter 7 and then equate the teams and pairings.

Any activity can also become unsafe if the rules of conduct are violated. It is your responsibility to make corrections as soon as you notice any potentially dangerous procedure violations. If misbehavior has been occurring for a period of time, and it leads to an injury, you would be held accountable. You should have had the supervision to be aware of it, and you should have remedied it. Only in rare situations would the elementary level teacher be absolved of responsibility due to the concept of *contributory negligence*. *Contributory negligence* is a legal term for situations where others may be held partially or totally accountable for their own actions. Take this as an example, a teacher gave clear warning to her sixth graders that swinging bats was dangerous and prohibited until everyone was spread out on the playing field. Then, out-of-the-blue, one of the students suddenly swung and injured somebody. If there was no good reason (past history or disability) to have suspected the child of this behavior, the teacher could hardly be thought neglectful; normal six-graders should be assumed to possess this much self-control. However, *contributory negligence* is not legally attributed to children less

---

[3] Broken teeth and noses have occurred in wheelbarrow races, and shattered kneecaps have resulted from piggyback relays. Even where the students have been size matched, the courts have ruled against teachers in such cases.

than seven years of age. This means that you should not feel confident that your warnings, no matter how clear they may be, will suffice to prevent inappropriate actions. Telling them not to swing the implements in their hands might be little more effective than telling them not to put peas up their noses.

3. *Safe play environment:* The teacher always has the duty to make activities as safe as possible. This means that the facilities and equipment must be made not just safe, but as safe as they reasonably can be. Always inspect the play space and look for things like wet spots on the floor, gravel on the pavement, or holes or sprinkler heads in the fields. Also, look for obstacles such as protruding bleachers, tables, chairs, or posts. Remove them if you can or establish boundaries to ensure adequate buffer zones. I am always amazed when the end lines and boundaries of relays, tag games and sports are immediately next to these all too solid, harsh realities. Finally, take heed to keep the facility uncluttered after activity begins; don't leave your clipboard, papers or computer message pad lying about. Watch for clothing articles that the children have the habit of leaving lying about.

The selection of equipment can have a major impact on safety. Always consider whether or not softer, lighter weight balls can be used. Yarn and nerf balls work great for many games. And it seems foolish to play softball with an official hard ball when softer ones are available that would be safer and probably much better suited to limited skills levels and play spaces.

The children's clothing has baring on safety. Pendulous garments and jewelry should be removed. From my experience, improper footwear is the greatest dress hazard because slipping and turned ankles can often result. Denying activity is the surest course and probably conveys a good safety message. Allowing participation in bare feet might be acceptable for some few activities. Performing in socking feet should be more unacceptable.

A legal term that relates to the environment is *attractive nuisance.* Occurrences of *attractive nuisances* would be leaving climbing ropes hanging, a mini-trampoline set-up, or a javelin lying about. Such items would be enticing to many children and must never be left available for unsupervised use. Make sure these kinds of things are not available before you get to the activity area and that they are put away before you leave.

Besides supervision, safe activities, and environmental factors, here are four other recommendations.

1. Have formulated in your mind a clear emergency care plan. It should include phone numbers, how the help of other school personal will be gained, and the basic first aid steps you should follow.
2. Do not force students to do activities they are afraid of. Make it clear that the choice of activity belongs to them. Although it can be frustrating when a child refuses to participate in a potentially beneficial activity, we should do no more than offer constant help and encouragement. Fear itself can make a task dangerous. Along the same line, we must honor all parental and doctor notes to be excused from participation.
3. Be cautious about having the children exercising when it is hot and/or humid. Children do not cope with heat stress nearly as well as do adults. Their sweating capacity is not as great and it is important to provide frequent activity breaks and regular fluid replacements. Overweight individuals have a larger problem with exercising in the heat because their surface area to mass ratios are smaller and hence heat dissipation is not as effective.
4. It is always our responsibility to warn participants of the *inherent risks* involved in activities. Make it a habit to tell or show the students what to watch out for and then check to see if they understood.

What Equipment Will I Need and How Might I Acquire It?

One of the themes of this text has been to maximize movement; this means a shift away from games and activities in which 30 students are playing with one ball or are impatiently lined up to await a turn on the tumbling mat or a shot at the basket. No, if high levels of activity and skills are to be attained it is requisite that we have play equipment for most every child in the class, ever as much as other academic subjects require books and writing paper. Nevertheless, the overall amount of equipment needed for a varied range of experiences does not have to be prohibitively great. First of all, there are many types of equipment for which it is not difficult to purchase or have enough made for each child. Examples would be bean bags, nerf balls, yarn balls, jump ropes, hula hoops, Frisbees, carpet squares, poly spots, paddles, birdies. With these items alone, and some creativity, there are endless activity possibilities. I have known teachers who have had parents or school personnel inexpensively make the likes of yarn balls, bean bags, jump ropes, hula hoops and wooden paddles. Equipment procurement is one of the areas where a formation of a wellness team could produce some dividends.

If you wish to introduce the children to certain sports, you should have a large number of sports balls and implements, ideally enough for every class member or one for every two students. Although these items are more expensive to attain, good accumulations of them may be feasible. Your physical education specialist and wellness team might be able to get donations from different sources. Remember that the sports equipment that might be most useful to you will not likely be "regulation" sized and weighted. I would like to have extra big, and soft, softballs; light weight fat bats, bigger and lighter volleyballs, junior size basketballs, soft-pliable hockey sticks, etc.

In addition to having the above for most everyone, I think you would find a good, easily portable sound system to be essential not just for dance type activities but also for general motivation and management purposes. A number of small cones would serve you well in delineating game and activity boundaries and target zones. Some type of jerseys are nice to lessen confusion in team games. A variety of longer length ropes make for a variety of group and double Dutch jumping challenges.

Finally, I would encourage you not to limit your equipment horizons. More expensive specialty equipment can sometimes be obtained through grants, civic organizations, and benefactors. Unicycles, rollerblading skates and accouterments, tumbling mats and crash pads, climbing walls, rope courses, hiking gear, pedometers, heart monitors, bicycles and helmets, and portable basketball hoops have all been gotten by other enterprising souls. Also, be aware that many school districts are now acquiring popular specialty equipment for shared use across schools. Have a look at the catalogs and web sites listed in the Annotated Resources section for other equipment and supply ideas.

When Should and Shouldn't Boys and Girls Play Together?

My view is that throughout the elementary years, there should be no gender segregation in regular school physical activities. We should be attempting to convey the message that we are friendly caring people, we don't discriminate on the basis of disabilities, race, gender or anything else. We treat everyone with respect and uncomplainingly play with the nearest person. And we should not foster stereotypical roles by suggesting that certain activities are more for boys or girls. Nor should we allow to go unchallenged talk of "throwing like a girl" or girls being better at dance or rope jumping. Let's provide male and female models for all children and not unnecessary limit anyone's aspirations. I would not require the assumption of boy and girl roles in dance or gymnastic activities and I would not encourage an us against them mentality by having all boys' teams playing against girl's teams.

As was made clear in Chapter 9, ability matching is needful in competitive physical activities, without it safety, enjoyment and skill development is threatened. At the intermediate level you will be seeing that some boys in your class will be significantly excelling the girls in sports involving physical power and aggressive play behaviors. However, I do not believe this should lead to separate boys and girls games. Overlap will surely exist in which some girls will be competitive with the better boys and more advanced than many of the boys. Let everyone appreciate this reality by matching solely according to ability.

Before leaving this topic, something should be said about the controversial issue of co-educational, after-school sports. Some people feel that up through sixth grade the teams should continue to be co-educational. Their reasoning is much the same as that made above for common, regular physical education experiences. However, there is another school of thought, with whom I concur, which believes that some fifth and sixth grade after-school sports teams are best separated. Basketball, soccer, softball and other sports with a premium on physical power will see many boys beginning to exhibit a decided advantage over the girls. Although there may still be some girls who are capable of competing with the boys at this higher level, it is not going to be as common as was the case in regular class play. The elective sports teams will be attracting a pool of the best boy performers and thus it should be expected that only a very select few of the girls will be able to keep up. The larger the student population the more likely this will be the result (Figure 10.2).

With boys and girls maturing much earlier than in past years, and most school sports programs drawing from larger populations, I would argue for the consideration of some fifth and sixth grade co-educational sports teams. I believe that co-educational sports will afford more girls the opportunity to participate and be leaders. But if we do organize separate teams, we have the duty of making sure the teams are given equal prestige and rights. Schedules, equipment, coaches' pay, and our support deserves to be equably distributed.

Figure 10.2. Bell Shaped Curves for the Motor Abilities of Two Populations

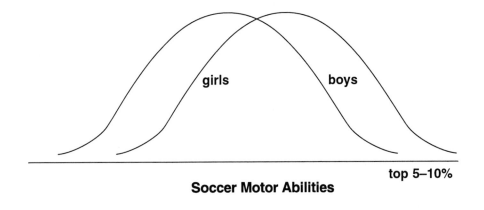

Soccer Motor Abilities

If fifth and sixth grade boys had a small physiological power advantage for playing soccer, we would expect the displacement of the bell-shaped curves as depicted above. Because the individual ability differences within the boy and girl populations would be greater than the between group differences, many of the girls would be expected to be able to out-perform a sizable segment of the boys. However, if only the top 5 or 10 percentage of the composite group were selected for a sports team, it could be expected that those elite performers would be all, or nearly all, boys.

I Have Been Urgently Asked to Coach Youth Sports. What Do I Do?

Of course, your decision as to whether or not to coach a youth sports team depends upon you and your situation. But perhaps I can provide some information to weigh. Probably the two most common factors arguing against taking on a coaching duty are (1) not having the time and (2) insufficient knowledge. Time undoubtedly is a concern for all and doing a good job of coaching will require a significant commitment. If you elect to coach, will you still have adequate time for work, family, and personal intellectual/physical development? It will not be easy but with good time management skills it may be possible.

A number of points can be made regarding your knowledge to do a good job. Firstly, I would say that your elementary education studies are a stolid foundation for dealing with young people in any context. Your training in educational philosophy, child development, and your close working with children will give you an advantage over many other coaches who lack this background. Also, the principles you have learned from this text should provide a sound theoretical basis from which to begin; you have learned about physiological training principles, effective demonstrating and feedback provision, how to go about modifying drills and games to promote greater activity and skill development, management techniques, discipline procedures, how to make activities enjoyable, and much more.

Although you might feel comfortable with your educational/pedagogical foundation skills, you may yet question whether or not you have enough knowledge in the X and O specifics of the sport. This is certainly a legitimate concern. It is not essential that you were an outstanding athlete or even that you played the sport, but you do need to know the fundamental techniques, strategies, and rules of the game. If you lack this kind of sport specific understanding it might be best to postpone your acceptance until you have upgraded these skills. There are a number of ways to acquire sports specific knowledge. A first step would be to talk to, observe, and if possible, assist an experienced master coach. Be aware too that there are many excellent texts and videos on the market for both beginning and experienced coaches.[4] Finally, you might wish to take a step further and earn some coaching credentials by attending certifying workshops or completing a university degree program. Local universities may give coaching workshops and/or offer a coaching minor degree program. Various coaching organizations provide workshops and certification courses. The National Federation Interscholastic Coaches Education Program (NFICA) would be one contact source (National Federation of State High School Associations, 11724 Plaza Circle, P.O. Box 20626, Kansas City, MO 64195, 1-816-464-5400).

A final point I would desire to make is that coaching can be a tremendously rewarding position. Sports are a highly valued experience in young people's lives and it is not uncommon for a coach to be listed as the person of most influence. This is a weighty responsibility that deserves to be held by the best society can provide. Sadly, we do not always have the best of role models as coaches. There is a high turnover rate in coaching (approximately two years is the average tenure) and thus inexperience is a recurrent problem. Also, because of the excitement of sports and the impressive images of sometimes dubious professional coaching behaviors, some youth sport coaches can be led to over stress winning at the expense of fun and educational purposes. We need to have leaders who will remember that it is full striving to win, not winning *per se,* that is most important, and that the welfare of the young athletes is what must always take precedence over winning. If you could be such a person, please coach, we need you.[5]

---

[4] Human Kinetics (P.O. Box 5076, Champaign, IL 61825-5076; http://www.humankinetics.com/) is the world's largest publisher in the area of coaching and physical activity. They have an impressive list of materials for all sports and aspects of coaching. Free catalogs are available upon request.

[5] Although the number of sports programs for girls have greatly increased in recent years, the number of women coaches is small, and has been significantly decreasing. The need for women coaches is great.

What Are Appropriate Physical Activities and Teaching Methods for the Pre-School Child?

You will find it enjoyable to teach physical activities to pre-schoolers. They are so full of energy and take such delight in games and moving. Frequent short bouts are good for their developing bodies and will make for more attentive students.

The very simplest of individual and partner activities will generally work best. Any games with more than one or two rules will not be understood; team play and competitions are too advanced for them. At this age it is good to have them experience all kinds of locomotor skills: walking, running, skipping, jumping, leaping, sliding, hoping, galloping. Doing these skills in different directions and patterns, and at different rates, will develop their motor schema of how to move and will serve as the foundation from which later sport specific skills can be built. Look back to Figure 8.14 for the NASPE Kindergarten Benchmarks.

Early childhood is also the time to begin learning the overlapping concepts of *body awareness*, *directionality* and *laterality*. *Body awareness* refers to the children knowing their body parts and how they move. *Directionality* refers to a comprehension of the orientation of one's body and body parts in space. *Laterality* is more specific and means knowing left from right and the relationships between them. In Figure 10.3 are some sample activities.

Preschoolers are especially fond of sing along activities, rhythmics and simple dances. They love to pretend and act-out things. Examples would be animals (chickens, horses, bunnies, elephant, ducks, frogs, cats, alligators); daily activities (waking up, getting dressed, washing body parts, brushing teeth, do exercises, running for the bus, carrying groceries); sports (skating, race walking, baseball, trampoline, swimming, dancing, soccer, basketball, volleyball); vehicles (airplane, bicycle, lawn mower, fire truck, row boat, unicycle). Manipulative games will also be enjoyable and beneficial for them; bean bags, streamers, beach balls, yarn balls, nerf balls and rhythms sticks work great. It would be good to have enough pieces of equipment for everyone so as to maximize skill development, but also keep in mind that they will tire quickly and will require frequent rest periods.

For a more comprehensive coverage of preschool activities and method suggestions I would recommend acquisition of the following small text: Hammett, C. T. *Movement Activities for Early Childhood*, Human Kinetics, 1992 (http://www.humankinetics.com/). The pecentral web site will also have a section devoted to preschool issues and activities.

Figure 10.3. Preschool Body Awareness, Laterality and Directionality Activities

Body Awareness Activities

put elbows together
touch both elbows
knees together
hands on top of head
back of hands together
touch heels together
raise your shoulders
hold one foot

touch one elbow
elbows to knees
knee to toe
elbows on hips
touch one shoulder
hands on ears
curl your body, extend it
jingles (head, hips, back, heels)

Laterality and Directionality Activities

stand in front of spot, back, left, right
hold spot in front, back, right side, over
stand on spot and face away, right side towards me
move away from your spot, forwards it
draw a square in air (triangle, etc.)
clap twice behind back
lie on your back, front, left, right
raise right arm, foot, elbow, shoulder, hip, knee
lean to left, right, forwards, backwards
bend left, right, backwards, forwards, sidewards
stand on left foot, toes, heel
stand on left foot and swing the right foot forwards, backwards
lift your right knee and left elbow
circle arms out in front, side, behind
turn knees towards each other, away, left, right

Questions for Reflection/Discussion

Name _____ Section _____

1. Some of us might have strong beliefs about physical contact between teachers and students. Some might feel that the guidelines limiting physical contact are foolish and preclude a warm, caring teaching atmosphere. Others might hold the contrary belief that restricting guidelines are definitely needed to protect children from those who may abuse their authority. How do you feel?

   _____

   _____

   _____

   _____

2. When is or isn't it legally acceptable teaching behavior to manually assist a student through a motor skill?

   _____

   _____

3. In which type of activity would inclusion of the special student normally be most difficult: *individual, cooperative, competitive*? Why?

   _____

   _____

4. Explain three modifications you could make to include a wheelchair bound student in a two-on-two volleyball game.

   a. _____

   _____

   b. _____

   _____

   c. _____

   _____

5. Cite three progressive stages of a soccer skill, moving from *environmentally closed* to *environmentally open*.

a. _____

_____

b. _____

_____

c. _____

_____

6. What are three basic legal duties teachers are expected to uphold?

a. _____

b. _____

c. _____

7. Imagine you gave each of your first graders a hockey stick and strongly give warnings not to swing them until everyone was spread out on the playground. Then, as you were talking to the class and preparing to lead them outside, one of them suddenly swung his/her stick and hurt another child. What would be the legal ramifications?

a. you would not be at fault because of *contributory negligence* on the part of the child

b. you would not be at fault because you had warned the students not to swing

c. you would be at fault because *contributory negligence* would not apply at this grade level

8. Which is a best example of the legal concept of *attractive nuisance*?

a. inappropriate dress of students or teachers

b. playing games that may be fun but which have little education value

c. teaching in an environment in which many distractions are present

d. unattended unicycles being left out

9. Which is generally true? Are the motor and physical activities between the genders normally larger or smaller than the abilities within the genders? What implications might this understanding have for gym class activities and for selective sports teams?

_____

_____

_____

10. Give examples of simple activities that would be teaching . . .

a. *laterality:* _____

b. *directionality:* _____

c. *body awareness:* _____

11. What is *With-it-ness*? _____

_____

Laboratory Exercises

1. Think of the first coach of young people that comes to your mind. Do you think that coach was in a position to have a significant impact upon the emotional/physical growth of the players? Do you think that someone in such a position should have more in his/her background than having played the sport (training in child development, educational philosophy and pedagogical techniques)? Why?

_____

_____

_____

_____

_____

_____

Some Activities to Help You Start

11

Warm-Ups

Cool-Downs

General Games

Tag Games

Relays

Activities to Music

Dance
Golden Oldies
Folk Dance
Square Dance

Cooperative/New Games

Individual Challenge Stunts

Cooperative Partner Stunts

Activities with Ropes

Activities with Hula Hoops

Activities with Beanbags

Activities with a Parachute

"I know of no more encouraging fact than this . . . If one advances confidently in the direction of his dreams, and endeavors to live the life he has imagined, he will meet with success unexpected in common hours."
H.D.Thoreau

"Nothing great was ever accomplished without enthusiasm."
R.W. Emerson

Hopefully you have gotten numerous activity ideas throughout this text, and more importantly, you have developed an understanding of how to create and evaluate your own. In this final chapter I will add some of my favorite selections in the categories of: warm-ups, cool-downs, general games, tag games, relays, activities to music, dance, cooperative games, individual challenge students, cooperative partner stunts, activities with ropes, activities with hula hoops, activities with bean bags, and activities with a parachute. All these activities have been effectively used by me or other teachers of elementary children. They have passed the *SOS Test:* they can (1) be played <u>S</u>afely, (2) keep everyone actively <u>O</u>n-task, and (3) <u>S</u>uccessfully enjoyed by all the children regardless of their ability levels. However, I do not guarantee that any of these activities will work for you. Unless effective management procedures have been established, the most commendable of games can be torn apart by unruly students. Also, you will need to further vary and build off of these suggestions to suit the specific grade level, skills, temperaments and interests of your students. You may have to alter them in light of your unique environment and equipment possessions. And finally, as I hope you have realized from studying this book, there are many pedagogical skills that make for a good teacher (*anticipatory set, the three-rule rule, teacher movement, effective questioning, proximity control, with-it-ness, varied reinforcement,* etc.). These skills will require months and years of patient and purposeful practice before fully effective games and lessons can be implemented.

Permit me to conclude by saying that I hope these following activities will, in a small way, add to what you have learned in this text and help you to begin an enjoyable career of teaching of physical activities. The quotes at the beginning of this chapter have been an inspiration to me. I truly believe that if you are determined and enthusiastic, you can make yourself into a master teacher. No other goal could be worthier. Thank you for your patient reading.

May the gods go with you. Upon your sword sit laurel victory and may smooth success be strewed before your feet."
W. Shakespeare

Warm-Ups

One Behind: This is a good simple one to do in your classroom as an activity break. You or a student leader does a series of exercises at the front of the class. The class follows suit but the trick is that they stay one exercise behind the leader. When the leader starts to do exercise two the class begin on exercise one. Stretches, isometrics, and calisthenics all work fine. I have not tried it yet but it might be fun to have the class delayed by two activities, or half the class behind one while the other half is two behind.

Astronaut drill: Everyone is locomotoring in a circle. It could be walking, walking with arm circles, walking with arm windmills, jogging, bear walking. Periodically groups are identified to go to the center of the circle and do a prescribed activity. The identified groups could be left-handers, those wearing shorts, those with birthdays in months which begin with a J, etc.

Partner warm-up: Partners stand back to back, one facing into the circle, the other facing out. The outside people jog a counterclockwise lap while the inside people do a prescribed activity such as curl-ups, lateral stretch, treadmills, sit and reach, rope skipping. When a jogger gets back home the roles are reversed.

High-tens: Students move around the gym in different directions to music. When the music stops, they give as many high-tens to as many different people as possible. They start locomotoring again when the music begins. Something like a five or ten second music break works well. Of course, activities other than high-tens could be specified (low fives, hand shake variations, foot-fives, etc.).

Over-unders: Half of the class is scattered about in push-up or crab positions. The other half of the class will be traveling over and under. When a person goes under a bridge, the bridge flips over into the crab position. When a person goes over a crab, the crab flips over into the bridge position. Give the class a set amount of time to see how many bridges and crabs they can go over and under.

Hall of the Mountain King: "In the Hall of the Mountain King" is a segment from the *Peer Gynt Suite* by Edvard Grieg. The music starts with a very slow tempo and gradually increases until it is extremely fast. The children are lined-up in the center of the gym and are to begin walking slowly in step with the beat. They first go forward 16 counts to the music and then backwards 16 counts. Their task is to keep up as long as possible to the increasing speed. Sometimes falls occur when going fast backwards. To avoid this problem and to create variety you can have them pivoting so that they are always moving forwards. Sliding to the left and right also works well.

I suggest you keep your ears attuned for other music that has an increasing tempo (Bolero, Cotton-Eye Joe, Dueling Banjos, etc.)

Cool-Downs

Electricity: Two lines sit facing each other, hands joined with their teammates on both sides. I start the message at one end by simultaneously squeezing the hand of the head person of each line. The students relay a hand squeeze down their line. When the last person in the line has his/her hand squeezed, he/she attempts to pick-up a ball or other object that is placed directly between them. It is a race to see which line can produce the fastest current. A rule is that everyone's eyes must be on the ball so as not to anticipate the coming message. False messages due to nervous twitches result in "short circuits" and points for the other team.

AC-DC: A hand squeeze message is sent around a circle of seated people in any direction. A person can relay the message to continue it in the same direction or he/she can reverse it back towards the sender. The "it" person in the center tries to locate who has the message. Set a short time limit so no one gets stuck in the center for an embarrassing length of time. A good variation is to have someone in the circle "who's the leader." That person is doing an activity which everyone else in the circle duplicates. The leader keeps trying to change the activity without being identified by "it." If this variation was being used as a cool-down you might have everyone in the circle seated, for more vigorousness they could be standing and doing things like jumping jacks and jogging in place.

Killer: Everyone mills around shaking hands with people they meet. One person has been secretly appointed the "killer." The killer winks at people he/she wishes to kill. Those killed do not die instantaneously but after a few seconds die a horrible shrieking death and drop to the floor. If someone thinks he/she knows who the killer is, he/she says "I have an accusation to make." If someone else says "I second it," both people count 1-2-3 and simultaneously point at the suspect. If they both point to the true killer the game is over. If they point to different people or to a non-killer, they must die the death of ignominious false accusers and the game continues. It is fun when everyone has been killed and you have a complete cool-down.

Sculpturing: Students are paired and one is designated the sculpturer and the other the clay. The task of the sculpturer is to gently bend the clay into an interesting shape. The task of the clay is to be pliable and to hold the positions as best as possible. It works well to have slow music playing and to frequently give a command for role reversal and partner switching. At the very end you might have everyone step back and have the sculpturers judge which are the most interesting shapes.

General Games

Rainbow run: This game is relatively complicated so it will be necessary to sit everyone down and carefully teach all the rules. It basically is a scavenger hunt type game. A wall chart is made so that small groups of children are working through differing sequences of colors. For instance, the first color for group A might be red. This would mean that the group members must run and look under the many cones spread over the gym or playing field. Under one of the cones is hidden a red magic marker which they use to check a recording card that everyone carries. After this, they run to an exercise wall where they perform the prescribed activity on the red sign. Finally, they return to the original wall chart to see what their next color assignment is and the whole process is repeated.

You could play the game until all groups had finished or you could cut the activity off at a set time limit. One important detail is that the markers must never be removed from their cones because that would make it impossible for the other groups to complete their assignments (I have known some teachers to tie the markers to the cones as an anchoring precaution). This game certainly has great possibilities for interesting variations. Colors could be just one of many coding systems (animals, geometric shapes, numbers, planets, etc.).

Card game: The class is divided into small groups. Each group has a stack of playing cards. The cards have been shuffled but each group has the same number of cards. The game is played by attempting to get through your cards as quickly as possible; each card has a designated activity that must be done before moving to the next. The activity possibilities are unlimited but I have provided a cooperative activities version below. Notice that some groups might be luckier than others in the card numbers they draw. This tends to increase the excitement and the more skilled students are not always the winners.

Face cards
Aces:	run two laps around the cones, hands joined
Kings:	race walk around the cones, hands joined
Queens:	one lap around the cones joined together in train fashion
Jacks:	slide one lap round the cones, hands joined
Joker:	everyone does 10 shoe juggles

Non-face cards
Hearts:	that number of partner push-ups (one partner has feet on shoulders of the other as they both do push-ups)
Spades:	that number of people through a push-up tunnel (the squad is in push-up position shoulder to shoulder, the end person crawls through, followed by the next, etc.)

| Diamonds: | that number of partner dips and curl-ups (one partner is in curl-up position, the other is in dip position with his/her hands on the knees of the curl-up performer) |
| Clubs: | that number of around the clocks (the squad standing in a circle with hands joined, they run around the circle and back as quickly as they can) |

Bird's nest: The class is divided in small groups. Each group has a "bird's nest" which might be represented by a cone with a hula hoop around it. Nine or so bins are located throughout the play space. Different objects are in the different bins (bean bags in one, nerf balls in another, jump ropes another, etc.). Each bin should have the same number of equipment pieces as there are total students.

The game simply has all the students running at once. Each student's assignment is to retrieve all nine objects, one at a time, and place them in his/her "nest."

Daytona speedway: The class stands around the perimeter of a square about 30 feet per side. The game is progressive in nature. To begin, two of the opposing lines walk across the square and back without touching anyone (this speed is first gear). Then the other two lines follow suit. Next the activity is repeated at a slow jog (second gear) and finally at a fast but controlled speed (third gear).

When these levels have been demonstrated without crashes and fender benders the entire progressive process is repeated with all four lines going at once.

Partner variations of this game can be fun. One child can drive his/her partner stock car fashion. The child playing the car might have his/her hand up as protective bumpers. Possibilities involve motorcycle events, Mac Truck races (groups of 4), or nighttime driving in which the vehicles have their eyes closed. Of course, nighttime events must be done in first gear.

Indianapolis speedway: This is a circular relay race. The class is divided into teams (pit crews or grease monkeys) who remain on the infield of a racetrack. When the race is started with a green flag one member from each team races counter-clockwise around the track to tag a teammate who then becomes the racing car. The teams are responsible for keeping count of the number of laps their team has completed. The race will have been set at 10 or 15 laps. When they have achieved this number they are to sit in a straight line and raise their hands.

To add further spice to the atmosphere the teacher introduces commands like "flat tires" "blow outs" and "crash & burns." When "flat tire" is called all the children in racing car mode must stop and do five jumping jacks before continuing onward. "Blow out" means three push-ups are needed. "Crash & burn" is yet more serious. The car crashes to the ground and their pit-crew rushes to their aid. They pick-up or drag the disabled car back to the pit-stop and then send the next car on its way.

I also like to further build upon the *anticipatory set* by playing race music, waving a checked flag, and having victory laps to cool down the engines.

Tag Games

Here are a few guidelines it is good to keep in mind when playing any tag game. (1) Have more than one person it. If only one person is it he/she may not be able to catch anyone and thus is placed in an embarrassing position. (2) Make sure boundaries are established and enforced. Without them the children will run far away and into dangerous areas. (3) Make sure the "it" people are easily identifiable to avoid confusion. Pennies, hats or large balls make for good distinguishing markers. (4) I also have a rule of *killing it before it dies.* That means I do not need to feel that the game must be played until the last person is tagged. After the children have had good exercise, but before their interest has waned, I terminate the game. By so doing the children will be eager to play the game another day.

Walking tag: Everyone has a partner. Within each pair one is designated the initial chaser (perhaps the taller of the pair, the one with the cleanest shoes, etc.). At the beginning command the "its" must spin once around before beginning the chase. As indicated by the name, walking is how everyone locomotors. When touched the tagged person spins around once and assumes the role of chaser.

The idea behind the spinning around is that it gives the fleeing person a chance to get a small lead. Requiring walking is also a good initial rule for minimizing collisions while still requiring a lot of activity.

Two good variations of this game are *couple tag* and *monster tag*. In *couple tag* pairs of students with hooked elbows play other pairs. Before initiating the chase the partners much pivot around in hooked elbow position. The chaser is the monster in *monster tag*. In this game I let the children reverse roles at anytime they wish. This role switching can be done by the fleeing student suddenly pivoting about and letting out a scream. This means he/she has metamorphosed into the monster. "Monster Mash" music goes well with all the screaming of the class.

Variants of basic tag: The format of basic tag has a few "it" people (as designated by balls, pennies, etc.) trying to tag any of the non-"it" people. When someone is tagged he/she is never long eliminated from the action. There are two concepts for accomplishing his/her re-entry.

Unfreezing oneself concept: *Jumping jack tag* or *push-up tag* would be examples. After being tagged, five jumping jacks or three push-ups will respectively get you back in the game. *Circuit tag* would see the tagged persons running outside the tag area where a circuit has been set-up. After navigating themselves through the circuit they flow back into the tag activity. *Samurai warrior tag* is an exciting one for the younger children. The teacher is the Samurai warrior, replete with robe and sword. Those who have been tagged go to the warrior to be saved. The warrior strikes the sword to the ground and simultaneously yells "Samurai warrior will save you!" Then the sword is swung over the heads and under the legs of those children, carefully of course. The children duck and jump and then return to tag.

Unfreezing others concept: Tagged people assume a stationary position signaling that they have been tagged and need to be rescued. In *tunnel tag* they stand with their legs apart and if some non-"it" person crawls through their legs they are enabled to re-join the game. In *shake-and-bump tag* the tagged individuals stand with their right arms out in front of them. They are unfrozen when someone comes by, gives their hand a shake and bumps hips with them.

Variants of Everyone it tag: In its simplest form everyone is "it" and tries to run about tagging everyone else. No one is eliminated, if you are tagged it only means that that person scored a point. There is much high intensity activity when everyone is "it" so usually the games will need to be stopped within a minute or so.

Beanbag tag is the same as everyone it tag except now the students score points by throwing their bean bags to hit somebody's foot. Requiring the beanbags to be slid or bowled is a good variation. *Bum tag* is the same as beanbag tag but now nerf or yarn balls are thrown at the backsides of others. *First aid tag* has everyone "it" at the start. When someone is tagged he/she is wounded and must hold that body part with one hand. He/she can still tag others with the free hand. When tagged a second time that wound also must be held. With no hands available for tagging those people are incapable of further tagging but are yet alive and can continue to run about. A third tag brings death.

Variants of multiplying "its" tag: These tag games begin with one or two people being "it" (remember the danger of having a slower student being it by him/herself). *One-arm bandit tag* has the "it" person chasing everyone else. He/she is identifiable because one arm is held behind his/her back. When anyone is tagged that person puts one arm behind him/her and also becomes a bandit. *Snake-pit tag* is a favorite of younger students. The snake pit is the area within the boundaries of the tag game. The boundaries are made more confined than normal because the "it" person is a snake and thus can only crawl and slither about. When someone has been touched (bitten) by the snake, he/she joins the snakehood. In *Home-on-the-range tag* the "it" is a pair of hand-in-hand students. The "it" pair represents a horse and rider. All else are steers out on the range valuing their liberty. When the horse and rider tags a steer they take it back to a corral area. After a second steer has been added to the corral the two steers form a horse and rider and join the round-up.

Relays

A few suggestions for relays. (1) Be a good official. If you are keeping track of times or comparing team performances, you must ensure that the skills are being done according to specifications. (2) Keep the finishing lines well away from walls so as to afford safe stopping distance. (3) Have a discernible finishing position. Sitting in a straight line with their hands up would serve well. (4) I prefer relays in which more than one person goes at a time and thus the amount of cooperation and on-task time is increased.

Train relay: The squads hook together in a straight line, hands on the waist of the person in front of them. They must not become disconnected throughout the race. At the turnaround on a down and back course it is best to simply turn around so that their order is reversed on the return trip (this avoids a dangerous whip cracking effect).

Circle-of-friends relay: The squads form circle-of-friends by joining hands around one of their teammates. The object is to race in this formation, taking the inner person down and back the course. This is then repeated for each member of the squad being given the escort.

Shuttle relay: The squads are lined-up, hands joined, with the center persons straddling a centerline. When the race begins the lines run or slide in one direction and then the other in a designated pattern. On a basketball court a good sequence is back and forth from foul line to foul line, baseline to baseline, foul line to foul line, and then back to center position.

Rescue relay: The object here is to move the squad from one location to another. The squad leaders are positioned at the opposite end of the play area. The race begins with the leaders running to their squad, grabbing the first member by the hand and taking them back to the other area. The squad leaders' task is done and they remain there. The first transported member goes back to get member number two and takes them back. This repeats itself until everyone has been transposed to the new location. To further increase activity and teamwork *Accumulative rescue relay* can be played. In this version the leader takes the first member back in the same fashion but then returns with the first member to pick-up the second member, and third member, etc. Clearly the squad leaders earn their running stars.

Reindeer relay: The squads are arranged with one member sitting on a carpet or blanket holding one end of a rope (this is Santa). The other team members hold onto the other end of the rope (they are reindeer). The task of each Santa is to deliver, one at a time, a number of objects (gifts) to a bucket at the other end of the gym. Rotating Santas and reindeer after each trip is fun. Keep the anticipatory set rolling with Christmas music and sleigh bells.

Activities to Music

Shoe aerobics: This is your basic aerobics class led by an instructor but with one difference, everybody has their shoes on their hands. With strongly beating music can you not imagine all the slapping of the soles together, over-the-head, behind the back, under the legs, crab walking, hands and knees, etc. It is not hard to think of things to do once you get started.

Any prop will do. *The Paper dance* is simply playing with some energizing music and a piece of paper. For example, how about putting on the fast paced "Let's Get Ready to Rumble" and then waving, swinging, fanning, turning, folding, wadding, tossing, and stomping the paper.

Shape museum: One half of the class assume original static shapes and hold them. The rest of the students jog around and through the museum of shapes. When a moving child finds an interesting shape he/she stops and creates a new shape in front of that person. That person says "thank you" and is unfrozen to join the joggers. The game continues in this fashion with half the class always posed in shapes and half the class moving. Mellow music generally works good.

A more vigorous variation of this game is called the *Dynamic shape museum*. The difference here is that the shapes are moving in place, jogging in place, jumping jacks, twisting, bending, and so on. More up-tempo music can be used.

Act-react: The teacher does a movement for a set number of counts (maybe 8 or 16) and then stops. As soon as the teacher stops, the class then mimics what they saw. As soon as they are done the teacher executes another movement segment and the game continues back and forth. Stationary movements such as jumping jacks and arm circles are the easiest with which to begin. Next, side-to-side and back-and-forth movements can be incorporated.

I have known dance instructors to progress to much more intricate movement skills and to increase their segments lengths to 32 or 64 counts. Also, they may even eliminate the lag time to create continuous leader and student movement. In other words, the instructor never stops moving and the followers replicate everything while remaining a set number of counts behind. You can see how this would be a good test of attention abilities.

4 wall game: It doesn't get much simpler than this and still be exciting. Signs are posted on the four walls. One day's example might be (1) head & shoulders, (2) arms, (3) hips & knees, and (4) whole body jump & bounce. When the leader shouts "one" the students turn as fast as possible to face that wall and begin moving their head & shoulders creatively in time with the music. When another number is called they quickly rotate to it and move the prescribed body part(s). Up-beat music should be used; "Whole Lota Shakin" is a good one that comes to mind.

Criss-cross game: Groups of children are at the four corners of a square. One group leads with an activity across the center of the floor. They may be individually sliding, skipping or crawling; or they may be hooked together as a team as they do some locomotor skill. When the opposite group sees what the approaching group is doing they duplicate it by weaving through them in route to the vacated corner. As soon as these groups have cleared out of the center the side groups follow suite.

The game continues in this manner with the children thinking up new movements and patterns. After one group has led the activities for five or six times the other groups should be given their chance at leadership. I have known this game to flow for an extended period of time. In introducing this game there is one point that may be worth making to the students; tell them that a considerate activity selection would be one that everyone in the class should be able to perform. For instance, leading with a handspring would be inappropriate because there will be some who cannot do it and maybe someone would be injured in making an attempt.

Me and my shadow: Everyone is moving in a line following whatever actions the head person initiates. When anyone wishes to begin a new activity he/she can separate from the line and begin a new activity. Followers can stick with the same leader, follow the new or chart their own course. This game usually results in a good mix of followers and leaders. I have learned that if you don't want a group always tagging after you the initiation of something akin to one-handed push-ups will result in a winged dispersal.

Partner mirroring is a similar game in which one partner faces and mirrors the actions of the leader. The command is frequently given to change leaders and to quickly find someone new to continue the game. *Small group mirroring* is the same game but with a group of about four students in a circle. They are numbered one through four and take turns being the leader. *Creative circle* is simply having the entire class in a circle with each child in turn assuming directorship. This game seems to work better after the children have had some leadership experiences in the less intimidating partner or small group versions.

Dance

Golden Oldies

There are many oldies but goodies that should not be forgotten. It is tough to beat *The Twist*, *YMCA*, *Limbo*, *Electric slide*, *The Stroll*, etc. Here are a couple of my favorites.

Bunny hop: You have been deprived if you haven't already done this in your salad days. The basic step is an easily learned one for probably third graders on. Two hopping side-touches are made with the right foot, two hopping side-touches are made with the left foot, then a jump is made forward (a jump is performed with both feet), a jump made backward, and then three forward jumps. I like to initiate the dance with everyone doing it on their own. Then, as the dance progresses people can start hooking together by grasping the waist of someone else. In the end you might have an interesting snake line. I have an Elvis Presly "I'm All Shook Up" tape that works great.

Hand jive: Here is the way I learned it.
Clap both hands to thighs twice
Clap hands together twice
Wave R hand twice over the L hand
Wave L hand twice over the R hand
Hit the R fist on top of the L fist twice
Hit the L fist on top of the R fist twice
Hitchhike the R thumb over your shoulder twice
Hitchhike the L thumb over your shoulder twice

Folk Dance

I like to adapt folk dances to match the developmental needs of the children. That means I feel free to change the skills involved to make them simpler, or more complex, or more physically demanding. Also, I like to get the activity initiated right away with little worry about all the slowing organizational aspects such as boy-girl pairings, group formations, and highly specific sequences of steps. Here is how you can do that with a couple of fun folk dances (music and complete instructions for these could be easily obtained where folk and children's music is sold).

Mexican hat dance (La Raspa): The basic step is called a "bleeking" step. This is where you jump up and place your right foot out in front of you with the heel touching the floor. Then you reverse and do the same with your left. The basic rhythm is easily established by the music: three bleeking steps (R,L,R), followed by a pause, three more "bleeking" steps (R,L,R), followed by a pause, etc.

To get immediate action, everyone attempts this step to the music (If first and second graders cannot do it you might see if they can simply jump up and down to the music's rhythm.). When the "bleeking" segment of the music is over the children could individually jog or skip randomly around until you cue them that the "bleeking" segment is about to begin again. If time and the skills of the children permit you can begin the expansion process: two quick hand claps can be added during the pause between the "bleeking" steps. During the locomotoring phase everyone can find the closest person for a partner to skip beside in a big, two-by-two class circle. During the next locomotoring phase you might ask for right and left elbow turns with partners.

You can see that the above procedure gradually leads to an approximation of the "official" dance. Sometimes it might be educational to get to a culturally correct version of the dance, but that does not always have to be the goal. I have taught a conditioning variation of this dance where all movements were done in crab position.

Troika (three horses): This is a popular Russian folk dance. The music has a good running tempo that gradually increases to a challenging speed. In the "official" dance everyone is in a big circle with groups of threes running counter-clockwise together. Sixteen counts of running is followed by some dishrag movements, a circling of the 3s with grapevine steps and stomping.

An effective progressive instructional approach is to have the children running solo to the music. Beginning variations might consist of directional changes, stomping during the easily recognizable ending beats, running with one or two partners. Slightly more complex elements might be added later: circling of groups of threes, dishrag movement in groups of three, grapevine circling of groups of threes, etc.

Macarena: I like to teach the macarena movements and then see if the students can do them while performing various locomotor skills: walking, jogging, skipping, sliding, galloping, cariocaing. Okay, if that is a piece of cake, add to the challenge with a muscular strength and/or muscular endurance version in a curl-up or push-up position.

R palm down, L palm down
R palm up, L palm up
R hand to L shoulder, L hand to R shoulder
R hand to head, L hand to head
R hand to L waist, L hand to R waist
R hand to R hip, L hand to L hip
Stand still and hula, hula, hula, clap

Square Dance

Scatter square dance is application of the same instantly active organizational progressions used in the other dances. The children dance their way through an expanding list of square dance skills that are intermixed with fun cooperative stunts and imitations (see Figure 11.1). To teach scatter square dance three things are needed. (1) A listing of activities on a large poster. This displayed referral list will make your calling easy and will help the rehearsal of the children. (2) A lengthy compilation of music. This can be either traditional square dance music or more popular country tunes. (3) A microphone system. This activity will work beautifully if your calls can be heard, but confusion worse than death will ensue if your voice is overcome by the music and the sounds of the stomping-clapping children.

You will find that calling scatter square dance is not difficult and can be delightful. Experience, and the children's input, will quickly suggest improvements and additions to your list. Having the children keep repeating the skill over and over until you decide what next to call helps them learn it better and provides you time to think what next to call.

Figure 11.1. Scatter Square Dance Call Sheet and Descriptors

1. Keep time to the music	head, shoulders, elbows, hips, knees, toes, walking in place
2. Hit the lonesome trial	moving in all different directions in time with the music
3. Wave to those you pass	
4. Say "Hi to you"	
5. Do Si Do a partner	arms are folded and partners walk around each other right shoulder to right shoulder
6. Turn a partner	right elbows hooked*
7. Circle up two with someone new	partner circles are done with two hands
8. Turn one by yourself	make some turns—don't let this one continue too long or dizziness results
9. Honor your partner	bows and curtsies—if this is too old fashion I suppose you could substitute something hip
10. Find a friend and promenade	moving with a partner hand in hand
11. Horse and rider	one person put hands on shoulders of another and rides his/her horse
12. Circle up 3, go back the other way	circle out direction and then the other
13. Hook up a horse & buggy	two people hook elbows and a third, with hands on their shoulders, drives
14. Right hand star	partners touch right hands in a raised position and walk forward around
15. Left hand star	partners touch left hands in a raised position and walk forward around
16. Shoot that star	from a star position the hands are pushed against each other and both sent away
17. Back up that star	walking backward

continued on next page

---

* I began by saying "swing" a partner but soon discovered that swings suggested a too vigorous action to the energetically disposed.

18. Birdie in a cage (duck, frog, etc.)	three people join hands in a circle around a fourth—that person is a bird, duck, frog, etc. and acts the part
19. Dive for the oyster	form a group of four, two partners stoop under the arms of the other pair and come back out
20. Dig for the clam	same dive for the oyster action by the other pair
21. Four leaf clover	two partners stoop under the arms of the other pair and then turn away from each other to end the group in a wrapped clover pattern
22. Follow the wagon trail behind _ & _	partners are promenading in a line behind a designated pair
23. Circle up that wagon train	everyone promenading in a circle
24. Follow the wagon train, make a tunnel, others go through	lead couple makes an arch which the others pass under
25. Circle up wagon train, all join hands in one big ring	
26. Circle to the left (and right)	
27. Go into the middle and come back out	
28. Go in once again, come back out with a great big grin	
29. Now into the middle and give a little shout	
30. Circle wagon train with your partner	
31. Inside person move up one	by moving in front of partners a single file circle should result
32. Face your partner, join right hands	you have set the stage for the Grand right & left
33. Grand right & left	past your partner, left hand to next person on your way, right to next, etc. until home
34. Weave	same as Grand right & left but with arms folded and passing shoulders
35. When home Do Si Do and promenade around the ring	remind them of this as they are enroute about the circle

Cooperative/New Games

Levitations: The entire class lies down on their backs with their heads on a line. The direction in which they are oriented is alternated so that if the first child has his/her feet in a northern direction and next child's feet are to the south. This results in people being ear to ear in what I call a zipper formation. The first command is to have all the lying down students extend their arms into the air to form a row of supporting hands. At one end of the line I have a volunteer whom I will gently place on those hands. That levitated person will be rigid, facing toward the ceiling, and prepared to be passed head first down the row of hands. I will move to the other end of the line to receive the child when the passing nears completion.

I have seen a number of variations to this game. Sometimes instead of lying down the students are seated in a row. They are all close together, facing the same direction with their hands above their heads. The levitated person is passed in the same manner but of course is somewhat higher above the ground. Because of the greater height there should be a spotter walking on each side of the column. Then, to take this game to yet new heights it is possible to have the class standing close together instead of sitting. This can be exciting in the extreme but might necessitate that there are more than one strong spotter on each side of the floating child.

Levitations can also be played with the children lying on their backs in a circle, their heads together and legs radiating outwards spoke fashion. After the levitating child is positioned on their circle of hands, they attempt to produce a rotating motion. Sometimes it is possible to get a fairly rapid ride.

Lap game: Begin by having the class stand in a circle. Everyone is facing the same direction, either clockwise or counter-clockwise. They are close enough together so that they can easily place their hands on the waist of the person in front of them. The instructor gives the command, "On my knees, please." On "please" everyone is to sit down on the thighs of whoever is behind them. If all do it together it will work. If someone hesitates you are likely to have a laughing collapse. When there has not been a collapse I will ask for the releasing of hips and the waving of hands. An almost sure way to end in a pile is to have everyone attempt to make three small, synchronized steps backwards.

Knots: This game works best with about 8 to 10 students per group. Everyone stands in a small circle and puts his/her hands into the center. Hands are joined with others. The only stipulation is that (1) you must not hold both hands of another person nor (2) can you be holding one of the hands of a person immediately on your left or right. After this positioning has been accomplished the group's task is to untangle themselves without letting go of hands. It usually is not easy but it should always be possible to make it into a circle or two links of a chain.

Blind run: Form two parallel lines facing each other, about 6 feet apart. Players stand in their lines at least two arms' lengths apart (forming a lane of about 25 feet is good). Once the lines are formed and people are paying attention, a person on one end of the lines runs between the lines from one end to the other with his/her eyes closed. The two people at the end where the runner winds up take care to let the runner know they have come to the end of the line by gently tapping on the shoulder or hip, and, if the runner continues, with the word "stop." The end people should not try to forcibly stop the runner. For a second or third turn, runners can spin around before running and periodically during the whole run.

Touch my can: The concept is simple but it can be challenging when you have a class of thirty or more students. Two people support a pop can between them by each pushing against it with one of his/her fingertips. The rest on the class join in with their fingertips. The objective is for everyone to be touching the can but without touching anyone else in the class.

Body surfing: The entire class, except for one surfer, lies face down in a line, shoulder to shoulder. When the instructor yells "surfs up!" everyone begins continuously rolling in the same direction. It is imperative that everyone remains close together so as to avoid gaps. With the current flowing the surfer gently extends onto the waves and is transported along in prone position. The surfer needs to follow a path near the shoulder level of the students and not slide down to the legs and feet.

If you felt it best to reduce the amount of body contact, a small gymnastic mat could be used as a surfboard.

Around the clock: The class joins hands in a circle. From here on all that is involved is having the group locomotor around the circle. For example, everyone slides once around and back, or jogs twice around and twice back. Challenges can be introduced by timing how long it takes them to jog around a back, three times. The game requires cooperation because some children will be slower than others and thus some must learn to moderate their pace if others are not to be pulled down or become unattached.

Individual Challenge Stunts

Ski boogying: Everyone stands next to a line. On command they begin to jump from side to side over the line as quickly as possible. I usually challenge them to do their maximum in one minute. Jumping 145 times is considered simmering, 160 warm, 175 cooking, and 185 hot stuff. Slanty rope challenges can be created by providing wider lines or objects to jump over.

Fish hawk dive: Everyone is given a piece of paper that they fold lengthwise in half. They place the paper on the floor, standing on end. Then they balance in front of the paper on one knee and foot. The task is to dip forward and pick the paper up with one's mouth; balance must be maintained even after the paper has been raised.

While others continue to practice, those who have achieved the skill are next required to lay the paper on its side and thus must dip lower to reach it. Beyond that, there is a standing variation called the *Crane dive.* This is tough but can be done by some.

Crazy walk: This is a task in which the children walk forward, but with a catch. The catch being that the free foot much come forward from around behind the support leg. With proper shifting of weight it is possible to place the swing foot ahead of the other and thus make slow but consistent transit. After some practice *crazy walk* races can be fun. One foot must remain on the ground at all times.

Blind stand: The task is simply or not so simply this. Stand on your toes, extend your arms out in front, close your eyes, and then hold that position. I consider 15 seconds simmering, 20 warm, 25 cooking, and 30 hot stuff. Try the one-foot version.

Human tops: Attempt to jump and spin halfway around (180 degrees) and land in good balance. Challenge them to do it in both directions. More advanced progressions would be 270s, 360s and one foot variants of them.

Foot drills: Place markings on the floor using tape or poly spots. All sorts of configurations can be laid out: circle, seven, Z, eight, triangle, etc. The task is to as quickly as possible do repeated, two footed jumps around the circle, up and down the seven, up the Z and back, etc. The spots need to be only about a foot apart and it is fun to keep the distances standardized so that self-improvement goals can be set and realized.

Cooperative Partner Stunts

Scooter: Two children sit facing each other. The feet of each are underneath the others bottom. They reach forward and place their hands on their partner's shoulders. After this positional unit has been achieved they attempt to begin rocking back and forth so that one's bottom and then the other's come off of the ground. If this can be done, one of the children must learn to slightly extend his/her legs when the other's weight is lifted and shifted backwards. With practice they will gradually get the feel of being able to progress across the floor. Eventually they might be ready for scooter races.

Pop-ups: Person 1 is in push up position. Person 2 crawls under the bridge formed by person 1 and stands up. Person 1 now flattens out on his/her stomach and person 2 jumps over the top of person 1. The progression continues and the idea is to see how many pop-ups the partners can do in a set time.

Partner-lean: Partners side by side with a partner. Each person's feet are together and as close to the other's as possible. Their inside hands are tightly clasped. The task is for them to lean away from each other until their joined arms are completely straightened. If the children do not slowly and cooperatively work against one another balance will be lost. When a fully extended position is held the instructor or another student should be able to pass between them.

Double top: Partners literally stand toe to toe. They tightly clasp one another's hands and in slow unison lean away from each other. After they have achieved a fully extended lean they are to begin to take tiny steps around each other. If a good lean has been established a fast marry-go-round spinning action is producible. Make sure they know to not let go of their partner, and make sure the grouping are well spaced so there is not a chance of them crashing into other human tops.

Seated cycling: Two children sit facing each other. They raise their legs so as to put the soles of their feet together. Next they attempt to establish a cycling leg motion, slow at first and then more rapidly. A good expansion of this skill is to add the hands so that they are maintaining both the hands and feet in a coordinated cadence.

Up and at 'em: From a standing position, partners hold a ball in between their foreheads. The challenge is to lower their bodies to a push-up and then prone position without touching the ball with their hands or dropping it. And then of course, the process must be reversed to a standing position again. *Partner ball carries* are also fun. Students attempt to move from one location to another. Negotiating obstacles can add excitement. Also, the ball carries do not need to be restricted to the head-to-head position. Consider head-to-back, back-to-back, shoulder-to-shoulder, etc. (Group carries are also great, five people carrying four balls, etc.)

Activities with Ropes

Ropes offer many options for enjoyable challenges for individuals and groups. It should not be too difficult to get individual ropes for each child (the best fit is when stood on the rope will come up to the armpits), a number of Double-Dutch length ropes (these are about 8 to 10 feet), and a big long, heavy duty one (about 25 to 30 feet).

Before beginning to handle the ropes a good warm-up procedures is to have everyone lay their rope in a circle on the floor. Endless exercises can be done around and through them. Many similar things can be done when lain in a straight line.

When the ropes are picked-up and being used, a good *home position* is for everyone to stand on the center of the rope.

Individual jump-rope challenges: The idea here is to make a sizable list of stunts for the children in work on, both in class and at home and recess. To meet the needs of all the students, the list should include easier stunts as well as advanced ones (Figure 11.2). Incentives can be provided for demonstrated improvements. For example, they could qualify for a "Skipper's Club" or participate in a jump routine.[1]

Jump routines: This is where you choreograph the children's jumping skills to music. For a beginning level group an effective formation is to have two line facing each other. For the first 16 counts or so, the members of the lead line do a step to the music (maybe the basic jumping in place). For the following 16 counts they stop while the other line follows their suite. The routine continues back and forth in this alternating manner. The advantage of this procedure is that it gives the lines time to rest and an opportunity to plan the next step. The skills can be kept fairly simple such as running in place, one foot jumping, or the boxer step. If some children have mastered only one or two skills there is no reason they cannot be assigned more fundamental movements than their teammates.

When higher levels of skills are possessed the skills and patterns can be made as demanding as you wish. The skills of cross-overs and double jumps can be add; patterns where the teams exchange positions and simultaneously travel in circles can be instituted.

Cooperative task assignments: A variety of partner and small group challenges can be designed. Figure 7.2 provides an example of a task style teaching approach. What is nice about this is that the different groupings of children can work at their own rate on different skills. Different skills can be added to those of rope jumping. For instance, a ball can be dribbled, passed, and shot at baskets. I usually set ten or fifteen jumps as being the criterion that is necessary before a skill is considered accomplished.

Double-Dutch: Even if you are not an experienced Double-Dutcher it might be possible to involve your class in this exciting challenge. Very likely there will be some students in your class, or the older grades, who both know how and would be eager to help with instruction. Another, simpler way of jumping duel ropes is the *egg-beater*. Two swingers hold a Double-Dutch length rope and two other swingers have their rope at a right angle to them, so that the ropes are crossed in the center. If the two groups begin swinging at the same time the egg-beater effect is achieved and one or multiple children can dare to enter the center for jumping. It looks harder than it actually is.

Long rope jumping: There are many things that can be done with a long rope. *Run throughs* are where the rope is swung and one child after another runs into and immediately exits on the opposite side. I like to have everyone continue jogging around so that the entire class creates a non-stop jogging circle. See how many laps can be completed.

Doing *paired run throughs* demands more cooperation and it also dictates that the pace of the joggers be increased. They will have to go twice as fast as the singles did if they expect to maintain a continuous flow through the rope. Because the outside partners have to run much faster than their partners I sometimes specify a figure 8 pattern; if a clockwise turn is followed on the first run through a counter-clockwise path will be taken on the next. To moderate the faster pace of the partner format, the skill can be changed to require the execution of one jump before the partners escape.

---

[1] I do not favor charting each student's progress on a publicly displayed chart. Although such a procedure will be motivating to some students, the lesser skilled can find it disheartening. I would rather everyone had a chart in his/her own portfolio and learned to focus primarily on self-improvement as opposed to social comparison.

Figure 11.2. Individual Jump Rope Challenges

Stunts

1. _____ Basic 1/2 time jumping of rope swung by others (50 times) (1/2 time jumping is a slow jump with a small bounce in-between)

2. _____ Basic 1/2 time jumping self-swung (50 times)

3. _____ Basic full-time jumping of rope swung by others (50 times)

4. _____ Basic full-time jumping self-swung (50 times)

5. _____ One foot jumping (50 times)

6. _____ Boxer step (50 times) (hopping on right foot twice, left foot twice, etc.)

7. _____ Bleeking step (50 times) (Bleeking is alternating heel touches)

8. _____ Running in place (50 times)

9. _____ Basic backwards spin (50)

10. _____ Criss-crosses (10 times)

11. _____ Consecutive criss-crosses (10 times)

12. _____ Double twirls (10 times)

13. _____ Consecutive double twirls (10 times)

14. _____ Consecutive under the legs (10 times)

15. _____ Egg beater jumping (20 times)

16. _____ Double Dutch jumping (20 times)

Conditioning Challenges

17. _____ Running one lap around the gym

18. _____ Running 5 laps around the gym

19. _____ Skipping one lap around the gym

20. _____ 2 minute basic jumping

21. _____ 5 minute basic jumping

22. _____ 10 minute basic jumping

Addition jumping is having someone jumping the long swinging rope and then others keep joining in. The object is to see how many can be jumping at once. I have seen whole classes of elementary children doing it with the instructor jumping with a small child on his shoulders. What do you think to be the maximum number of elementary age jumpers?[2]

Jumping the shot: This game also makes use of the extra long rope but it does so in a much different manner. A heavy rubber ball or a number of bean bags are placed in a sock which in turn is tied to the end of the rope. The instructor or instructor's aid kneels in the center of the floor and begins to swing the rope over his/her head much like a cowboy lariat. Gradually more rope is let out so that the end of the rope with the sock is traveling close to the ground. The children who are positioned beyond the circumference move in until they must start jumping over the rope as it swings past. If most everyone is being too hesitant I have required that they join hands in a circle around the swinger. This draws everyone into the action and maybe you will be able to have the whole class jumping in wave fashion.

With more skill and daring students can intersperse tricks in between the jumps (touching the floor, hitting the deck, 3 jumping jacks, etc.).

It is also possible to *run against the current* or *run with the current*. *Running against the current* means the student(s) run inside the circle in direction opposite the spinning rope. Frequent leaps are necessary. *Running with the current* might sound easier but is actually harder. You have to be really fast to get around and out before the rope catches you and if you don't make it in time the timing of your leap is more difficult.

Activities with Hula Hoops

As with ropes or other implements, the number of games and activities that can be done is limited only by our creativity and that of the children. I like to begin with each child having a hoop to warm-up around, over, and through. A good *home position* for hoops is on the floor with the student standing inside it.

Spinning: The easiest spinning is around the wrist and forearm. With practice the non-dominant arm can be used, it can be transferred back and forth from arm to arm. Different locomotor skills can be done at the same time. Perhaps they can learn to pass the hoop from their arm to that of another, while they are skipping.

Spinning can also be done around the neck, waist, and ankle.

Hoop imaginings: The younger children especially like to pretend. Here are some ideas: hoops above heads—angels, hoops in front of face—mirrors, hoops hanging on ears—world's largest earring, hoops in front—race car steering wheels, hoops around necks—plow horses, hoops around waist—zooming, swooping spaceships.

Twirling: The hoop is set on end and is given a vigorous wrist snap so that it twirls on end for a period of time. All the children will be able to do this to some degree. While the hoop is twirling the children can see how many jumping jacks or push-ups they can do. They can locomotor around it: running, sliding facing in, sliding facing out, etc. Partners can start their twirls at the same time and run around each other's hoops. The whole class can start on command and see if they can give high 10s to five different people and still get back home to catch their hoop before it stops wobbling.

---

[2] Two hundred twenty children did 13 jumps.

If a child waits until the hoop starts to wobble toward the floor, he/she can jump into the hoop and out again without being "bit" by it. A goal might be to see how many times you can enter and exit before it stops.

Rover: Producing a "Rover" hoop will be difficult for many students but there will be others who can learn it. In this trick you are throwing the hoop out ahead of you with a wrist snap that imparts backspin to it. If enough spin has been applied the hoop will come back home to you like the good dog Rover being called. If some of the students can get hoops rolling like this they and others can practice running beside and around it, straddle jumping over it, or even diving through it. I have had some students diving back and forth through one as many as eight times before it stopped.

Musical hoops: This game is much like the old familiar musical chairs. The hoops are lying about the floor as the children weave about them to music. When the music stops everyone scrambles to get inside a hoop. If you like you can remove a couple of hoops so that two students will be caught without a hoop. Adhering to our rule of not eliminating people from activities I would suggest merely giving them a point and then letting them continue in the action. There are a variety of positions which might be assumed in the hoops: one foot balance, crab position, two body parts touching inside the hoop and two outside, three in and one out, etc. It is also fun to call numbers indicating how many people are to swiftly get inside of one hoop.

Hoop drills: Squads of about six children each are lined up. In front of each squad is a row of six or seven hoops, spaced approximately six inches to a foot apart. The challenge is to traverse through the hoops in a variety of ways without stepping on the hoops. For example, the squad leader might leap through all the hoops so that he/she is stepping only inside each hoop. His/her squad members follow immediately behind. It works best if the leader has traveled some distance beyond the last hoop to permit room for the following students to finish their leaps. When they have been given this much room you can have the last student turn around and lead the same activity back through with the squad now in reverse order.

Besides leaping through the hoops the assignment might be to: slide, skip, weave, or follow some hop-scotch pattern (one, two, one, two; one, two, three, one, two, three). Connecting the squads together increases the challenge: sliding with hands joined, train fashion with hands on hips, train fashion while weaving about the hoops, etc.).

Of course these drills can be turned into relay races in which the teams compete against their own times or the other squads. Generally, with enough variety, it will not be necessary to add this competitive element. Also, I have found that racing through the hoops greatly increases the chance of someone tripping. Taping the hoops to the floor or using floor markings would be the more prudent and safe thing to do.

Poison hoops: This game can be played in a whole class circle or in separate squads. When in a squad formation everyone is in a line with his/her hands joined. A pile of hoops are lying in front of the first person. The leader picks-up one hoop with his/her free hand and wiggles the hoop through his/her body to the next person. The next person, without the use of hands wiggles and sends it on down the line. The group's task is to convey all the hoops from the head person to the last person, and back again.

I have also heard of this game being played where everybody is lined up facing the same direction. They are connected by reaching one of their hands backwards between their legs and the other hand forward to grasp the hand coming from between the legs of the person in front of them. Oh what a tangled web we weave . . .

Activities with Beanbags

I have suggested games with beanbags in other places of this text so I will introduce only a couple new ones here. I good home position for beanbags is balanced on top of heads. This certainly restricts fidgeting.

Quick hands: Partners are seated crossed legged facing each other. A beanbag is placed directly between. When the teacher calls "ready" students place their hands on their thighs. When the teacher calls "right," "left," or "both," the students react by grabbing for the bag with the appropriate hand or hands. Sundry starting conditions can be stipulated: hands on hips, over eyes, behind back, on head. Also, there are other possibilities besides the seated position: push-up and curl-up position.

Put and take: One person is in push-up position facing his/her seated partner. The seated person has a beanbag resting in each hand; palms up. On a signal the push up person reaches up and takes one bean bag and puts it on the floor, then reaches up with the opposite hand and removes the second beanbag. When both beanbags are on the floor, the push-up person reverses the procedure by sequentially moving the bags from the floor to the hands. The object is to see how many can be moved in a given time period.

Activities with a Parachute

I strongly encourage you to consider getting a parachute. There are endless everyone-active activities you can do with them. The students love playing with it and it lends itself to a managed environment because everyone is holding on to a designated position.

To gain access I suggest first checking with your physical education specialist. If you need to purchase one they are not expensive and last for many years. The catalog references I listed in chapter 7 will have them in various sizes. Small ones big enough for six people will be 15–20 dollars while extra large ones with 36 handles will be approximately 350 dollars.

Merry-Go-Round: Everyone holds with L or R hand and walk, hop, slide, gallop, run, etc. Run while holding the chute like a kite.

Ocean Waves: Everyone holds the chute with both hands and shakes it. They will gladly do it and it will not take long for them to tire their arms. They can do this while moving also.

Circle the Ball: Place a playground ball on the raised chute. Make the ball roll around the chute in a clockwise or counter-clockwise direction. Try it with two balls, a large beach ball, or cage ball.

Popcorn: Place a number of bean bags (6–10) on the chute. Shake the chute to make them rise like popping corn. When I do the same thing with jump ropes I call it *Poison Snakes*.

Team Ball: Divide the chute players in half, so each team defends half of the chute. Using two to six balls, and variety, try to bounce the balls off the opponent's side.

Umbrella: Everyone holds the chute with both hands and raises their arms in unison. Then, a moment later, they lower their arms (remaining in position).

Mushroom: Everyone raises the chute and walks forward; everyone lowers the chute and returns.

Fly Away: With the chute inflated, youngsters take one step forward. On command, they release the chute and it remains suspended in the air for several seconds. On command the class reaches for the ribs again. Care must be taken that the chute is not released too soon.

Ghost Town: Starting in the forward bend position, youngsters inflate the chute on command. They take three steps toward the center, stand still, leave go of the chute, and allow it to settle down on them.

Face Museum: Make an umbrella, pull it to the ground with everyone putting his/her head inside. It is fun to make faces. I have called this a *Rogue's Gallery* but may be you will not want to.

Amusement Ride: Make an umbrella, pull it to the ground with everyone sitting on the edge inside of the chute. Make it into an amusement or space ship ride by rocking forwards, backwards, and sidewards.

Mountain of Air: Youngsters umbrella the chute and then quickly bring the edges to the floor to trap the air (this time they are remaining on the outside). Students whose number has been called then crawl across the top until the air is all out.

Circular Dribble: Each child has a ball. The object is to run in circular fashion counter clockwise, holding onto the chute with the L hand and dribbling with the R hand. The dribble should be started first, then on signal, each starts to run. If a ball is lost, the child must recover the ball and try to hook on at his or her original place.

Run for it: Have the children around the chute and count off by fours. Start them running, holding the chute in one hand. Call out one of the numbers. Children holding the number immediately release their grip on the chute and run forward to the next vacated place. This means that they must put on a burst of speed.

Passing Under: Children have numbers. When called they run, hop, skip, etc. under the chute to a new vacated position. In addition to numbers it is fun to designate movers on the basis of things like hair color, white socks, shorts, handedness, or everyone with two ears.

* *Individual stunts:* go under and do 5 jumping-jacks, 2 push-ups, or may be both the jumping-jacks and push-ups.

* *Cooperative activities:* go under and shake hands with 2 people, or jumping high 10s with 3 people, or a patty-cake sequence.

* *Stunts with props:* go under and do 3 jump ropes, or hula hoop three revolutions (this results in some hoop collisions), or dribble behind your back, or pick up 5 bean bags.

Tug-Of-War: Divide class into two equal teams. On signal, they pull against each other and try to reach a restraining line. Another tug-of-war that is often more enjoyable for primary-age children is an individual pull, where all children tug in any direction they desire.

Horse and Jockey: Youngsters are paired off and standing evenly around the chute with the "horse" holding the chute waist high and legs in a straddle position. The "jockey" is in a squat position facing the "horse." On a signal all jockeys scramble between the horses' legs and speed away to the right running all the way around the chute and back to their horse. In the meantime, the horses have inflated the chute and then placed themselves on all fours, still holding the chute so the "jockeys" can mount their "horse" as they return back to the starting place. The first jockey to run around the chute and mount his horse is declared the winner. Partners can then exchange places.

Jaws: This makes for a good culminating game because it is a favorite and everyone ends up in a big laughing pile. The game begins with everyone sitting with the chute pulled tightly up to his/her chin. One person, the shark, swims about under the chute in search of prey. When the shark grabs some unfortunate's leg he/she gives a scream and is drug beneath the surface. Now there are two sharks and the waters become more and more dangerous.

Air Conditioning: This makes for a good cool down. Some of the children lay down under the chute and the rest of the fans them with air by repeating umbrellas.

The Big Sleep: This is the ultimate cool down. Everyone lays down under the chute with the edge pull up to his/her chin. I guarantee you will hear some snores.

Rhythms: Since many rhythms are by nature in a circular formation, the parachute lends itself very well to rhythms adaptations. In some instances it helps to overcome the stigma of "dancing" since the outcome seems to appear very different. Old standbys are things like the Hokey Pokey and Green Sleeves. Blow I have described two simple, well-known folkdances. By doing these I think you will see how easy it would be to do with others.

✳ *Pop! Goes the Weasel:*
    - count off by 2's; hold parachute in R hand
    - walk 12 steps then make umbrella
    - 1's pop under and move ahead one person
    - REPEAT

✳ *La Raspa (Mexican Hat Dance)*
    - Chorus
        Hop on L with R heel forward
        Hop on R with L heel forward
        Hop on L with R heel forward
        REPEAT 8 times
    - Umbrella up for 8 counts; umbrella down for 8 counts (REPEAT)
    - Chorus
    - Umbrella up of 8 counts; umbrella down for 8 counts (1's run under and exchange positions)
    - Umbrella up of 8 counts; umbrella down for 8 counts (2's run under and exchange positions)
    - Chorus
    - 16 count gallops with R hand on the parachute
    - 16 count gallops with L hand on the parachute
    -Chorus
    - Ripples (32 counts)
    - Chorus
    - 16 count gallops with R hand on the parachute
    - 8 count-put parachute to the ground

Questions for Reflection/Discussion

Name _____ Section _____

1. What would be a good activity idea to add to those presented in this chapter?

   _____
   _____
   _____
   _____
   _____
   _____

2. What may you have liked most about the text?

   _____
   _____
   _____
   _____
   _____
   _____

3. Can you think of a way in which this text could be improved?

   _____
   _____
   _____
   _____
   _____

This is a core of the resources that I have found to be especially useful. Many of them have been referred to in the text but there are others that have not. The list has been kept brief so that these important ones do not get lost in a crowd. Of course, most of these references have linkages if you wish to research further.

Web Sites

www.pecentral.org
This is the largest and most used web site for health and physical education teachers. It has just about everything you will want: lesson ideas of all kinds, assessment ideas, preschool physical education, instructional resources, health and physical education products, books and music, top web site links, and much more.

www.pelinks4u.org
This site is a smaller version of pecentral.org but can be particularly useful to those teaching in the State of Washington. It is located in Central Washington University and hence can keep people updated on conferences, workshops, and state political happenings.

www.fns.usda.gov/tn
This is where you will find the USDAs "Team Nutrition" Program. They have all kinds of ways to help you teach sound nutrition to kindergarten through high school. They have lots of free resources, lesson plans for different grades, overheads, posters, student workbooks, etc.

www.eatsmart.org
The Washington State Dairy Council sponsors "The Nutrition Education People." Not only do they have free and low cost materials, they have trained regional workers who will visit your school to provide sample lessons and in-service

training. Their materials and lessons are designed to satisfy state academic learning requirements.

www.pbs.org/teachersource/health.
This site it called the PBS Teacher Source. It is a more general site with lessons and activities in all fields. Besides Health and Fitness there are the areas of Arts and Literature, Science and Technology, Social Studies, and Early Childhood. They are all worth a visit.

www.aahperd.org
This is the home of *the American Alliance of Health, Physical Education, Recreation and Dance (AAHPERD)*. This is a big organization with an extensive web site. Here you will have a wealth of information in such areas as coaching, recreation, health, physical education, adaptive physical education. This is where you will find all the particulars of the *Fitnessgram* and *Activitygram*. Also, they will have interesting information such as position statements on things as diverse as "activity recommendations for toddlers and preschoolers" and "the proscription of battleball" and "a code of ethics for coaches."

www.wahperd.com
The Washington Alliance of Health, Physical Education, Recreation and Dance (WAHPERD) is the state level of *AAHPERD* organization. It can be primarily helpful in keeping you aware of events happening within the state. *Jump Rope for Heart* and *Hoops for Heart* programs are examples. This organization also puts on an annual state conference that has much to offer.

www.sportscoach-sci.com
This is ISBS Coaches Information Service. The site is mainly for those in the coaching profession, but it has good information on a variety of sports. Specific sports have different sections that contain articles.

Books

Hellison, D. *Teaching Responsibility Through Physical Activity*, Human Kinetics, 1995. (1 800 747-4457)
Don Hellison teaches students with behavioral problems. From his experiences he developed the *Personal and Social Responsibility Model (PSRM)*. It has been proven to be an effective guide for teaching affective behaviors.

Launder, A.G. *Play Practice: The Games Approach to Teaching and Coaching Sports*, Human Kinetics, 2001. (1 800 747 4457)
This book introduces many fun and effective drills and game modifications. A large range of sports is covered. I especially recommend this book for coaches of team sports.

Siedentop, D. *Sport Education: Quality PE through Positive Sport Experiences.* Human Kinetics, 1994. (1 800 747 4457)
This book gives ideas how to modify sports to make them more educational. It also explains how to use the contextual aspects of sports to make the sports experience more challenging and fun. Practical experiences of teachers at a variety of grade levels, with a wide variety of sports, are offered.

Sweetgall, R. *Pedometer Walking,* Creative Walking, Inc. (2001)
This book, and others by Rob Sweetgall, provides good ideas for fun walking activities and lessons. Visit his web site (www.creataivewalking.com) for pedometer ideas and other resources. I also liked his older book *Walking for Little Children*.

Poppen, J.D. *201 Games for the Elementary Physical Education Program.* Parker Publishing company, 2002.
Jerry Poppen was probably the first to publish a book with activities that were designed in keep everyone active. If you like his ideas he has a number of other publications and resources. There is not a web site but his address is Action Productions, 11311 88th Ave. East, Puyallup, WA. 98373 (253 845 3627). Another of his book that I have found particularly useful *is Fitness Zone Ahead: Resource Material for Elementary Physical Education Programs*, 2nd Edition, Action Productions, 2000.

LeFevre, D.N. *Best New Games,* Human Kinetics, 2002 (1 800 747-4457)
If you like the concept of new games this is a good resource with which to start.

Carnes, C. *Teacher's Guide for Awesome Elementary School Physical Education Activities*, The Education Company, 1990.
Cliff Canes' book simply has a lot of good everyone-active games for elementary children. If you like them you might want to check out his *Awesome Jump Rope Activities Book*.

Catalogs

Human Kinetic Publishers (www.humankinetics.com)
This is the world's largest publisher in the area of coaching and physical activity. They have an impressive list of materials for all sports and aspects of coaching. Free catalogs are available upon request.

SPORTTIME, 1 Sportime Way, Atlanta, GA, USA 30340 (1 800 444-5700)
They have endless physical education and coaching supplies and equipment. Also things like music tapes and CDs.

WOVERINE Sports, 745 State Circle, Box 1941, Ann Arbor, MI 48106 (1 800 521-2832)
They have endless physical education and coaching supplies and equipment. Also things like music tapes and CDs.

THINGS FROM BELL, P.O. Box 135, East Troy, WI 53120, (1 800 432 2842)
They have endless physical education and coaching supplies and equipment. Also things like music tapes and CDs.

NASCO, 4825 Stoddard Rd., Modesto, CA 95356-9318 (1 800 558-9595)
They have endless physical education and coaching supplies and equipment. Also things like music tapes and CDs.

Journals

Journal of Health, Physical Education, Recreation and Dance
(www.humankinetics.com)
This is an AAHPERD publication. Its purpose is to promote high-quality programs in health, physical education, recreation, dance and sport. It has articles on what is happening in these areas.

Strategies: A Journal for Physical and Sport Educator
(www.humankinetics.com)

This is another AAHPERD publication. It strives to share "best practices" of field professionals in sport and physical education. It offers many practical activity and teaching/coaching methods ideas.

Teaching Elementary Physical Education: The Independent Voice of Elementary and Middle School Physical Educators
(www.humankinetics.com)
This resource provides many practical activity and teaching methods specifically designed for elementary and middle schoolteachers.

Glossary

Actively waiting: The instructional procedure of prescribing some activity to children as they await their turn to perform a game skill. For example, having everyone continuously walking during the course of a game of "Duck, duck, goose," would reduce downtime.

Activity Pyramid, The: An activity program that will promote the development of all the health related components of physical fitness. At its base is an hour at day of light activity. The second tier consists of aerobic activities 3 to 5 times per week. The third tier consists of 2 to 4 days per week of muscular strength and flexibility training. The peak of the pyramid represents a minimizing of sedentary practices.

ACTIVITYGRAM: This is part of the FITNESSGRAM test. The children plug in their physical activity patterns for three days and a computer printout provides an evaluation and feedback. It will explain what components of physical fitness they seem to be training and which might need further attention.

Aerobic Activities: Activities that result in a heart rate between 60 and 80 percent of maximum. It should be understood that any movement will improve the aerobic system. Less intense activity will produce smaller gains and more intense activity will yield greater gain but may be difficult to maintain.

Aerobic fitness: Refers to "with oxygen." The body's ability to supply adequate amounts of oxygen, over a period of time, to working muscles and other organs.

Anaerobic fitness: Refers to "without oxygen." The body's ability to sustain repeated short bursts of highly vigorous activity. The body does not have time to take in sufficient oxygen to meet the large demands of the muscles and must utilize other chemical methods to match the performance demands.

Analysis paralysis: A situation in which the student is overloaded with so many feedback suggestion he/she cannot incorporate any change.

Antagonistic muscles: Muscles that work against each other or produce counter movements. For example, the muscles in the front of the leg (quadriceps) work to extend the knee, the muscles in the back of the leg (hamstrings) work to flex the knee. When strength training it is recommended that antagonistic muscles receive equal training in order to avoid postural and injury problems.

Anticipatory set: Attempting to build up interest in the skill or activity to be performed. Interesting names can make a game sound more exciting, giving reasons for the drill can make practice more purposeful.

Attractive nuisance: A legal term for leaving unattended, inciting and potentially dangerous facilities and equipment. An example would be leaving a pool door unlocked or gymnastic equipment set up.

Authentic evaluation: Measuring sport skills under game conditions rather than in isolated drill situations. Such assessment determines not just if the performer processes the skill but also whether or not he/she appropriately applies it.

Awareness talks: A talk given before physical activities are begun which explains your affective behavior expectations.

Back-to-the-wall Principle: The teacher generally positions him/herself near the perimeter of the activity area. This is considered a good pedagogical strategy because it allows the teacher general supervision of all the children. Also, this positioning is important when an address needs to be made to the class; if the instructor is towards the middle of the class the students to the rear may not be able to hear.

Ballistic stretching: Stretching characterized by bouncing and lunging to reach as far as possible. Now days this procedure is considered effective but risky due to the potential injury to connective issues.

Behavioral weaning procedure: A change of habit ultimately requires the individual taking responsibility for his/her own actions. In the beginning instructors may want to regularly involve students in the new behavior and accustom them to it. But following this it is good to have the students beginning to carryout some of the assignments on their own. Eventually it moves from partly instructor directed to totally student directed behavior.

Body awareness: Knowledge of one's body parts and the manners in which they can be positioned and moved.

Body composition: The body's percentage of body fat relative to lean mass. A healthy range of body fat for young males is usually between 3 and 15 percent; the range for young women is usually between 12 to 25 percent.

Challenge approach to fitness testing: This approach is like the *traditional approach* of carefully measuring performances and giving recognition for excellent performances. The key difference is that it is an extra-class activity for only those who volunteer to take the challenge.

Children's Lifetime Physical Activity Model (C-LAM):
    Minimal standard: Children should be receiving at least 30 minutes of moderate level activity on a daily basis.
    Optimal standard: Children should be receiving at least 60 minutes of moderate to vigorous activity on a daily basis.

Children's Walk/Run Formula: For a rough estimate of how far young children might be expected to walk simply divide the child's age by three. For example, a good distance for a six-year old would be around two miles.

Circuit training: A teaching method in which various activity stations are located around the play space. The children rotate from station to station in accordance with some pacing commands.

Compressed morbidity: The concept that continuing to follow good exercise/health practices will tend to reduce the period of time an elderly person might expect to be ill and lacking independence.

Competitive games and sports: Activities where players or teams attempt to outperform the opposing player(s).

Conditioning exercises: Movement experiences primarily done to derive physiological benefits. Calisthenics would normally fall into this category as would weight training and stretching exercises.

Congruent feedback: Feedback which relates directly to the objective or learnable piece of the lesson.

Contextual aspects of sports: There are many features associated with institutional sports: seasons, affiliation of teammates, formal competition schedules, record keeping, festivity, and culminating events. Some authorities downplay these characteristics for fear of *hypercompetition*, others think that they can add to the joy of sports without impairing the educational goals.

Contributory negligence: A legal term for situations where others may be held partially or totally accountable for their own actions. Teachers have a legal duty to provide students with a safe learning environment. However, because of unexpected irresponsible behavior, the students themselves can sometimes be held partially or entirely at fault *(contributory negligence* is not legally attributed to children under seven years of age).

Cool-Down Principle: Light to moderate paced activities or stretching exercises following more vigorous exercise. These are thought to gradually return the physiological state to a normal level and reduce the possibility of ensuing muscle soreness.

Cooperative activities: Activities where partners, small groups, or the entire class attempt to work together to accomplish a physical goal.

Critical period: Some recent research is suggesting that lack of motor skill experiences prior to around 12 or 13 years of age might have permanent affect on brain development. If skills are not learned during the early years it may never be possible to achieve a high level of performance.

Criterion referenced fitness tests: Arbitrary cut-off levels are set and the children are judged to meet or fail those standards.

Directionality: Knowledge of the orientation of one's body and body parts in space.

"Doing" goals: These are goals in which the individual is determined to perform an activity, the outcome of the activity is only of secondary importance. For example, I have a goal of doing at least a 45 minute aerobic workout on a daily basis; I am not especially concerned about whether or not I am covering a greater or lesser distance.

Dose effects: Generally speaking, small amounts of exercise will produce small benefits in fitness and protection from hypokinetic diseases, larger amounts of exercise will tend to produce greater benefits. It should be cautioned that more is not always better; at very high intensities and durations exercise could become counter-productive.

Effective Questioning Strategy, The: First pose the question and then pause to allow time for thinking of the answer. Then select different students. By following this procedure it is hoped that you will be able to get all the students rehearsing the answer. If volunteers are always allowed to answer some of the other students may learn to not concentrate.

Eighty-Percent Success Rate: When children are learning new skills it is desirable to have designed the situation so that they will have a success rate of around 80 percent. High success will increase their liking for the activity. If the task is too easy some level of challenge and interest is lost. Learning must involve some struggle.

Eliminate the elimination: This concept is rather self-explanatory; it means that teachers should not select games which eliminate people from the action for any significant amount of time.

Environmentally closed skills: A skill for which the environment is stable and predictable, allowing time to prepare the movement. Hitting a stationary ball while standing still would be an example.

Environmentally open skills: A skill for which the environment is unpredictable or unstable, preventing advance planning of the movement. Running and attempting to catch a thrown pass would be an example.

Exercise deficiency: The body's natural response when it is not regularly exercised; a feeling of tiredness, malaise, lethargy.

Expansion Principle: This is a teaching technique of starting a game with a few simple rules and then making further additions latter on.

Fat phobia: An excessive fear of having too much fat in one's diet. Something like 20 percent might be a good minimal guideline for fat intake. Fat plays an important role in neurological functioning, connective tissues, skill care, and organ protection and insulation.

Fifty-Percent Activity Standard, The: When in the gym and on the playground we want to keep children moving, that is the way they will improve fitness and develop motor skills. A basic goal might be to have children moving at least 50 percent of the time. This means that we must establish good time saving management techniques and design activities and games in which everyone is active. Evaluation of many teachers shows that the children are active only about 10 to 30 percent of the time at best.

F.I.T. Principle: F.I.T. is an acronym for frequency, intensity, and time. This principle can serve as a guideline for developing each of the components of physical fitness. Frequency refers to how often someone needs to exercise, intensity to how hard or vigorously they need to do so, and time relates to how long the activity should persist. For example, to reduce one's body fat ratio a good procedure would be to exercise daily (frequency), at a low to moderate rate (intensity), for one hour (time).

FITNESSGRAM: This is a health related physical fitness test. The students are given personalized printouts of whether or not they achieved a "healthy level" of fitness for each of the health related components. Among other things, the test includes sit-ups, push-ups, trunk-lifts, sit-and-reach, the PACER aerobic test, and the ACTIVITIGRAM to measure typical daily activity levels.

Five-A-Day: The Food Guide Pyramid recommends 5 to 9 servings of fruits and vegetables everyday. This is a motto for remembering to achieve the minimum of that standard.

Five Philosophies of Competitive Sports, The: Everyone who instructs children in competitive sports no doubt thinks he/she is teaching good ethical and sportsmanship lessons. And yet it is clear that unethical practices sometime occur in sports and that the coaches/instructors condone and teach vastly different behaviors. The reason for these differences has roots in the philosophies of those leaders. There are five basic philosophies of competitive sports ranging from very altruistic to very egocentric: (1) reflects a concern for the welfare of one's opponent, (2) views sports as a physical challenge, (3) views sports as both a physical and mental challenge, (4) considers winning to be of paramount importance, and (5) thinks of it as all out war.

Flexibility fitness: The ability of the joints to move through a full range of motion.

Food Guide Pyramid: The USDA's guidelines. The base is made up of foods high in complex carbohydrates such as breads, cereals, and pasta. The second tier is also high in the complex carbohydrates and fiber that is found in fruits and vegetables. The third tier consists of meat and dairy products. The peak of the pyramid recommends a minimizing of sweets.

Found activities: Everyday things we can do to increase the amount we move: walking to the store, taking the stairs, getting up from our desk, etc.

Fundamental motor skills: These are basic movement skills such as running, skipping, throwing and kicking. It is hoped that children will acquire these skills during the primary grades so that they have a sound foundation on which to build later sport specific skills.

Games Approach to teaching sports: The skills of the sport are taught within the context of the game. The idea is that the skills learned in isolated drills will not later be applied to the game situations. Rather, the sports must be simplified so that the skills can be learned and applied during play.

General feedback: Providing encouragement or disapproval about the overall performance in a non-specific manner. For example, comments like "Great going" or "That was not as good" might not convey clear information about what was exactly good or bad about the performance. Nor might head nods or a frown.

General supervision: This is where the instructor has positioned his/herself so that the actions of all the children in the class can be monitored. Teachers are legally responsible for maintaining this degree supervision of their classes.

Global good: A situation in which the instructor overuses the same reinforcer "Good." It is advisable that instructors learn to employ a variety of different expressions and gestures rather than falling into the habit of repeating the same one over and over.

Health fitness: The minimal level of physical fitness for which everyone should strive throughout their life span. It would allow them to carry out their daily activities without pain or significant restrictions.

Health Related physical fitness tests: Tests in which the focus is on the components of fitness most connected to long-term health. Aerobic cardiovascular fitness and body composition would certainly be emphasized.

Heart-Rate monitors: These devices consist of a chest strap which picks-up and transmits the heart beat and a wristwatch which gives a digital display of it. They are being used by more and more physical education teachers in their classes. Normally a few students take turns wearing them in class to get an understanding of exercise intensity involved in different activities.

Holistic evaluation: This refers to evaluating the overall composite performance of the activity. When applied to sports it means an assessment that will take into account all aspects of successfully playing the game. For example, the evaluation of a child's soccer played ability would take into account the goodness of his/her techniques, strategies, knowledge of the rules, and affective behaviors (sportsmanship, enthusiasm, etc.).

Home position: Establishing at the beginning of a lesson where the children should position their piece of equipment when you are talking. The designated position should be out of their hands so that juggling movements are not occurring.

Hydrogenation: Certain food processing results in hydrogenated fats. These have been found to be particularly susceptible to clogging of arteries and hence it is considered wise to minimize them in our diets. They seem to be as much or more of a problem than saturated fats.

Hypercompetition: Making games and activities more socially competitive by stressing such things as scores, rankings and giving special recognition to top performers.

Hypertrophy of muscle: When muscles are exercised an increase in the cross section of the fibers will occur. The more intense the overload the more the effect. Children and older adults do not have as such of the needed hormones to produce this occurrence as do young adults.

Hypokinetic diseases: diseases and disabilities associated with an inactive lifestyle. Examples would be cardiorespiratory diseases, type II diabetes, excessive body fat, lower back pain.

Individual activities: Activities where everyone works independently and non-competitively on his/her own.

Inherent risks: Anytime people participate in movement activities there exist the possibility of physical injuries occurring. It is the responsibility of teachers to inform the students of the dangers that are involved and take steps to minimize them to the best of their ability.

Instant activity: An activity that the children perform when they first enter a gymnasium or other play space. These can serve the purpose of a warm-up and review of skills.

Interval training: Repeating a vigorous activity a number of times with short rest or recovery periods interspersed. This is an especially effective training procedure for the components of fitness that require high intensity efforts such as anaerobic fitness and muscular strength.

Isometric training: Muscular strength or endurance training in which the resistance is stationary. Supporting oneself in a bent arm hang would be an example.

Isotonic training: Muscular strength or endurance training in which the resistance is moved through a range of motion. Curl-ups and bench presses would be examples.

Kill it before it dies: The instructional practice of terminating a game before the children begin to lose motivation for it. By so doing they will always be eager to play it again at another time. Adherence to such a policy demands that the teacher possess a large number of alternate activity possibilities.

Labor saving devices: All the modern conveniences that serve to reduce the amount of moving that we do: elevators, automatic doors, attached garages, electric can openers, etc. They can be thought of as "exercising costing devices."

Laterality: Knowledge of left and right sides of the body and the relationships between them.

Learnable piece: Focusing a lesson on one observable objective which everyone can accomplish or review. For example, "As we are dribbling soccer balls today I am going to be looking for fast moving-happy feet."

Learned helplessness: Through repeated efforts which result in repeated failures, the person adopts a belief that he/she is not in control of his/her fate. Effort is futile so why try.

Long slanty-rope Principle: The concept of designing class activities so that everyone can participate at the same time, and each student will have the activity's difficulty level adjust to his/her needs. Having a long rope strung across the gym would allow all the children to simultaneously practice jumping the rope; if the rope was sloped from very low to quite high, they could select to jump the rope at the height commensurate with their unique ability.

Maximum Heart-Rate: The fastest speed the heart rate will achieve when exercising at highest exercise intensity. This can be estimated by subtracting one's age from the number 220. For example, a 20-year old might be expected to have a maximum heart rate of around 200 beats per minute. It can be seen that with aging the heart loses some capacity to beat fast.

Mini-games: The instructional concept of organizing a number of simultaneously played small-sided games rather than one mass-on-mass game.

Morbidity: A period of ill health.
> *Compression of morbidity:* A reduction in the period of ill health during the latter years. A typical sedentary individual can expect to experience 11.5 years of ill health and dependent living during old age; that figure can be shrunk to around a year when the person has trained the different components of fitness throughout the years.
> *Expansion of morbidity:* Medical advances which significantly increase the length of our lives but which have a lesser effect on our quality of life will result in an extension of ill health during the latter years.

Multidisciplinary Approach, The: The point here is that you can not do it all yourself and you need to find help. You will not be able to change the lifestyles for your students by yourself. But you will be more successful if you organize a support group or "wellness team." If people from different disciplines (administrators, lunch personnel, specialists, parents, etc.) combine their efforts significant changes are possible.

Muscular fitness: This system can be divided into two basic components.
> *Muscular strength:* The amount of resistance someone is capable of moving. Training to be able to do a pull-up would be an example.
> *Muscular endurance:* The ability of someone to repeatedly move a resistance. Paddling a boat across a lake without the arms giving out would be an example.

Muscular hypertrophy: An increase in the circumference size of muscles, generally produced by strength training.

Norm referenced fitness tests: Everyone's test results are compared with others to derive percentile rankings.

Obese: Thirty percent more body fat than what would be ideal for an individual.

Outcome goals: Goals that are focused on outcomes relative to the performance of others. For example, winning the championship or making the first team. They are only partially under the performer's control.

Overcorrection: This is a technique for correcting misbehavior. The first step is to inform the child what was wrong about his/her behavior and what the correct behavior would have been. Next, if necessary, his/her is required to practice the correct behavior once or repeatedly. This procedure can also be used for groups.

Overexposure: This is the concept that sometimes school repeatedly introduce the same sports to the children each year without ever going into much depth. The result is that the children never get very proficient at any of them. The converse view is that we might be wise to spend more time on some activities before moving on to others.

Overuse Principle, The: This is the concept that more exercise is not always better. The body will normally improve and adapt to the stress of exercise, but if the stress is too sudden and too intense, breakdown can be a consequence. Gradual progress and adequate recovery time is the key to avoiding overuse problems.

Overweight: Twenty percent more body fat than what would be ideal for an individual.

PACER: This is part of the FITNESSGRAM physical fitness test. It is a test of aerobic fitness in which the children run back and forth between lines that are 20 meters apart. Music paces them at a gradually increasing tempo. There are healthy zone criteria established for children from fourth to twelfth grade.

Pedometers: These are inexpensive devices ($20–$35) that are worn on the belt. They measure the number of sets taken and can translate that into miles covered and calories burned. Many physical education teachers are using them on their students both during class and outside of it. They are good for measuring the total amount of activity children and adults get throughout the day.

Perceived Exertion Scale (1–10): A scale which allows people to simply estimate the intensity of their aerobic activities. Levels 4 through 7 represent a good training zone for sustained aerobic activity.

Performance fitness: A high level of physical fitness which will allow an individual to reach his/her fullest potential. He/she could safely enjoy various physically challenging sports and recreations; and could derive many psychological benefits such as better self-concept, body-image, and anxiety reduction.

Performance goals: Goals that focus on one's own performance rather than on an outcome comparison with others. For example, striving to achieve a certain race time or improving one's technique. These goals are largely under one's control.

Performance related physical fitness tests: Tests in which the focus is on the components of fitness most connected to sports performance. Muscular power and anaerobic cardiovascular fitness would certainly be emphasized.

Personal approach to fitness testing: Informal self-testing is done by the children. The emphasis is on children learning how to assess themselves and to set subsequent self-improvement goals.

Personalize: This is the practice of relating one's direct experience with an activity. For example, telling the children how and how often you do aerobic exercises might give your instructional advice more weight and relevance. Better than telling people what they "should" do you are telling them what you do.

Personal-Social Responsibility Model (PSRM): A hierarchical listing of six levels of personal-social functioning (ranging from irresponsibility to applying caring concepts beyond the instructional setting. Developed by Don Hellison.

Physical activities: A continuum of movement experiences from highly organized competitive sports to informal endeavors such as leisurely walking or gardening. Normally we participate in these because we enjoy something about the activity itself.

Physical guidance: This is a instructional procedure in which the performer is moved through the correct technique. Oftentimes the instructor will physically move and position the student. Devices such an arm brace to keep the elbow straight could also be considered as a physical guidance tool.

Positive transfer: A situation in which learning one skill will aid the learning of another skill. For example, having developed a sound fundamental throwing technique will facilitate the learning of the specific skills of pitching a baseball or throwing a football.

President's Challenge, The: This is a physical fitness test that offers awards for various achievements. There are awards for achieving in the 80th percentile or the 50th percentile on all the items. There are also awards for participating in the testing process and for logging a good level of regular physical activity.

Principle of individual differences: Due to genetic factors individuals have great differences in their capabilities for performing motor and physical fitness tasks. With all other factors held constant, some people may be two or three times stronger or faster than someone else. And on the other hand, that person might be more gifted in other components of fitness and motor abilities.

Process evaluation: Assessment of one's amount and manner of participating in an activity. Tracking how many times someone exercised during the week would be a process evaluation.

Product evaluation: Assessment of ability to achieve an environmental outcome. Measuring how many push-ups one can do is an evaluation of a physical fitness product, measuring how many baskets can be made in a certain time period is an evaluation of a motor product.

Proximity control: The teaching technique of moving closer to a child who is misbehaving or who you suspect might begin to misbehave. The thinking here is that your mere presence may be sufficient to stop the behavior and hence nullify the need for more disruptive corrections.

Readiness: Refers to whether or not a child is physiologically or psychologically mature enough to benefit from physical training.

Reasonably prudent: This is the legal standard the teacher must follow with regards to the children's safety. All movement activities have some level of inherent risk but activities which can be seen to pose a foreseeable danger should not be conducted.

Reflection time: Time when you get the children to think about the affective behaviors displayed in class. Discussion times can be set aside during class.

Residual calorie burning: The higher than normal body metabolism which occurs following vigorous exercise. This effect typically dissipates rather quickly and seldom can be detected beyond an hour or so.

Reversibility Principle, The: Physiological adaptations to exercise are not long maintained following the cessation of training. A crude estimate might be a 10 percent decline of capability each week until the return to baseline.

Rubrics: These are a listing of the criteria expected to be demonstrated. They are being more widely used to assessment the attainment of both motor and affective skills. For example, the instructor may be looking for four different aspects of a skill technique and evaluating each of them on a 3 or 5 point scale. Use of rubrics greatly reduce the subjectivity of assessment and provide learners with defined objectives.

Sandwich Principle: Keeping feedback positive by saying something good about performance both before and following the corrective statements. For example, "Good ready position, but remember that we need to hustle so as to be directly under the ball. I like the way you are calling out your shots."

Saturated fats: These are typically found in high levels in meat and whole diary products (milk, cheese, egg yokes, lard, butter). They are considered to be major contributors to the development of cardiovascular diseases and dietary guidelines recommend that they should account for no more than 10 percent of caloric in-take

Scaffolding: Gradual adding to a previous day's learning. For example, "Yesterday we learned and practiced the proper way to catch a ball. Today we will see if we can use that skill as we are running."

Sedentary: Not engaging in any exercise beyond that which is required at work.

Self-efficacy: Believing that you are capable of accomplishing a specific skill. For example, "I believe that I can do a cartwheel." If someone lacks self-efficacy he/she is unlikely to attempt or long persevere at a task.

Slave market approach: This is a method of picking teams by having captains select the people they want. This is not considered a good approach because it is not very rapid, and more importantly, it can be a discouraging experience for those students are consistently last to be chosen.

Slippage: This is where students will gradually discontinue compliance to class rules. Too prevent this from occurring, the teacher needs to remind the students when failure to follow class rules is first noticed.

SOS question: To judge the goodness of a drill or activity use the SOS acronym in this order; Is the Safe? Is everyone On-task? Is everyone being Successfully challenged? If you cannot answer yes revision is in order.

Specific feedback: Providing encouragement or disapproval about performance in a qualitative manner. For example, comments like "That was a good follow-through," or "You are forgetting to stay tucked," convey clear information about exactly what was good or bad.

Specific supervision: This is when the teacher is directly present at the site of an activity and can quickly regulate or stop the action if necessary. This level of supervision is legally required when a child is performing a dangerous activity.

Specificity of motor abilities hypothesis: The concept that people possess many different independent motor abilities. Some abilities will aid the performance of certain skills, other abilities will effect different skills. The implication is that most people will have motor abilities which could enable them to proficiently learn certain types of skills.

Sport Education Model, The: This model sees that competitive sports can be a fun and educational part of the school day. All children can learn valuable motor skills and affective behaviors form competitive sports when the rules and equipment are modified to suit their needs and when there is an opportunity full and equal participation. Also, enjoyment can be increased by including the contextual aspects of sports such as league schedules, record keeping, tournaments and festivities.

Sports arms race: Universities and high schools are ever increasing their efforts to improve the success of their athletic teams. Both training and recruitment of players is becoming fiercer. To make these squads younger and younger players are feeling the pressure to train harder and to specialize year round.

Sports specialization: There exists a clear trend in this country for student/athletes to specialize in one sport at younger and younger ages. They are more likely playing just one sport and training for it year round. The driving force behind this is the increasing competitiveness of school and university sports programs.

Sports specific motor skills: These are specialized skills such as serving a tennis ball or performing a head spring. Although not a sport skill, doing Country Western two-step is a specialized skill built upon a foundation of fundamental motor skills.

Spotlighting: The technique of stopping practice to allow a skillful student to give a reviewing demonstration. It is generally thought a good idea to have more than one student demonstrate because it takes some of the pressure off of them and it more likely will result in a sound demonstration.

Stages of Change Exercise Model: In this model it is recognized that people do not normally move directly from non-exercisers to exercisers. In the beginning people might not be even thinking of exercise, then they start to contemplate it, then they actually start making plans, then they begin, eventually they may maintain it. Collapses and relapses are possible throughout the process.

Static stretching: Stretching that is done slowly and gradually. The person moves to the limit of the joint and then holds that position or only very gradually extends it.

Target Heart-Rate Zone: A guideline for aerobic training is to exercise at 60 to 80 percent of one's maximum heart rate. Within this range is the target heart-rate zone. If should be realized the improvements in aerobic fitness will occur outside this range. The gains will not be as great at lighter intensities and it may be difficult to maintain activity above this range.

Task mastery goals: These goals do not focus on a comparison of performance with that of others. For example, the goal might be to achieve a certain performance outcome such as making 3 out of 10 foul shots. Or it could be a "doing" goal such as practicing 10 minutes everyday.

Teacher movement: A recommended strategy in which the teacher circulates about the play space while giving instruction and supervising activities. This allows one to provide more personal feedback and encouragement.

Team-size rule of thumb: To achieve educational appropriateness, the number of players on a team should be equal to or less than the grade level of the children. When team sizes are larger the game becomes too complex and the amount of activity per child is greatly reduced.

Ten-Thousand Step Criteria, The: This is a common standard set to increase the amount of daily activity children or adults get. Pedometers are used to record the steps. Ten-thousand will put a person up around 5 miles of walking.

Ten-Year Rule, The: It is thought that approximately 10 to 12 years of regular, quality practice is required to achieve peak performance in complex sports such as basketball, tennis, and soccer. This seems to be true for other motor skills such as playing a musical instrument.

The 80-20 Diet Ratio: This means that the Food Guide Pyramid is not an unmerciful diet. It allows for 20 percent of your calories to come from treats if you are more vigilant with the other 80 percent.

Three-rule rule: This means that an instructor can explain a game in three rules or less. When a game has more rules than this the explanation will become lengthy and some of the children will not retain everything.

Three Thousand Five-hundred Calories Requirement, The: When all else is equal, it requires the burning of 3,500 calories to lose one pound of body fat. This is comparable to walking about 35 miles.

Time-out procedure: Disciplinary technique commonly consisting of four steps: (1) A first misbehavior warrants a warning, (2) recurrence of misbehavior results in removal to a time-out area of the student's self-determined length, (3) the third infraction results in another time-out period of a duration determined by the teacher, and (4) a fourth infraction brings removal from the class.

Traditional approach to fitness testing: Everyone is required to take the test. Performances are carefully evaluated and distributed to everyone. Good performances are recognized.

Traditional approach to teaching sports: The skills of the sport are taught in drill separate from the game. The idea is that the sport cannot be successfully played first without mastering the skills involved.

Trainability: Refers to the body's physiologically ability to adapt to exercise stresses. Pre-pubescent children do not have the mature physiological mechanisms possessed by young adults and thus do not respond as well to exercise.

Transfer: This is the effect learning one skill has on the learning of another skill. Transfer can be positive, neutral, and sometimes, but infrequently, negative. Learning fundamental motor skills in the early grades will have positive transfer to the children's later learning of sports specific skills. Learning skills in isolation sometimes does not result in much positive transfer to the game because the children might not recognize how they are applied.

Tropical oils: Palm and coconut oil. These two vegetable oil are high in saturated fats and thus are an exception to the rule that vegetable oils tend to be high in unsaturated and low in saturated fats.

Two-Minute Warning, The: This is a reminding motto that we should normally keep our talks short when explaining games and activities in the gym and on the playground. The children are ready to move and will likely not remember long, complex directions. Two minutes in a good criterion to stay under.

Unsaturated fats: These are typically found in vegetable oils such as olive, corn, and peanut. They are considered to be a better type of fat than the saturated version because they are not associated with the development of cardiovascular diseases.

USDA's Food Guide Pyramid: A guide for eating which stresses a balanced diet, with emphasis placed on carbohydrates and with fats, oils, and sweets playing a minor role.

Veganism: A meatless/fishless diet which also precludes diary products (milk, eggs, cheeses, butter, lard).

Vegetarian Food Guide Pyramid: Guidelines for a meatless/fishless diet which includes dairy products and eggs. Legumes, fruits & vegetables, and whole grains form the base on food to be eaten at every meal; seeds, plant oils, milk, soy, and egg whites are to be eaten daily; eggs and sweets form the peek to be eaten occasionally or optionally

Warm-up Principle: Light to moderate paced activities or stretching exercises before more vigorous exercise. These are thought to gradually increase blood flow and hence guard against muscle, tendon, and ligament strains.

When I say . . . Principle: The teacher technique of prefacing instructions with the words "When I say . . ." The idea is to tell the students how you want an activity to be performed before giving them the command to begin. This avoids the tendency of the children to rush off and begin an activity before you have specified how it should be done.

With-it-ness: is a term for the teaching skill of being able to attend to more than one thing at a time.

"Yet" Principle: When a child resignedly says he/she cannot do something, the instructor responds by saying "yet."